THE CAR

ALSO BY BRYAN APPLEYARD

The Culture Club: Crisis in the Arts

Richard Rogers: A Biography

The Pleasures of Peace: Art and Imagination in Postwar Britain

Understanding the Present: Science and the Soul of Modern Man

The First Church of the New Millennium

Brave New Worlds: Genetics and the Human Experience

Aliens: Why They Are Here

How to Live Forever or Die Trying

The Brain Is Wider Than the Sky:
Why Simple Solutions Don't Work in a Complex World

Bedford Park

THE CAR

THE RISE AND FALL OF THE MACHINE
THAT MADE THE MODERN WORLD

BRYAN APPLEYARD

PEGASUS BOOKS
NEW YORK LONDON

THE CAR

Pegasus Books, Ltd.
148 West 37th Street, 13th Floor
New York, NY 10018

Copyright © 2022 by Bryan Appleyard

First Pegasus Books paperback edition July 2023
First Pegasus Books cloth edition September 2022

ISBN: 978-1-63936-466-4

10 9 8 7 6 5 4 3 2 1

Printed in the United States of America
Distributed by Simon & Schuster
www.pegasusbooks.com

For Ada Shun-Shin

Contents

Everything in life is somewhere else,
and you get there in a car.

E.B. White

Introduction

THE LAST SPACE OF FREEDOM

Cars – internal-combustion-engined (ICE), driver-controlled vehicles – are scheduled to die in 2030. They will then be 145 years old. The policy of governments and companies is to replace them with EVs, electric vehicles, which will then be replaced by AVs, semi- or fully autonomous vehicles. Not long thereafter, 'smart cities' will control urban and suburban traffic movement and 'smart motorways' will control the rest.

These new vehicles might still be known as cars. But, apart from obvious similarities like wheels and bodywork, they will be something quite different. EVs do not need gears – this alone transforms the experience of driving whether you are used to an automatic or a manual gear change. But, in any case, they are just one step on the road to AVs in which the skills of the driver become increasingly redundant and, finally, irrelevant. AVs will be another step on the road to machines that nobody can seriously describe as cars – mobile living rooms or offices or even, according to IKEA's AV designers, cafés or hotels. The world made by cars, the cars we have known, loved and hated, the cars that engaged our feelings and senses, that gave us previously unimaginable forms of freedom, is ending.

In their brief ascendancy cars have dominated every aspect of public and private life – environmental issues from global warming to pollution of the air we breathe, politics by the power of their industrial wealth and their transformation of societies and lives, and, finally, they have occupied the summit of consumer society as the ultimate objects of desire. They have also permanently changed our understanding of space, time and nature.

The ICE car is the defining product of the industrial age that began in the early eighteenth century. To drive one is to be connected to steel and oil, rubber, plastic and glass, and a fabulous electro-mechanical ballet of sparks, cylinders, gears and springs, all operated by the movements of the driver's feet and hands. Giant factories employing thousands of workers have built these vehicles ever since Henry Ford opened the Highland Park plant in Detroit in 1910. Cars are, as management theorist Peter Drucker put it, the 'industry of industries'.

Various technologies – the personal computer, the mobile phone, the stirrup, aircraft, freight containers – are routinely said to have changed the world. But none of them has intruded so imperiously, so ruthlessly into the life and landscape of our planet as the car. Cars have redesigned cities and conquered the countryside, etching the landscape with networks of roads, service stations, parking lots, fast-food outlets, shopping malls and motels. They have remade industries and globalised economies. They have turned what were once strenuous journeys by foot or horse into almost effortless, air-conditioned voyages along smoothly metalled roads. They have subdued the wilderness and turned it into an 'attraction'.

There are 1.4 billion vehicles – including buses and trucks – on the world's roads. They cruise the rural land they seized, they fill city streets, consigning pedestrians to a narrow strip of pavement allocated to the activity of walking. The thousands of tons of metal, fuel and fumes that occupy the road are now barely noticed. This astonishing annexation of urban space has become normalised – it has become, like the ground, the sky, the air, a condition of our existence. Perhaps that is why people seldom say cars changed the world; it would be like saying oxygen changed the world or asking a fish for its opinion of water. Or perhaps it would be more accurate to say cars *made this* world, the one in which we now live.

Cars have also remade people. They are the ultimate prosthetics, extending human capabilities across physical and mental dimensions. They allow us to move at hitherto unimaginable speed with unprecedented freedom and to do so in a steel cocoon replete with sophisticated comforts.

Cars take us out into the world while simultaneously sustaining our solitude. By replacing maps and providing the rudimentary facts of place names and road numbers, satellite navigation systems have relieved us of the burden of knowing where we are. By seating us in a closed box, cars have relieved us of the burden of others. The car, unlike the horse, the carriage or even the train, is a world of its own, a physically and psychologically sealed zone. This was noted by that most mordant observer of late modernity Michel Houellebecq in his novel *The Map and the Territory* (2010). He called the car 'one of the last spaces of freedom' for humanity.

In this free zone we are released from the conformity demanded by the eyes and judgements of others. One survey found that two thirds of Americans sing in their cars. As though, remarks Matthew Crawford in his book *Why We Drive*, 'we were in the shower!' Crawford also notes a special kind of peace that descends on the lone commuting driver because he does not have to do anything else but drive. Alone in their automotive prosthetics, humans find a fulfilment that is elsewhere denied them.

Then there is the sheer joy of driving. Researchers into human happiness have been surprised to find that people derive enormous pleasure from driving. This is reflected in the tactile, sensuous and dynamic delights celebrated in contemporary car advertising. Beyond that there is the thrill of speed, of control, the giddy feeling of connection with the road, the gears, the tyres, the clutch, the engine, and the combination of aggression towards and cooperation with other drivers, the exhilaration of risks taken and avoided, and cyclists, road hogs or boy racers defeated, of toying with the law over speed limits or amber lights, of corners well taken.

This internal freedom is matched by the external freedom provided by the car. Freedom was the unique selling proposition of the very first cars: freedom to roam, to make your own way into, as Henry Ford put it, 'God's great open spaces'. Before the car, humans were either restricted to slow, punishing walks from their homes or to cities full of horse shit and disease. The car was not only human-liberating, it was also, in usurping the horse, at least to begin with, environment-improving. This was a new form of freedom, which, in turn, was elevated to a more generalised political and social freedom, the right to go or be anywhere, to move, to drive. 'Drive free or die' is the motto of Jalopnik.com, an automotive website, 'drive' having become synonymous with 'live'.

But the case for the prosecution has become ever more compelling. The car is now accused of limiting freedom. It denies freedom to those deprived of their land by the construction of highways and to victims of accidents and pollution. It also denies freedom to nature, to the wilderness. We regard the wilderness as good and define it as a place untouched by humans, something distinctively *other*. We may stare in wonder at the Grand Canyon but it does not stare back. The rational outcome of that is that we should leave the wilderness alone by making it inaccessible to human invasion. Instead, we cut roads through the mountains, deserts and jungles with rest stops, viewpoints, explanatory signs. Cities, meanwhile, are now choked with cars and littered with machines and buildings that feed them with fuel or allow them to park.

Most ominously for the car is the realisation that the fire that makes it run also emits carbon dioxide which warms the planet. It is now seen as complicit in the ultimate freedom-denying crime: rendering large parts of the earth – or the entire planet – uninhabitable.

Already the young are turning away. The number of teenagers seeking driving licences is, for the first time, falling. They are perhaps distracted by other technologies or by the efficiency and relative cheapness of ride-hailing systems. Ride-hailing turns movement into a service – you need no longer have a car exclusively for your own use. Within a few years owning a car might seem as eccentric as owning a train or a bus. Or perhaps it will simply be illegal.

And so by 2030 the death sentence will have been passed on ICE cars. Their crimes will be judged to outweigh their delights. The freedom and the joy of driving these fabulous machines, the love of their beauty and the subtlety of their responses to the human touch, their lover-like moods and need for constant care, will all be discarded in favour of something less sublime and less free but, we may hope, less damaging to humans and their planet.

There will be a gain in freedom from the social and environmental crimes of the car and, as the algorithms take hold, a loss in the freedom to drive however, whenever and wherever we want. This may seem a fair trade-off but less so when seen in the wider context.

It is no accident that Google is one of the leading developers of driverless cars. For the big tech companies to justify their inflated share prices they must continue to deliver rapid growth and their only credible source of growth is ever more information about consumer habits. Driverless cars in smart cities will shed rivers of such information. If nobody is driving and the car has become a mobile entertainment or shopping space – and assuming the tech monopolies have not been broken up – it will have become the most potent device for enforcing what Shoshana Zuboff has called 'surveillance capitalism'.

From an even wider perspective, liberal democracy is in decline and autocratic majoritarianism – the suppression of the individual in the name of the collective – is on the rise. Having sustained industrial capitalism, the surveillance systems in AVs and smart cities will move on to the sustenance of unelected and unaccountable central control. The destruction of automotive freedom will have many unintended consequences.

This is a book about, more than any other country, America. America's ascendancy has coincided with the reign of the car and her decline might well coincide with the last days of the car. Americans did not invent the car but, from 1908 until the rise of Japan in the sixties and the recent ascent of China, the car story has been dominated by America. This is not simply because the USA was, for so long, the biggest producer; it is also because it is the supreme automotive myth-maker and storyteller. America has created and controlled the global imagery and sounds of popular culture through which cars have been celebrated and their stories told. My own absorption of these sounds and this imagery has meant that all the greatest drives of my life have been on American roads.

My intention is to document a way of life that is now passing away. I wish to celebrate the immense drama and beauty of what is soon to be lost, of the genius embodied in the Ford Model T, of the glory of the brilliant-red Mercedes-Benz S-Class made by workers for Nelson Mandela on his release from prison, of Kanye West's 'chopped' Maybach, of the salvation of the Volkswagen Beetle by Major Ivan Hirst, of the absurd automotive wonders released by Detroit in its golden age, of Elvis Presley's 100 Cadillacs, of Bertha Ringer's theft of her husband's car, of the crazed genius of Soichiro Honda and the infinitely measured genius of Taiichi Ohno, of the platonic perfection of Gordon Murray's T50, of Pierrot le Fou and his Gang des Tractions Avant, of the Rolls-Royce Silver Ghost and the BMC Mini and even of that harbinger of the end – the Tesla Model S and its creator Elon Musk.

This book is a mosaic of stories and characters. A strictly linear form would not be true to the multifarious history of the car with its connections to politics, economics and art as much as to engineering, industry and consumer society. Only by setting these themes side by side is it possible to understand the world the car made, because in this world everything touches everything else.

PART ONE

MAKERS

Bertha Ringer

Chapter One

THE FIRE INSIDE

1

Jo the crossing sweeper is a character in Charles Dickens's novel *Bleak House*. In fact, he is barely a character at all, more of a spirit born of the filth in which he lives. He is a boy, 'dirty, ugly, disagreeable to all the senses . . . a common creature of the common streets . . .'

Jo is a nobody, an unnoticed street dweller; only in his appalling, harrowing, beautifully written death does he become a somebody. It is then that Dickens, magnificently robed in genius and righteous anger, steps out of the fiction to address his audience: 'Dead, your Majesty. Dead, my lords and gentlemen. Dead, right reverends and wrong reverends of every order. Dead, men and women, born with heavenly compassion in your hearts. And dying thus around us every day.'

Bleak House was published episodically between 1852 and 1853. At that time London, like many other rapidly developing cities around the world, was descending into hell. The Industrial Revolution had led to an explosive urban expansion. The cities could not cope. In London human filth was everywhere – the Thames was clogged with it. In 1858 hot weather caused the 'Great Stink', a smell of raw sewage so terrible that the curtains of the Houses of Parliament had to be soaked in chloride of lime so the members could continue their debates without retching. An engineer, Sir Joseph Bazalgette, stepped forward, first to narrow the Thames with embankments and thereby accelerate the flow and second to build a vast network of sewers. Over decades, human waste was gradually controlled.

But, as the pressures of modernity continued to increase, it became clear that human excrement was not the only problem. It was not even the worst problem.

Writing in 1958 about his boyhood in London in the 1890s H.B. Creswell, an architect, exclaimed, 'But the mud! And the noise! And the smell!' All of which, he said, were caused by horses. The filth formed banks along the pavements of even the most fashionable streets and when wet formed a 'pea soup' that would be flung up in sheets by passing carriages. This soup was temporarily cleared up by 'mud carts' into which men in thigh boots, oilskins and sou'westers ladled the muck which, each day, would return.

By 1900 there were 11,000 single-horse Hansom cabs in London and thousands of horse-drawn buses, each of which needed 12 horses a day. Transport in the city needed a total of 50,000 horses; on top of that there were the horse-drawn deliveries. Horses eject between 15 and 30 pounds of excrement a day; 50,000 horses would thus deposit over 500 tons daily. In 1894 *The Times* suggested that by 1930 every street in the city would be covered by 9 feet of horse excrement. By the same date it was estimated that Manhattan, with 130,000 horses working daily, would be covered up to the level of third-storey windows.

Also equine traffic jams could be as bad as anything achieved by cars. In 1838 a journalist, Edouard Kollof, described a bewildering variety of horse-drawn vehicles on the streets of Paris: 'Cabriolets, fiacres, deltas, lutétiennes, tilburys, barouches, calèches, coupés, landaus, gigs, curricles, four-horse post-chaises, six-horse diligences.' There were many accidents caused by broken axles and spooked horses. Paris, concluded Kollof, was becoming hell for both horses and pedestrians. The noises made by horses' hooves, wagon wheels and, especially, the crack of drivers' whips threatened to destroy the mind of the great philosopher Arthur Schopenhauer. He said the sound of whips 'slides through one's brain and shatters one's thoughts'.

Like cars in the twentieth century, horses in the nineteenth were an environmental hazard, the cause of traffic chaos and death and, also like cars, they remodelled cities with their demand for stables and food.

Jo, the crossing sweeper, was a casualty of the chaos caused by the urban horse. He was employed to brush away the filth to make channels for pedestrians, especially women in their long ground-brushing dresses and skirts. This was not an official job; sweepers survived, just about, on tips from any passer-by who took the trouble to notice and reward them. Most, like Jo, must have died young of diseases caused by equine excrement.

Dickens roused Christian consciences; Bazalgette built sewers. But, as the nineteenth century passed, the horse-shit problem became not only more urgent but also more soluble. Engineers – some geniuses, some crazed extroverts, many tinkering introverts and even a few women – were thinking that, surely, there must be something better than this.

2

In the Wonderwerk Cave, Northern Cape province, South Africa, fragments of burned bone and plant ash were recently found. These were 1 million years old and they proved that hominids, our pre-human ancestors, had controlled fire. They could warm themselves, cook food and, by setting fires, they could transform the landscape.

Three hundred years ago humans began to use fire to heat water to produce steam that could, in turn, provide mechanical power. Just over 200 years ago humans began to invent ways of putting the fire inside, rather than outside, their engines. Then, in the course of the nineteenth century, the internal-combustion engine (ICE) was found to be a superbly efficient and effective way to power wheeled vehicles.

The parts of the ICE were assembled over a period of at least 2,400 years. In South-East Asia at some point before 350 BC the fire piston appeared, a machine of compression and ignition that caused a piston to move up and down. Evidence of hand cranks from 200 BC have been found in China. Cranks with connecting rod mechanisms were in use in the Byzantine Empire in the sixth century. The great Muslim scholar and inventor Ismail al-Jazari created a twin-cylinder pump with a crank and connecting rods in the thirteenth century. Fire was introduced in the seventeenth century when gunpowder was first used to drive pumps.

It was all beginning to come together and finally did so in a number of locations, most curiously in France in 1807 when Nicéphore Niépce, the inventor of photography, sailed an ICE-powered boat on the River Saône. From that point onwards the development process accelerated until the car was created.

The car engine is, in principle, simple. Air and fuel are mixed, compressed by a piston and then ignited by a spark. This forces the cylinder downwards causing a crankshaft to rotate. At least one valve is required to let in the air-fuel mix and another to release the exhaust fumes. Precise timing is required as well as air and fuel intakes, an exhaust system and an electrical system to produce the spark. In a diesel engine, ignition is produced not by a spark but by the heat of compression. When multiple cylinders are involved the number of parts increases rapidly. The whole needs to be cooled by air flow or pumped water. Gears are also required since the ICE does not, like an electric engine, deliver all its power at once – its output needs to be guided upwards or downwards by the driver or, latterly, by automatic transmission.

The containment and control of fire inside the engine created the age of the car. Between 1885 and 1908 the birth pangs of this age were marked by furious, uncoordinated activity, first in Europe and then in America. Three questions needed to be answered: how should an automobile be powered – steam, electricity or internal combustion? What was the best automobile design? What was the automobile for? The first was effectively answered by 1910. The second in 1901 by the Mercedes 35hp. The third was answered in 1908 by the Ford Model T.

3

The photographs show a handsome, strong-willed woman, her features slightly boyish. The clothes are respectably feminine but her expression has an ironic, critical look as if she always knows better. In one shot taken in old age she wears a wry expression which seems to say, 'I told you so.'

Bertha Ringer was born on 3 May 1849 in Pforzheim, a city in south-western Germany. She died not far away in Ladenburg on 5 May 1944. Her long life thus covered the unification of Germany in 1871 and the two world wars of the twentieth century. In later life she became an admirer of Hitler and, in return, Nazi propaganda honoured her as a 'brave German mother'. Her destiny was decided when, on 27 July 1872, Bertha married Karl Benz, a prodigious 27-year-old engineer.

The photos of Karl show something quite different. His hair is swept back and he wears a fulsome, 'imperial' moustache. In every shot he looks stern, purposeful, sometimes angry, and the eyes stare fiercely into the future. But, in this, there is unworldliness. He was born on 25 November 1844; he died on 4 April 1929 and was thus spared the rise of Nazism.

Bertha's family was wealthy, Karl's was not. He was, however, a born engineer. As a child he disassembled five of his father's pocket watches to study the mechanisms. Subsequently he considered becoming a locksmith but then he turned to locomotive engineering; his father, who had died when he was two, had been an engine driver. In 1871, after a series of career variations, he founded an engineering company in Mannheim.

But the unworldliness detectable in the photos meant that he was a poor businessman and his partner in the company, August Ritter, was not much better. Bertha was by now Karl's fiancée and her dowry was used to buy out Ritter. After a few more business ups and downs, Karl joined a firm of local bicycle repairers to produce static-gas – or, as we know them, internal-combustion – engines. This went well and gave Karl the freedom to indulge in his real passion, the construction of a horseless carriage. He succeeded in 1885.

The Benz Patent-Motorwagen, a three-wheeler, was first seen in public on 3 July 1886 when Karl drove it through Mannheim at about 8 miles per hour (mph). St John C. Nixon, an English car historian writing in 1936, imagined the scene of the excited people and Bertha running behind 'clapping her hands in admiration'.

This, according to Nixon and, subsequently, the world, was the first true motor car – a viable machine with a four-stroke internal-combustion engine. It was certainly the first car to be put up for sale; it cost about $4,300 in today's money. The patent had been registered on 29 January 1886. This document is now celebrated by true believers as the birth certificate of the car.

This may not be quite fair. Also in 1885 and also in Germany, Gottlieb Daimler and Wilhelm Maybach built a two-wheeled vehicle, known as the Reitwagen, driven by a single-cylinder, four-stroke engine. It was intended as a demonstrator, though later it was said to be the first motorcycle. The following year they produced a four-wheeled ICE vehicle. They had bought a horse-drawn coach – an Américaine – pretending it was a birthday present for Daimler's wife. In this was installed a vertical single-cylinder 'Grandfather clock' engine. Being a four-wheeler it appears more advanced than Benz's three-wheeler; on the other hand it was a converted horse carriage – a genuine horseless carriage – so it could also be said to be more antique. As a stagecoach-type carriage with an engine instead of horses, pedants were free to argue that it was not, in fact, a car. But it was, and if history had decided that four wheels were a prerequisite of the car, Daimler and Maybach would have been the winners.

None of which matters to the official – and widely advertised – story of the car's origins, because Karl Benz had married a public relations genius.

Karl was meticulous but Bertha was impatient. By the time he arrived at the Mark III Benz Patent-Motorwagen she would have been wondering why her husband's car was not the worldwide sensation she correctly thought it should be. She decided to take a trip. Maybe she really wanted to visit her mother; perhaps her sons, 13-year-old Richard and 15-year-old Eugen, were, like later generations of teenagers, enthralled by the possibilities of a road trip. But it is more likely that Bertha wanted to free her husband from an excess of caution and humanity from its dependence on the horse. In which case, the first road trip was a brilliant publicity stunt indeed.

And so at 5 am on Sunday, 5 August 1888 Bertha and the two boys set out from the family home in Mannheim in her husband's car. They drove to Pforzheim, some 66 miles to the south.

This story has been told and retold so many times with so many added layers of myth and marketing that it is difficult to be sure of some of the details. Was the trip, for example, Bertha's idea or the boys'? Was Bertha even driving when the car left Mannheim?

Such minor uncertainties, however, cannot diminish the importance of this moment or, rather, the idea of this moment. This was the first long-distance road trip in what we would now call a car – an automobile with a four-stroke internal-combustion engine. Again, incontestably, Bertha is the heroine of this story, pushing the machine uphill, fixing it on the road and, in the process, proving herself a gifted engineer. But this was not merely the first road trip;

it was the first answer to the question what is a car for. Her answer was to visit relatives.

Karl is said to have known nothing of the plan until, on rising, he found a note telling him what they had done. He was horrified. Both Richard and Eugen could drive but neither had been allowed to do so unless accompanied by their father or his foreman. There were also potentially serious religious and legal issues. The Vatican had declared that an automobile was a devil's or witch's carriage; people were advised not even to look at such a machine. In addition, the Grand Duchy of Baden had banned any such machine from public roads and police had been stationed outside Karl's home and workshop, forcing Bertha to leave by an alley at the rear. Karl would later negotiate a deal whereby he could drive at 3.7 mph inside Mannheim's city limits and 7.5 mph outside.

When Bertha telegraphed news of their arrival in Pforzheim, Karl begged them to return. A few days later they drove all the way back to Mannheim, this time avoiding the steep inclines which, on the southward journey, had reduced them to pushing the car. The round-trip distance was astounding – 120 miles at a time when most automobiles had managed little more than a few yards.

Bertha's talent for foresight and planning served her well on the journey. The engine of the Mark III developed a mere 2 horsepower (hp) and attained a maximum speed of 10 mph; nevertheless, the car only managed 25 miles per gallon. As the capacity of the fuel tank was just 1.3 gallons, it was clear they would have to refuel. Bertha seems to have anticipated this and, at Wiesloch, 20 miles south of Mannheim, she persuaded the local chemist – Herr Ockel at the Stadt Apotheke – to sell her a large quantity of ligroin, a form of petrol then used for cleaning. The Stadt Apotheke is still celebrated as the world's first filling station.

Further south it became clear that the brakes – simple wooden blocks – were failing because the wood had been polished by use to a frictionless sheen. Bertha stopped at a shoemaker and bought some leather which she attached to the blocks. She thus invented the brake pad. A failing drive chain, meanwhile, was fixed by a local black-smith. She used a hat pin to unblock the fuel line and her garter to insulate the frayed wire to the spark plug. The cooling system was evaporative, which meant it had to be continually replenished from rivers and streams.

The trip was, in short, a frenzy of improvisation and invention. Nevertheless, as proof that a horseless carriage could work it was conclusive. When Karl's car subsequently appeared at the Munich Imperial Exhibition, it was a sensation. After the failure of a static display to attract much attention at the Paris Exhibition in 1887, he knew he had to show the car in motion. After some wrangling with the Munich police, who initially refused him permission to drive around their streets, it was agreed that if he drove no more than two hours a day, the police would do nothing to enforce the local law.

Everywhere his car went a crowd followed, as the *Münchener Tageblatt* reported: 'Without any sign of steam or other visible means of propulsion, human or otherwise, the vehicle proceeded on its way without difficulty, taking all the corners and avoiding all on-coming traffic and pedestrians. It was followed by a great crowd of breathless pedestrians, and the astonishment of everyone can easily be imagined.'

This urban astonishment contrasts markedly with the reported responses of rural folk suddenly exposed to Karl's Motorwagen. Children fled screaming from their houses with mothers dashing after them to save them from this clattering beast.

Along Bertha's route some might have heard of Karl Benz's machine – apparently the blacksmith who fixed the drive chain had heard of it and he was very excited to get a chance to work on the car – but most would not. This majority would have been disorientated. How could this machine move? What was the infernal noise it made, that explosive chatter? And why was a woman driving it? No wonder Catholics spoke of devilry and witchcraft. Even to the most secular minds it would have seemed like magic and to the most thoughtful it would be a sign that their way of life was coming to an end, that they were about to be absorbed into a larger world of which they knew, as yet, nothing.

4

Perhaps as a result of this sensation, the car's predecessor, the Mark I Benz Patent-Motorwagen which Karl built in 1885, became known as the first proper car. But though Daimler and Maybach might not have been credited with being the first, the character of these men determined the motoring future. Benz was a cautious man, reluctant to innovate. Daimler was an engineer and entrepreneur. He said 'The best or nothing at all' and he seems to have meant it. Along with Maybach, he went on to create a succession of ever better cars until his death in 1900. In 1901, with Daimler's son Paul, Maybach built the first car named Mercedes – the 35hp – the architecture of which laid down the basic plan of most future cars.

Nevertheless, Nixon's conclusion on the basis of engineering and biographical evidence was that Karl Benz was indeed the inventor of the car as we now know it. This is helpfully reinforced by the fact that Benz's company was merged with the one founded by Daimler to form Daimler-Benz in 1926. Daimler had, since 1900, been regarded as too Germanic sounding so, from 1901, the company's boss, Emil Jellinek, named the cars after his 12-year-old daughter Mercédès. This brand name continued after the merger.

And so the mighty Mercedes-Benz can now claim ownership of Bertha's road trip and, through lavish corporate videos, entrench the status of the Patent-Motorwagen as the first motor car. Would Karl now be regarded as the maker of the first car if Bertha had not driven to Pforzheim? Perhaps not. The engineering justification of Karl's primacy is not quite enough; it is the story of Bertha that seals the deal.

Bertha Benz long outlived her husband and she went on to claim her central role in the invention of the car. 'Before me,' she said, 'no automobile existed.'

5

It wasn't true. If Bertha had said 'car' she would have had a point, but automobiles, meaning self-propelled machines, had been around for some time. Indeed, the ancient Greeks could have got there first if they had adapted Hero of Alexandria's *aeolopile* – a sphere full of water that spun when heated as the steam escaped from two jets – to create forward motion. Centuries later somebody finally did this. The polymath Ferdinand Verbiest, a Flemish Jesuit missionary, built an *aeolopile*-powered toy trolley for the Chinese emperor Chien Lung in 1672. The steam jets drove a turbine which in turn drove a pair of wheels. With one load of coal it could run for an hour but, sadly, it was only 65 centimetres long and so incapable of bearing a driver or passengers.

Forty years later, in 1712, the Industrial Revolution was launched when Thomas Newcomen developed a steam-powered pump to clear tin and coal mines of water. The world was catapulted into the great technological acceleration amidst which we still live and into the geological epoch known as the Anthropocene. For 200 years this acceleration was to be powered almost exclusively by steam.

In France in 1770 Nicolas-Joseph Cugnot, an army officer, built yet another vehicle with a reasonable claim to be the first automobile. His *fardier à vapeur* – steam wagon – was a monstrous three-wheeler that managed about 2.5 mph and had to stop every 15 minutes to generate more steam. It was wildly unstable, an attribute which earned it the honour of being the first automobile to be involved in an accident when the *fardier* collided with a stone wall.

Never mind, steam seemed to be the future. Starting with Richard Trevithick's elegant steam carriage in 1802, the first half of the nineteenth century produced a menagerie of not so elegant steam vehicles, including Dr Church's steam coach of 1833, described by historian Rodney Dale as 'a marvellous construction, in outline and ornamentation something between a gypsy van, a merry-go-round and a ship's saloon'.

The evidently highly creative and energetic business of steam-powered, road-going automobiles was, however, snuffed out in Britain by government meddling in the form of road tolls. Parliament also passed the disastrous Locomotive Act of 1865, known as the Red Flag Act. This restricted the speed of self-propelled vehicles to 4 mph in the country and 2 mph in the town. In addition, a man with a red flag would also be required to walk in front to alert pedestrians and keep the way clear of horses and carriages. The speed limits were lifted by acts in 1896 and 1903 but by then the damage to the British car industry had been done. Germany was to be the father of the car, as Karl Benz put it, and France – or Bertha – the mother.

Steam was joined by electricity in the 1880s. In 1888 Walter Bersey, the Elon Musk of his day, developed a new form of battery that powered an electric bus. He went on to create an electric taxi service in London. In 1899 a fabulously named, rocket-shaped electric car – La Jamais Contente – driven by the Belgian Camille Jenatzy, known as Le Diable Rouge, became the first road vehicle to exceed 100 kilometres per hour.

As David Nye observes in his book *America's Assembly Line*, even as late as 1900 internal combustion seemed to be a distant third in the automobile race. Only 20 per cent of the 5,000 cars in the USA were powered by petrol; the rest were electric or steam-powered – 'Only in retrospect does the victor in this contest seem obvious.'

In 1906 a Stanley Steamer – produced by two brothers who had switched from photography to automobiles – set another world record. On Ormond Beach in Florida they hit 127.7 mph, a record not broken by any automobile until 1911 and by a steam car until 2009 when the British-built Inspiration – a 7.6-metre-long, three-ton machine – reached 151 mph at Edwards Air Force Base in California.

In America steam cars outnumbered any other form of self-propelled vehicles in the early 1900s and steam production continued through the twenties. The last private steam car was the 1932 Doble Model F, capable of 90 mph.

Through it all, ICE made steady gains. By early 1908 *Cycle and Automobile Journal* reported there were 166 makers of 'pleasure' – i.e., non-commercial – automobiles in America, 151 of which were making ICE cars, 11 electric and four steam.

As sociologist Rudi Volti has suggested, the advantages of ICE cars were not purely technical, they were 'social, cultural, and even psychological'. His point is that early automobiles were not meant to provide everyday transportation – 'They were all sports car in the sense that speed, adventure, and the appeal of technological novelty were among their key attractions.' Electric cars were neither exciting nor adventurous and were, in any case, seen as cars for ladies.

Steam cars, meanwhile, required intimidatingly high levels of vigilance from the driver which perhaps made them a little too exciting and adventurous. ICE was the compromise choice and by 1910 it had triumphed.

Even narrowing the field down to that one form of propulsion does not make it any easier to unmask any competitors that might unseat Karl Benz. There were a number of convincing mid-nineteenth-century contenders – notably from Étienne Lenoir and Alphonse Beau de Rochas in France. The latter worked out the principle of the four-stroke engine in 1861, 16 years before Nicolaus Otto patented the idea in Germany and won historic naming rights.

The Otto Cycle, which should be known as the Rochas Cycle, is still the driving principle of most cars in the world. In a two-stroke engine the piston compresses the fuel–air mixture and then both ejects the exhaust and draws in the fuel in the down stroke. In a four-stroke engine the fuel is drawn in, compressed, ignited and exhausted in four separate strokes.

Meanwhile, in 1863 Lenoir's internal-combustion-powered, perversely named Hippomobile – horse carriage – was driven from Paris to Joinville and back, a round-trip distance of 22 kilometres. This is a strong claimant and, indeed, a month before his death in July 1900 Lenoir received an award from the Automobile Club de France that credited him with being the 'builder of the first car in the world'.

Even earlier there was an Englishman, Samuel Brown, who had road-tested a vehicle with a 'gas vacuum' – i.e., internal-combustion – engine by driving it up Shooters Hill in south-east London in 1826.

Most poignantly there was Siegfried Marcus in Austria. He has often been said to be the true inventor of the modern automobile. At the 1898 Vienna Commercial Exhibition it was clearly stated that his first car was made in 1877. Much later, this was in fact exposed as a non-steerable handcart.

His claim has never really caught the imagination. First, though an engineer of genius, he was destructively prolific. He was granted 38 patents between 1857 and 1896 – these included a fast solidifying compound for filling teeth – and he was, among other things, a dentist. Having invented something, he tended to move on. 'He lacked,' as one motor historian put it, 'grit and determination.'

The second reason was that he was a Jew. Until March 1938 Marcus was routinely celebrated in Austria as the inventor of the automobile. In that month Nazi Germany annexed Austria and he was removed from history. The Reich Ministry of Public Enlightenment and Propaganda ordered that henceforth reference books were 'to refer to the two German engineers Gottlieb Daimler and Karl Benz as the creators of the modern automobile, not to Siegfried Marcus'.

The rediscovery of the second vehicle that Marcus built in 1950 restored his reputation, not least because it worked. But his claim to be the inventor of the automobile is invalidated because this machine seems to have originated in 1888.

So who really was first? Was there a predecessor to Benz's tricycle? It is hard to say. There were too many contenders and so many different engineering issues to be resolved. As a result, the creation of the car does not look like a flash of genius but like a film of an explosion, reversed and in slow motion. Somehow, from the chaos of smoke and inwardly accelerating parts, the car emerges.

Perhaps it is simplest to agree with the American engineering academic John Lienhard that 'no one person invented the automobile'. The car is a fortuitous compound of parts refined by many inventors and engineers.

For a later generation of automobilists, a generation that had glimpsed the monstrous scale of the car's ascendancy, this was frustrating. It certainly frustrated one of the most stylish and informed of all motor writers, St John C. Nixon. A natural storyteller himself, he *needed* an inventor, a clear human origin of the story of modernity's greatest invention. He worked on the assumption that justice required the existence of such a being. Writing in 1936 he expressed his astonishment that nobody seemed to care about the inventor of the car, the machine that had 'revolutionised the whole face of human existence as perhaps no other scientific invention in this or in any other age'.

And so he anointed not only the inventor of the first true car, Karl Benz, he also placed what he considered the first true driver, Bertha, on a pedestal where she remains to this day.

6

Stepping back from the characters, claims and confusions of these early years, a much larger picture emerges of the birth of the car. Context is everything and it is perhaps more truthful to say that the car was an invention not of a person but of an era, of a time, the late nineteenth century, of two countries, France and Germany, and of a culture, modernism. The era was La Belle Époque, which overlapped with the American Gilded Age. Both were products of peace and plenty – economies were growing rapidly as industrialisation spread. But the car came a decade later to the USA, so its early years were entirely European.

Like the equivalent English term, Golden Age, La Belle Époque is

almost always used nostalgically. It covers the period between the end
of the Franco-Prussian War in 1871 and the start of the First World
War in 1914. From the perspective of that empire-shattering carnage, La Belle Époque would indeed have looked like a lost paradise.
The empires of Europe were still intact; in the arts and philosophy,
especially in Paris, there was a frenzy of innovation and a seemingly
unending supply of creative genius; peace, at least at home in rich
Europe, reigned; finally, and most importantly, a second Industrial
Revolution seemed to be under way. This was all accompanied and
celebrated by a cultural frenzy.

Bertha's ride was a modernist act. The artistic and philosophical
fireworks of La Belle Époque were the birth pangs of the artistic,
literary, political, scientific and cultural movement we now call modernism. This movement still dominates our ways of thinking. Like
the Renaissance, modernism's scale and variety make it impossible
to define with any precision, but certain themes are clear and all of
them were in the air when Bertha and the boys set off for Pforzheim.

In that same year, 1888, Friedrich Nietzsche wrote *The Antichrist*,
the most brutal and brilliant assault on Christianity. This was, in
part, inspired by that bible of modernity, Charles Darwin's *Origin
of Species*, published in 1859, which showed humanity's kinship
with animals.

'We no longer derive man from "spirit," from "godhead,"'
Nietzsche wrote, 'we have put him back among the animals. We
regard him as the strongest animal because he is the most cunning:
his intellectuality is a consequence thereof.'

Claude Monet had, five years earlier, moved into his house in
Giverny where, with his paintings of water lilies, he called into question what and how we see and know. Three years earlier Georges
Seurat had painted his pointillist masterpiece *A Sunday Afternoon
on the Island of La Grande Jatte*, a painting derived in part from
the science of colour but which also seemed to show a social world
frozen in time as if waiting for something to happen. And it was no
accident that, in 1863, the artists – among them, Courbet, Manet
and Pissarro – whose work had been rejected by the Paris Salon
called their alternative exhibition the Salon des Refusés (exhibition
of the rejected).

A decade earlier Otto von Bismarck had united Germany, creating
the state that would dominate the European politics of the twentieth

century. America, the state that would dominate the world after 1918, was absorbing immigrants and conquering the native lands to the west. US industrial supremacy was already casting its shadow over British imperial power and would, from 1908, overthrow European dominance of the car industry.

Between 1850 and his death in 1879 the great Scottish physicist James Clerk Maxwell had laid the foundations of the modernist physics of quantum theory and relativity, both of which, like the lilies of Monet and the brutal atheism of Nietzsche, revealed a world beyond our conventions of seeing and knowing.

Sigmund Freud was working on 'nervous disorders' and was soon to publish *Studies on Hysteria and the Interpretation of Dreams*. We knew little of this new world and, Freud showed, even less of ourselves.

Karl Marx died in 1883 having written *Das Kapital* and, with Friedrich Engels, *The Communist Manifesto*, the handbooks for twentieth-century revolutionaries.

Photography was well established by the time Bertha set off. In the same year as her ride, Louis Aimé Augustin le Prince had made the first moving pictures. The car and the cinema were siblings – they grew up together, nurtured by technology.

In 1886 Fyodor Dostoevsky published his last masterpiece, *The Brothers Karamazov*, a prolonged wrestling match with the Christian faith that Nietzsche, two years later, was to condemn as the religion of cowards. In 1888 Henry James published *The Aspern Papers*, one of his greatest works, and, on 26 September, T.S. Eliot was born. In 1922 he was to publish his masterpiece, *The Waste Land*, the ultimate expression of the anguish of literary modernism.

As Bertha deployed her garter as insulation and invented brake pads ancient certainties were being abandoned just as the horses were soon to be made redundant by cars. The salons, the academies, all the taste-dictating institutions were being overthrown by modernists of genius. It was a dizzying and ecstatic but alarming moment. The world seemed to be casting off from its moorings and setting out for uncharted waters.

History is chaos and any event can be connected to any other event. But, in the present, we know things the inhabitants of the past did not. Today we can see that Bertha stole Karl's car as modernism was being born. We can also see that modernism made the world in which we live and that it was dominated by one technology more than any other – cars.

Cars made movement the new age's sorcery. Speeding through a landscape created new ways of seeing and being that were celebrated in impassioned paintings by the Italian futurists of the early twentieth century. Seurat's frozen figures took to the road and then to the air after the Wright Brothers showed it was possible in 1903. What was available to be seen – not just places but perspectives – was expanding. And, thanks to the open road rather than the fixed railways, such seeing would eventually be available to millions.

The futurist painters were right: the car was indeed the supreme expression of modernism and it was to keep that role for more than a century. But, like modernism, the car was Janus-faced. Some forms of modernism – notably in the visual arts, especially architecture – were wildly optimistic; others – primarily literature – were predominantly pessimistic. The pessimists saw the darkness that lay beneath modernism. They saw the loss of a transcendent religious world and its replacement by an unconsoling materialism. Matthew Arnold, in his poem 'Dover Beach', saw this loss as 'a melancholy, long, withdrawing roar'. The immaterial realm of meaning and purpose had gone to be replaced by the material flames of modernism.

Either there was enthusiasm for the new world that was sweeping away the old or there was anxiety about the nature of this world, an anxiety that was to be vindicated by two world wars in the twentieth century, both the most murderous in history and both products of modernism. Equally, the car has been seen as a force of creation and destruction, a liberation or a revelation of the limitations of human power over nature.

But the car, even in the form of Bertha's wild ride, was not the sole precursor of a new way of life, of modernist movement and speed-blurred landscapes. It was preceded by one unconditionally optimistic modernist device.

7

The son of the inventor of the Maxim gun and early automobile maker Hiram Percy Maxim, in his book *Horseless Carriage Days*, published in 1936, asked himself why cars had not emerged before

1880. His answer was that there had not been enough bicycles around to demonstrate the joys of swift and free movement. In other words, the car needed more than technology; it needed an idea, a purpose, a justification for its existence. The bicycle provided that idea.

To modern minds, the Benz Patent-Motorwagen may be the first car but it does not look like a car; it appears to be nothing more than a rather large tricycle, a machine with two large rear wheels and one much smaller front wheel. Tricycling had been a craze in Britain in the 1870s – these machines felt safer and more comfortable than the penny-farthing bicycles, the 'high-wheelers', favoured by the young and fashionable.

Benz evidently preferred this format to the horse-drawn carriages on which Daimler was to hang his drive trains, perhaps thinking he was being more modern. The horse-drawn carriage was an ancient vehicle; the bicycle was not. In truth, the bicycle is the true fore-runner of the car – not mechanically but imaginatively. It planted the idea of free individual movement along open roads in the public imagination.

One crucial side effect of the bicycle craze of the 1890s was a rise in popular demand for better roads. In the eighteenth century the French had led the way with plans for a national highway network for military purposes. The British followed in the early nineteenth century when two great Scottish engineers – Thomas Telford and John McAdam – devised new ways of creating smooth road sur-faces. The road-building programme that should have ensued, how-ever, ran out of, so to speak, steam with the advent of railways. But good British roads returned as a cause when it became clear that cyclists needed them.

The bike, strangely, was, like the car, introduced to the world in Mannheim. As with the car, it has uncredited and possibly fraudu-lent predecessors.

The first verifiable bicycle was made by Baron Karl von Drais in 1817. Drais was, like Siegfried Marcus, a prolific and formidable inventor. He built the first typewriter, the first meat grinder, a peri-scope and a stenograph machine. But his name lives on because of the bike. One attractive theory is that he invented his machine after his experience in 1816, the 'Year without a Summer'.

The dreary weather was caused by the eruption of Mount Tam-bora in the Dutch East Indies in April of the previous year. This darkened the skies around the world and the baron's horses died of starvation thanks to the ensuing crop failure. Thousands of horses were slaughtered to save food for humans. It was, symbolically if not actually, the beginning of the end of the horse.

Drais determined to create an alternative form of transport – 'a machine sparing horses and their costs'. In this he was a modern man, a child of the Enlightenment. The pre-Enlightenment mind would have tended to shrug off the misfortune of Tambora and blame God; the post-Enlightenment mind decided to do something about it. Unlike God, of course, such a mind could do absolutely nothing about volcanos.

Drais's solution was the *Laufmaschine* (running machine) which he unleashed on Mannheim on 12 June 1817. He rode about 8 miles at 5 or 6 mph. The machine was steerable and had two wheels and it was propelled not by pedals but by the rider's striding feet. It was a success, but there was a problem. Horse-drawn carriage wheels had cut deep channels in the road, making balance for cyclists difficult or impossible. They took to the pavements, endangering pedestrians. As a result, several cities – Milan, London, New York, Calcutta – banned the *Laufmaschine*.

Drais, a revolutionary liberal and an adventurer, fled Baden for Brazil for political reasons in 1822, returning to Mannheim five years later. He subsequently renounced his title in the name of the revolution and died in poverty in a house that was, astonishingly, perhaps providentially, two blocks away from the home of Karl Benz.

The dandy horse, as the *Laufmaschine* came to be known in English, was certainly a breakthrough, in that it showed balancing on two spinning wheels was possible, but the bicycle was not to attain maturity until the appearance in Coventry of John Kemp Starley's Rover Safety Bicycle in 1885, the same year that Karl Benz produced his Mark I Benz Patent-Motorwagen. This was more or less the bike as we now know it and it was – and is – a sensation.

Cars of the time – and for many years afterwards – now look distinctively antique. Starley's Rover in its final form looks both familiarly contemporary and strikingly elegant. It has a lean, leaping, spidery look with high handlebars, a steerable front wheel, two equally sized wheels and a chain drive to the rear wheel. In purely aesthetic terms it is closer to a modern Ferrari than to anything produced by Daimler or Benz.

The word 'safety' in the name of this machine was crucial. The previous, most popular form of the bicycle was the penny-farthing, the enormous front wheel of which made every pedal stroke more effective. Standard bikes have a wheel diameter of around 0.7 metres; the front wheel of a penny-farthing was typically 1.5 metres across. This more than doubles the top speed from 8 mph to 17.5 mph. On the other hand it caused terrible injuries if the rider fell off, as many did. The Rover solved the problem of gearing up the rider's pedal strike not with an enormous wheel but with a pedalled gear that was larger than the gear driving the wheel.

The Rover was a huge success and it launched a worldwide boom in bike sales. Again, the history of the imagination trumps that of engineering. The bike opened new vistas of the eyes and the mind, but also of human possibility.

'Every time I see an adult on a bicycle, I no longer despair for the future of the human race,' said the novelist, commentator and, at the time, optimistic modernist H.G. Wells. Wells also wrote a novel on the subject, *The Wheels of Chance: A Bicycling Idyll* (1896), in which the hero – a gauche young shop assistant named Hoopdriver – spends his holiday on 'a great cycling tour along the Southern Coast'. The timid Hoopdriver is freed by the ecstasy of movement, the joy of gliding through an English phantasmagoria:

> There were miles of this, scores of miles of this before him, pine-wood and oak forest, purple, heathery moorland and grassy down, lush meadows, where shining rivers wound their lazy way, villages with square-towered, flint churches, and rambling, cheap, and hearty inns, clean, white, country towns, long downhill stretches, where one might ride at one's ease (overlooking a jolt or so), and far away, at the end of it all, — the sea.

Note the quasi-cinematic style of the description; the spectacle unrolls like a film strip. It is the movement of modernity.

With the car still in its slow and noisy infancy, this was, as Wells saw, a portent of the future – fast and free movement available to the masses. Railways might have provided the sense of speed and the cinematic movement of the passing scene but they could not provide the freedom. Railway engines could carry tons of coal and a substantial external fire but no efficient, rapid and manoeuvrable vehicle could have emerged from such technology. For a brief, shining moment the bicycle was the supreme liberator. The bike went far beyond the horse or the train. It was freedom. But the car could do better.

8

Just as Wells was writing *The Wheels of Chance*, the car in Britain was preparing to free itself of Parliament's frenzied attempts to legislate the future out of existence. Those 'Red Flag' acts had put punitive speed limits on any horseless vehicle and stipulated a man with a red flag should precede them. It has been suggested that the British love of animals was the inspiration for these ruinous pro-horse laws. This is unlikely; horses, at the time, were treated appallingly. More plausibly, the motoring journalist L.J.K. Setright suggested it was something more sinister. Parliament was packed with MPs with shares in railway companies who feared the effects of the car on their investments.

The first flamboyant sign that Britain was ready to embrace the automotive age came when the Hon. Evelyn Ellis, formerly of the British Embassy in Brussels, imported a rather fine Panhard Levassor, sometimes claimed, improbably, to be the first car seen in England. By boat and train it had arrived in Micheldever in Hampshire from where Ellis drove it in July 1895 to Datchet, now in Berkshire, then in Buckinghamshire, a journey of, at the time, 56 miles which took 5 hours 32 minutes.

'Cyclists,' reported Frederick Simms, the engineer who accompanied Ellis, 'would stop to gaze enviously at us as we surmounted with ease some long hill.'

In 1878 the man in front had been relieved of the necessity of carrying a red flag, but the damage was done. The acts crushed British steam power and held its engineers back from competing with French and German car makers for the crucial decade from 1885. Finally, in 1896, the year after Ellis's grand gesture, the Locomotives and Highways Act introduced a 12 mph speed limit – though local authorities were given the power to go up to 16 mph. Among the motoring classes, this was called the 'Emancipation Act' and a celebration drive was promptly organised.

On the foggy, damp morning of 14 November 1896, a multitude of petrol heads assembled for a celebration breakfast in London. It was organised by one Harry John Lawson (more of him later). A red flag was symbolically torn apart. Nevertheless, safety remained important to the organisers, not for the health of the public but for the health of the motor industry – 'Owners and drivers should remember that motor cars are on trial in England and that any rashness or carelessness might injure the industry in this country.'

Meanwhile, the cars were being prepared. A witness, Charles Jarrott, described the scene:

French mechanics and German inventors, with enthusiasts of all nationalities, were mixed up in indescribable confusion. Huge flares were being carried about from one machine to another to assist in lighting up the burners for the cars, which at that time were innocent of electric ignition. An occasional petrol blaze was seen through the fog which filled the hall, making the scene resemble a veritable inferno. In addition to this, the noise from the motors, which, after desperate efforts, the various persons interested had succeeded in getting started, prevented the merely human voice from being heard.

The competitors then gathered at the Metropole Hotel at the corner of Northumberland Avenue and Whitehall Place and they set off on the first London to Brighton run at 10.30 am. This first one was entitled the 'Emancipation Run'. It survives as an annual event – the London to Brighton Veteran Run.

What happened next has been muddled by conflicting accounts. Some entrants, far from heading to Brighton, only intended to drive a short distance from the start. There were also rumours that some cars were transported on a train, being spattered before they arrived with cosmetic mud. Exactly who started and how many legitimately finished has proved, I was told by the Veteran Car Club of Great Britain, 'an impossible task for historians'.

Apart from the cheating, quite a few cars failed to start and Jarrott recalled seeing a miserable and violently inclined French mechanic 'keeping off the crowd with the aid of a particularly vicious and formidable-looking starting-handle'.

At Reigate, roughly the midpoint of the run, an enterprising wheelwright had put up a sign that read 'Motor-Cars repaired while you wait'. The breakdowns and the limited number of finishers damped the ardour of the crowd, many of whom had seemed to believe that 'horses would be superseded forthwith'. Far from it; horse dealers and saddlers 'relapsed into placid contentment'.

The official programme listed 58 starters but some say only 33 actually began, perhaps the remainder having failed to start. The two most significant – and generally agreed upon – finishers were two Duryea 'carriages' listed in the programme. Driven by the brothers Frank and Charles Duryea, these were built in Springfield, Massachusetts. It was the first appearance of American cars in Europe.

In the American journal *The Horseless Age* it was noted that the British had been sneering at the quality of American cars. 'The record of the Duryea wagon in the London-Brighton outing is a sufficient commentary on that,' the *Age* sneered back.

It was, indeed, sufficient. In four years it would be the twentieth – the American – century and in twelve years the world would be overrun by Ford Model Ts. The 1896 London to Brighton Run might not have killed the horse. But it certainly introduced the world to its American executioners.

9

Sadly, the run failed to announce the arrival of Britain as a significant car manufacturer. In 1900 France produced 4,800 cars, America 4,192, Germany 800 and Britain 150. This was in spite of the best efforts of the run's organiser, Harry John Lawson, who, being only 5 feet tall, was known as the Little Man.

A whole range of famous British car brands – Humber, Sunbeam, Singer, Rover and Hillman – had emerged from the British bicycle business. Rover cars were the direct descendant of John Kemp Starley's Rover Safety Bicycle. Lawson was no different. He had invested in numerous cycle companies before establishing the British Motor Syndicate in 1895. His plan was, as a motor writer named Herbert Osbaldeston Duncan put it, to 'corner the British side of the motor industry by buying up all past, present and future patents in the expectation of running across some "master" patents'.

This was a terrible business plan not least because Little Harry was so desperate for patents that he kept paying over the odds. He was said to have 'paid away £10,000 as the ordinary man would a £5 note'. But he did at least help to establish Coventry as Britain's Detroit by buying the Coventry-based Daimler Motor Company, which owned the right to produce Daimlers in Britain, from Frederick Simms. The company had, when bought by Lawson, not produced a single car. In fact, neither he nor Simms seemed to have much interest in actually making cars – an omen of the difficulties that were to beset the British industry 50 and more years later.

Lawson's company became the British Motor Syndicate and in 1896, with characteristic impetuosity, he declared a first dividend of 10 per cent, explaining that 'The public has begun, however slowly, to wake up to the fact that a horseless carriage is a necessity.' He was boundlessly optimistic: 'We are celebrating the birthday of the most wonderful industries that God ever blessed mankind with . . . each large town will have its own manufactories, and Nottingham carriages will vie with Birmingham carriages for lightness, elegance and speed.'

It was bound to come unstuck and it finally did in 1904 when Lawson received a 12-month sentence for fraud. He died in 1925 leaving behind just £99.

Luckily, there were real engineers and businessmen on hand to rescue the British industry from this mess, notably Frederick Lanchester – once described as 'the most accomplished gentleman ever to be wasted on the motor industry' – and Herbert Austin, who, remarked historian Jonathan Wood, 'was never slow to ignore any idea, particularly if it belonged to someone else'. In fact, the first car he built – in 1896, which had rapidly become an *annus mirabilis* for British motoring – was a straight copy of Léon Bollée's *voiturette* (miniature car), which had appeared in the previous year. It was a demonstration vehicle and would, if sold, have infringed a whole range of Bollée patents. These patents were bought up, like everything else, by Lawson's British Motor Syndicate.

Austin, who had fled boredom at home in Yorkshire by decamping to Australia with his uncle, arrived at cars via sheep. There he met Frederick Wolseley, patent holder of a sheep-shearing machine of dubious utility. The company making this troublesome device was transferred to London in 1889 and Austin, now with a reputation for engineering and design, was made general manager. In this role he was forced to accept a deluge of defective parts for the shearing machine.

One thing led to another and, having proved his point with the *voiturette* and with Wolseley having resigned, he talked the company into making cars. He came up with the Wolseley Autocar Number One, which looked like an elongated Benz Patent-Motorwagen. But, crucially, he also came up with a four-wheeler just in time for the Automobile Club of Great Britain's One Thousand Mile Trial in 1900 – 'an attempt to demonstrate that the motor car was not merely the toy of the wealthy dilettante . . . but a commercial reality capable of accomplishing long distances day after day' as *Motoring Annual* described it.

This was another attempt, rather more successful than the 1896 London to Brighton Run, to convince the British people to give up their horses. The course ran from London to Edinburgh and back. There were 83 entries and 65 starters; 35 – a surprisingly high number – made it back to London. A Wolseley, driven by Austin, won a prize from the *Daily Mail* for being first in the *voiturette* class.

Austin's car ambitions having become too much for the sheep shearers, he left to become a manager at Wolseley Tool and Motor Car Company created by the Vickers engineering group. This also went wrong. Vickers grew impatient with Austin's stubborn attachment to his increasingly outmoded engineering. He left in 1905 to form the Austin Motor Company at Longbridge just outside Birmingham. This was Austin's apotheosis. He died in 1941 but the company endured as a key pillar of British car manufacturing until it collectively chose to commit suicide.

The problem was inward-looking complacency. In 1945 Sir Stafford Cripps, the new and very left-wing president of the Board of Trade, lectured car makers on the necessity of exporting 50 per cent of British cars, the country at the time being catastrophically broke. 'Poppycock' and 'tripe' cried the complacent ones to which Cripps responded, 'I have often wondered whether you thought that Great Britain was here to support the motor industry, or the industry was here to support Great Britain. I gather from your cries that you think it is the former.' He was more right than anybody could have imagined at the time.

Nevertheless, in 1932 the UK overtook France as the world's largest car maker and in 1950 she overtook America as the world's largest car exporter. One early sign that this was all going to fall apart was the merger of Austin with Morris Motors in 1952 to form the British Motor Corporation. From there it was all downhill. BMC became the British Leyland Motor Corporation in 1968. This produced excruciatingly awful cars like the Morris Marina and the Austin Allegro in the brief interludes of peace in a prolonged war between management and trade unions. Government subsidy kept this automotive absurdity afloat, which meant, as Margaret Thatcher, echoing Cripps, pointed out in 1986, every family in Britain had been forced to give British Leyland £200. Thereafter Britain continued to mass-produce cars but almost entirely under foreign ownership.

But there was a benign legacy from those early years – local British engineering genius and excellence. The first was represented by Frederick Lanchester, a terrible businessman but a physicist, singer and poet as well as an engineer. His range of inventions were spectacular – notably, he invented the torsional vibration damper, which made six-cylinder engines possible. That and a whole range of other innovations are still in use to this day. He died in 1946 – 'blind, childless and, for a time, forgotten', in the words of Peter King.

Excellence was represented by Henry Royce, who, in 1906 in partnership with Charles Rolls, produced a chassis that became the foundation, a year later, of the Rolls-Royce Silver Ghost, named by *Autocar* magazine as 'the best car in the world'. More of the Ghost later.

10

Even as late – in automotive terms – as the turn of the century the roads of the United States were among the worst in the world. Fewer than 9 per cent were surfaced, usually by a layer of gravel. The rest were dust which turned into mud after rain and into frozen ruts in winter. French and German roads, in contrast, were the best in the world.

The state of American roads had been a hot political issue even before the arrival of the car. The Good Roads Movement had been founded in 1880, primarily for cyclists. It became the National League for Good Roads at a meeting in Chicago in 1892. A journal

– *Good Roads Magazine* – was published and a pamphlet addressed to farmers.

'You will agree with me that your roads are bad,' wrote the pamphleteer Isaac B. Potter. 'You may not know they are the very worst in the world; but you have never seen or heard of worse ones; nor, alas, perhaps of better.'

A hero of this movement emerged in the form of Horatio 'Good Roads' Earle. He became Michigan's first state highway commissioner. He promised to conquer the 'Mighty Monarch of Mud' and, in the end, he did.

Meanwhile, American car makers were a long way behind the French and the Germans. Seven years after Karl Benz patented his first car and five years after his wife's road trip the first American gasoline car company was established. This was the Duryea Motor Wagon Company in Springfield, Massachusetts. Soon after the company was formed, the *New York Times* reported that something astonishing had happened on the streets of Springfield: 'A horseless carriage – so-called because it has power of locomotion independent of horse or any other beast – is to be seen almost any day in Springfield's streets. That [it] is practicable and serviceable is shown by the fact that it has made four long trips from one city to another. It is the invention of C.E. and J.F. Duryea.'

The Duryea brothers had first built their 'Motor Wagon' and demonstrated it on Taylor Street in 1893. In fairness, this wasn't, as is often claimed, the first gasoline-powered car in America. The historian James Flink lists five cars that preceded the Motor Wagon – but these 'made no lasting contribution to the implementation of the automotive idea in America'.

The Duryeas had been inspired by an article in the *Scientific American* magazine about Karl Benz's car. The *New York Times* report, two years later, was probably based on the news of the establishment of the Duryea Motor Wagon Company.

'The Messrs. Duryea,' concluded the article, 'are confident of getting their machine taken up by capitalists in a short time, and expect in a few days or weeks to consummate a deal by which it will be put on the market in a short time. They think that many machines of the kind will be made in the country before long.'

Their confidence was overstated. By 1898 the Duryeas had produced only 13 cars for sale; Benz sold 600 cars in 1899. But in 1895 the brothers were not alone, though internal combustion did not yet dominate the market. A leading automobile maker of the time was Locomobile, which made only steam-powered vehicles before it switched to ICE in 1903.

Nevertheless, in 1895 enough basic cars were being produced to stage the first ever motor race on American soil – the *Chicago Times-Herald* Race. It was on a 52-mile course on the Chicago lakeshore. There were 83 entries, but only six turned up – four cars and two motorcycles. The first attempt was disrupted by police officers who would not allow two of the cars to be driven into the city – they had to be towed in by horses.

The race was finally run on 28 November, Thanksgiving Day. There were three Benz cars, one of which dropped out after hitting a horse. Only two finished, the Duryea and, an hour and a half later, a Benz. In view of the poor weather – 38 degrees and snow drifts – the fact that anybody finished was hailed as a triumph of the car over the horse. Unfortunately, the winning Duryea, surely the first great American car, was later 'destroyed through a workman's misunderstanding'. The second-place car – a Benz driven by Hieronymus Mueller – survives in a museum in Decatur, Illinois, named after the driver.

For years afterwards many Americans persisted in believing that the Duryea brothers had built the first petrol-powered car. Indeed, when Charles Duryea died in 1938 the headline of the *New York Times* obituary said he was 'Credited With Building First "Gasoline Buggy"' and the intro proclaimed him the 'father of the automobile'.

In spite of this dubious display of American exceptionalism and in spite of the fact that it was, by European standards, primitively engineered, the Motor Wagon was a decent car. St John Nixon drove one in 1905 and pronounced himself 'much impressed by the suspension and general comfort'. But fraternal discord led to a break-up of the company. The brothers went their separate ways and Duryea was not to be the name of one of the great car corporations of America. Perhaps the Duryeas' problem was that they were not in Detroit.

11

Hazen S. Pingree was mayor of Detroit from 1889 to 1897. He became a hero of the Progressive Era, which lasted from 1896 to 1916, and was after his death named as one of the ten greatest mayors in American history. It was a period of reform and assaults on political corruption and corporate greed, of campaigns for women's suffrage and, for some, a chance to prohibit alcohol. Pingree did not support that last cause: rumours that he was a temperance supporter were dispelled by his insistence on drinking red-eye whiskey with the Irish voters. He was an avid reformer, raising the profile and the respectability of this port city. And, though he would not have known it, he laid the urban foundations of the greatest industrial system the world had ever seen. In that context his most percipient project may well have been the improvement of the city's streets, which the *Detroit Journal* had described as '150 miles of rotting, rutted, lumpy, dilapidated paving'. In summer a discarded cigar butt would cause the pitch and resin in the streets to catch fire. After Pingree, Detroit became a useable city for the creators of the American motor industry.

But I doubt that he met Henry Ford, who test-drove his first car in Detroit in 1896, nor knew of the city's first car-manufacturing plant, opened by Ransom Eli Olds in 1899. Pingree died in London of peritonitis at the age of 61.

Détroit is French for strait and the settlement was established as Fort Ponchartrain de Détroit by the French explorer Antoine de la Mothe Cadillac in 1701. It had previously been inhabited by the Native American Iroquois Confederacy. This theme of Frenchness persisted, as we shall see, all the way down to the naming of American car types and models. The British occupied Detroit in 1760 and it was taken from them by the Americans in 1796. In 1827 it adopted the not entirely confident city motto *Speramus eliora; resurget cineribus* – we hope for better days; it will arise from the ashes.

In fact, for Ransom Eli Olds that is exactly what happened. His original car company was established in another Michigan city, Lansing. But the company was bought by a copper miner named Samuel L. Smith, whom Olds met on the platform of Detroit station, on the condition that he moved to that city. The first factory was gutted by fire but rose from the ashes to manufacture one of the first great people's cars – the eccentrically named Curved Dash Oldsmobile, which was produced from 1901 to 1907.

Olds was a radical. He aimed for simplicity – a one-cylinder runabout weighing about 500 pounds and selling for $500 that could be easily repaired. In fact, the Curved Dash weighed 700 pounds and sold for $650. It was, nevertheless, a big success. The Curved Dash was a little gem of a car that could have made its creator a colossus of American motor supremacy before Henry Ford and Alfred Sloan.

The dash was the dashboard, a term taken from carriages for the board intended to protect driver and passengers from muck 'dashed' up or produced by the horses. Cars still being in thrall to carriage design at this date, dashboards were included and the one on Olds's car happened to be curved. So this great car was named after its most trivial design feature.

A test drive from Detroit to New York in less than eight days at once brought in 1,000 orders. Almost 20,000 were to be produced in total. In 1938, one George C. Green drove a 1904 model across the United States. In 1946 he did it again: 'It's the only car I have that knows the road. The others – you have to *steer* them.'

Olds and his Curved Dash were the great forerunners of the Detroit ascendancy. A year after production ended in 1907 everything changed. General Motors bought Olds Motor Works and Henry Ford launched the Model T.

12

Emil Jellinek was, like many car-crazy males in these stories, an extrovert and an adventurer. Born on 6 April 1853 in Leipzig but brought up in Vienna, he was the son of a distinguished rabbi. He performed poorly at school and he was a natural prankster. He was the family's black sheep; both his brothers were serious types, one becoming a linguist, the other a law teacher. Aged 17, he ran away from home and became an official on the State Railways. This ended badly when, aided by a driver, he stole a train.

Thanks to family connections, he entered the Austrian diplomatic service in Morocco and then Algeria, where he began to trade in tobacco. Settling in Oran, he married and fathered two boys. He moved back to Austria, where his daughter was born – Mercédès Adrienne Ramona Manuela Jellinek. He came to believe her first name brought him good luck and in 1903 he changed his own surname to Jellinek-Mercédès. *Mercedes* is the plural of the Spanish word *merced*, which means mercy.

I find the most reproduced photograph of him intensely moving. Decorated in assorted orders and honours of the Austro-Hungarian Empire, with a pince-nez and extravagantly waxed moustache, he looks like a character from a novel by two of his greatest compatriots, Stefan Zweig and Joseph Roth. The empire was dying and – perhaps this is my imagination – he seems to be wearing its regalia as a kind of nostalgic prank. Jellinek did, in fact, die in 1918, the same year that the empire was dissolved.

Appropriately, like Roth and Zweig, he became an exile. His diplomatic career – almost as inexplicable as his job on the railways – had led him to become, by accident or design, Consul General in Nice. There, with his family, he occupied a large mansion on the Promenade des Anglais, which he christened the Villa Mercédès, and he set up a car business. His enthusiasm for his daughter's name knew no bounds. He had a yacht called *Mercédès* and then a motorboat called *Mercédès W.N.* and, finally, another yacht, called *Mercédès II*.

With the start of the Great War it all began to fall apart for the great prankster. The French accused him of spying and seized all his assets. He fled to Geneva, where he died.

His daughter Mercédès was an aspirant Bohemian and very artistically inclined. Aged 20, she married Baron Karl von Schlosser at a grand ceremony in Nice. They had two children. When ruination in Nice loomed, they moved to Vienna, where Mercédès left her family and married another baron, this time a sculptor, Rudolf Weigl, a consumptive and a heavy drinker. He died soon after. Mercédès died of cancer, aged 39, in 1929. She was buried in Vienna next to her grandfather, Rabbi Adolf Jellinek.

In the midst of all this chaos, excess and catastrophe Emil was responsible for one of the world's most important cars, the one that settled the problem of the optimum design for a car. In fairness, this question had more or less been answered in 1891 when, in France, René Panhard and Émile Levassor built a car with an engine placed vertically at the front and the crankshaft running parallel with the length of the vehicle and power going to the rear wheels. This was known as Le Système Panhard.

But it was Emil who masterminded the perfection of this design. He was only a dealer but he went to enormous lengths to specify the cars he sold. From the Daimler Motoren Gesellschaft (DMG) he acquired two 28 hp Phoenix racing cars which he entered in a race in Nice. But Gottlieb Daimler died in March 1900 and the mechanic William Bauer was killed on the first curve of the Nice to La Turbie race. Thereafter DMG was wary of racing but Emil continued to demand cars.

Specifically, he wanted more power, a lighter engine, a longer wheelbase and a lower centre of gravity. He was, in effect, asking for an almost wholly new type of car. It was not entirely original, but Emil's ambitions took the Système Panhard to new heights of engineering perfection.

Wilhelm Maybach, technical director of DMG, was to be the designer in tandem with Gottlieb's son Paul. Emil ordered 36 cars at an extravagant price. The car was to be named Daimler-Mercédès – the first, but far from the last, appearance of his daughter's name on a car.

Miraculously, Maybach pulled it off and Emil received his first delivery in December 1900. The car, now known as the Mercedes 35hp, was low, light and fast, the engine was aluminium, the main bearings were magnalium, the clutch was automatically adjusting, the valves were controlled by the camshaft . . . I could go on. This car was, according to L.J.K. Setright, 'more than merely ambitious: it was authoritative'. It was, in short, the first truly modern car.

In races it achieved 53 mph and beat everything in sight. 'We have entered the Mercedes era,' announced the director of the French Automobile Club. The touring four-seater version became a success-ful family car for the wealthy.

Karl and Bertha Benz had been the future for but a brief moment. Emil Jellinek, Wilhelm Maybach and Gottlieb Daimler, Karl's great rival, and his son had stolen the moment from them. Their 35hp was a masterpiece. But it still did not quite answer the outstanding question: what is a car for?

13

Certainly, cars would transport people horselessly but where to and where from? And which people? And why did they need to move at all? Historically most people have lived and died within a few miles of where they were born. Industrialisation had driven people from villages to the cities but once in the city they would seldom see the countryside. Cars, when they arrived, were for the rich and adventurous; the poor and home-loving couldn't afford them and neither did they need them.

In 1900 the question 'What is a car for?' was to produce one massively self-indulgent answer of great ingenuity from the French. There were few cars on the road in that year and they tended to belong to the rich, the obsessed and the tinkerers. The rest of the population were in the habit of crying 'Get a horse!' as the cars of the day rattled by. In spite of the success of the London to Brighton Run in 1896, various race spectaculars in the United States and the ever-improving cars from Germany, culminating in the Mercedes 35hp in 1901, automobilism remained a niche interest.

This was a problem for the two Michelin brothers – Édouard the engineer and André the marketing guy – in Clermont Ferrand. They had a rubber factory at which, in 1889, a cyclist arrived with a tyre problem. It was a pneumatic tyre and fixing it was made all but impossible, as it was glued to the wheel rim. Nevertheless, Édouard was enthused by the concept of pneumatic tyres. He devised one that required no glue, upon which Charles Terront won the world's first long-distance cycle race – the 1891 Paris–Brest–Paris. Michelin pneumatic tyres were fitted onto a car, a Peugeot, in the 1895 Paris–Bordeaux–Paris race.

But large-scale production of car tyres was their aspiration and so, in 1900, they found they had to confront the problem of how to convince people to buy and drive cars. There were only 3,000 cars on French roads at the time. Plainly there needed to be many more.

The brothers' rather startling solution was the Red Guide, intended to offer information about hotels, restaurants and, crucially, pharmacies that sold gasoline, as there were then no petrol stations. Previously, travel guides had been based on train journeys but, as one ad for the guide in 1924 said, 'With a car, no more 5am trains. With a car there is more opportunity for the pleasant things of life.'

The first Red Guide was 399 pages long and 35,000 copies were printed, a very ambitious print run in view of the extreme scarcity of drivers that needed to be guided. But the Michelins were nothing if not ambitious – 'This work came out with the century,' proclaimed André, 'it will last as long.' He was, unusually for a marketing man, right.

One slogan for the guide in 1908 was 'With Michelin one knows exactly where one is going'. Not only did the book get you there, it kept you there by telling you what to do when you arrived. The guide *presupposed* the car.

But it did not democratise the car. The Michelin Man, a fatty made of tyres, was created by O'Galop – real name Marius Rossillon – and first appeared in public in 1898. It was a very bizarre poster. The Man of Tyres is wearing a monocle and holding aloft a glass full of various tyre-bursting – nails, shards of glass – road hazards. '*Nunc est bibendum*,' it says – a quote from Horace, meaning now is the time to drink – then, 'That is to say cheers. The Michelin tyre drinks obstacles.' Bibendum – it later became his name – was plainly an upper-class high-lifer. The guide itself has remained upmarket, with its precious rating system for the best restaurants in the world. One drove, it became clear, to eat.

It must have worked. By 1903 France was the world's leading car maker, producing 30,124 cars; the number produced in America that year was 11,235. But the point was that these were still small numbers, because cars remained the preserve of the rich and the enthusiast. The guide was an ingenious way of disseminating the idea of the car, but nobody then had the right car to sell to the people.

That was to appear eight years later in that city named after a French explorer – Detroit. There, from this chaotic story of movement and modernism, of bicycles, cars and characters, and of the fire inside, was to emerge the one indisputably great machine, the car that was to lead the reshaping of the world in its image.

Henry Ford with a Ford Model T

Chapter Two

MECHANICALLY UNCANNY

1

On 4 March 1906 the *New York Times* carried an article headlined, 'Motorists Don't Make Socialists'. It was a response to an anti-car speech made by Woodrow Wilson, then president of Princeton University, later President of the United States.

'Nothing,' he had said, 'has spread socialistic feeling in this country more than the use of automobiles. To the countryman they are a picture of arrogance of wealth with all its independence and carelessness.'

Various distinguished automobilists were outraged, pointing out that many farmers, who could not possibly suffer from the arrogance of wealth, now owned cars and that all the evidence suggested that capitalism, not socialism, was being advanced by cars.

'The very opposite of President Wilson's statement,' said John Farson, a Chicago banker and president of the American Automobile Association, 'is practically true in the farming districts of the West. The small machines that have been built in such large numbers recently and that may be purchased for from $750 to $1,250 are being used to a large extent in the West . . .'

This was nonsense. About 25,000 cars were produced in 1906 in America, a country of 100 million people. Wilson was right that cars were still toys of the rich; they were overwhelmingly sports and leisure vehicles. But soon it wouldn't matter. Both arrogance and socialism were about to be swept aside and the farmers were to be given their own cars by one man who made one car. In 1923 3.1 million cars were made in America and 1.8 million of them were Ford Model Ts.

It is said that late in life Henry Ford was being interviewed by a reporter who suggested that perhaps his views were now out of step with the modern age. 'Young man,' Ford replied, 'I invented the modern age.'

The quotation is probably too good to be true. Nevertheless, it is at least in part true. Henry Ford was one of the two inventors of the core features of twentieth-century modernity. He invented and refined mass production and thereby created a mass market of consumers; Alfred Sloan at General Motors invented and refined the techniques of marketing to the masses. In their hands cars remade the world.

2

To the casual contemporary gaze the Ford Model T just looks like a comical old car: black with a high, ungainly passenger box – men kept their hats on in those days – a small engine compartment, prominent lamps, mudguards and running boards, all bolted on without a thought of aerodynamic efficiency. It is a car that, especially in coupe form, seems to be walking on tiptoes. This two-box design – engine bay and passenger compartment – immediately evokes cars from the early twentieth century right through to the thirties and the forties. It was preceded by the tricycle or horseless-carriage styles and succeeded by the three-box style of the saloon/sedan with a large boot at the rear. That, in turn, was to be succeeded by the two-box sport-utility vehicle.

The striking thing about the T is the transparency, the naked display of its own construction. The workings of the car are almost all visible and it looks as though it could be taken apart with one screwdriver and one spanner. Other cars of the period made some effort to look like integrated wholes; the T flaunts itself as a compilation of parts. And, indeed, parts defined the consumer experience of the car. By the 1920s, when sales were at their peak, the Sears Roebuck catalogue offered 5,000 accessories that could be bolted on to the family T, including a 'de-luxe flower vase of the cut-glass anti-splash type'.

The car inspired affection in its owners. The T rapidly acquired nicknames: Tin Lizzie, flivver – a word of indeterminate origins – or jalopy, which might be derived from Jalapa, a Mexican town where many old cars were sent to be turned into scrap.

The T, as it aged, became comical because of its illusory appearance of fragility. In the Laurel & Hardy film *Slippery Pearls* (aka *The Stolen Jools*) Ollie is driving a T and Stan is in the passenger seat. In the rear seat is a smart-looking man in a hat. A siren is wailing. Stan attempts to push a button on the dashboard but Ollie slaps his hand away. The car pulls up and, once again, Stan reaches for the button. This time he is unimpeded and the button is pressed. There is a sharp cut away so we can see the whole car just as it collapses into its constituent pieces. All three are flung backwards. Stan recovers looking confused and Ollie wearily readjusts his bowler hat. The smart man in the back rises from the wreckage, dusts himself off and, as if nothing had happened, as if cars were expected to fall apart when they parked, says, 'Thank you, boys, where'd you be when I need you?' 'Right here,' says Ollie, pointing downwards at the now immobilised wreckage.

The film was made in 1931, four years after the end of Model T production. Stan and Ollie's machine certainly looks like a Tin Lizzie – unkempt, fragile – though the totality of its collapse goes way beyond anything that might have been expected of any ordinary jalopy.

But such jokes were only possible because by then everybody knew about the T. It was eulogised and sung about. In a way never achieved before or since, the word 'car' meant this car; it had a cultural presence greater than any music or film star. In 1922 E.B. White was just out of college and looking for something to write about. That same year Scott Fitzgerald and Ernest Hemingway had gone to find themselves in Paris – a very retro move, as if old Europe were still in charge. White chose, modernistically, to drive across America in a T, an experience that became two essays – 'Farewell to Model T' and 'From Sea to Shining Sea'. He did not see the T as a jalopy; he saw it as a technological masterpiece and, most importantly, a new way of life: 'Mechanically uncanny, it was like nothing that had ever come to the world before . . . My generation identifies it with youth, with its gaudy irretrievable excitements.'

That last sentence tells us to look more carefully at this car. It was not always a cranky old-timer, an eccentric jalopy. On the contrary, it was once about youth and gaudy excitements. It compares with sixties cars like the Ford Mustang or the BMC Mini, emblems of both the threat and the charm of youth culture. But the message of the T was more astounding than the symbolism of either of those two cars. For what it said, in the still horse-drawn year of 1908, was: everybody can have a car. When production ended in 1927 and the 15 millionth T rolled off the production line, it was clear that everybody could, indeed, have a car.

Considered as a business proposition the T was absurd. Produced between 1908 and 1927, it was the only car then made by the Ford Motor Company. Any contemporary executive would say this one-product strategy was madness, a ludicrously high risk. But to Henry Ford in his most puritan mode the T was perfect, the only car people would ever need, and, for a surprisingly long time, he was right. He even intended it to last a lifetime, another commercial madness – the ideas of planned obsolescence and annual model upgrades were yet to infect the car industry. The final madness was that he kept reducing the price; the first basic T cost $825, the last $360 after having dipped as low as $260. Again, he was right: he still made money. Other cars have since sold more – the Toyota Corolla in various iterations sold 44 million, the Volkswagen Beetle 22 million and so on – but the Ts were sold in their millions when there were very few cars in the world. And, more to the point, there was only one Henry Ford.

3

In his memoir, *My Life and Work* published in 1922, Ford quotes a speech he made in 1907. It is a summary of the T's business plan:

> I will build a motor car for the great multitude. It will be large enough for the family but small enough for the individual to run and care for. It will be constructed of the best materials, by the best men to be hired, after the simplest designs that modern engineering can devise. But it will be so low in price that no man making a good salary will be unable to own one—and enjoy with his family the blessing of hours of pleasure in God's great open spaces.

But this wasn't Ford; it was Samuel Crowther. Crowther, a journalist, 'ghosted' the memoir as well as three other Ford books. Here Ford seems to be quoting himself, but this is a writer's, not an engineer's, paragraph – clipped, precise and rousing. I would be prepared to bet that the word 'multitude' in the first sentence is Crowther's oblique reference to a famous line from Walt Whitman's 'Song of Myself' – 'I am large, I contain multitudes'.

And Ford did contain multitudes. His lifespan is neatly bracketed by two of the most momentous events in American history. Born in 1863 four weeks after the Battle of Gettysburg, the most decisive and bloody battle of the Civil War, he died in 1947, having witnessed the defeat of Japan by the first and so far only deployment of nuclear weapons in war.

In opinion and attitude he could be all things to all men. He was a vicious anti-semite and then, for a time, he wasn't; he was puritanical and yet extravagant; he was a man of peace and then of war; he was a philanthropist and a cruel hoarder; he loved his son Edsel and he tortured him; he was an enlightened boss but he became a global emblem of cold, grinding capitalism. Anything, good or bad, about Henry Ford can be contradicted except the ambition and the work. Two hundred years before he was born, the poet John Dryden captured Ford in a couplet:

> A man so various, that he seem'd to be
> Not one, but all mankind's epitome . . .

He was a populist of genius. One biographer, Steven Watts, writes of 'a love affair between a pioneering automaker from Detroit and common Americans that transcended all reason'.

In 1919 Ford pursued a libel case against the *Chicago Tribune*, which had called him an 'ignorant idealist' and 'an anarchistic enemy of the nation' because of his opposition a few years earlier to President Wilson's decision to send the National Guard to the Mexican border to prevent raids by Pancho Villa's guerrillas. The *Tribune*'s defence was that Ford was an ignoramus.

On the witness stand Ford did indeed display remarkable ignorance – he thought the American Revolution had occurred in 1812 and that chilli con carne was a large mobile army. He was widely mocked, but he didn't care. In fact, he revelled in the scorn, as it put him in touch with the common man. 'I rarely read anything except the headlines,' he said. 'I don't like to read books; they muss up my mind.'

He was admired for his lack of pretension and his insistence that he was too busy working to educate himself. Those who mocked him could be dismissed as snobs. Preachers offered prayers to deliver him from these people, and farmers and labourers sent him letters of support. As a result, what would have been embarrassing to a lesser man became for Ford an assertion of his status as an American folk hero. He won the case.

The populist simplicity of the values evoked in Crowther's paragraph and proved in the court case is deceptively straightforward: family, good and accessible products, simplicity in use, low price and, crucially, 'God's great open spaces'. That last attribute is the only one that offers an answer to the question, what is a car for? It also points to the most striking of Ford's paradoxes: in providing access to God's open spaces, the car would threaten their continued existence.

But that unfortunate side effect was only to become apparent years later. For Ford the creation of the greatest of all 'people's cars' was entirely consistent with his homespun values. Values that for him were embodied, first, in his mother and, second, in *McGuffey Eclectic Readers*, school textbooks published between 1836 and 1960. These imparted not just basic education but also the values of honour, integrity, temperance, kindness, hard work, patience and so on. The books stayed with Ford throughout his life. In 1934 he moved the log cabin where William Holmes McGuffey was born to Greenfield Village, his outdoor history museum in Dearborn. He had also created the largest private collection of McGuffeys in the USA. 'The McGuffey Readers,' he said, 'taught industry and morality to the youth of America.'

Ford might not be the most successful car magnate of all time – that title surely goes to Alfred Sloan of General Motors – but he was certainly the most interesting. Sloan's memoir, *My Years with General Motors*, is, as the title suggests, paralysingly dull; everything Ford – or Crowther – wrote, said, thought or made, for good or ill, was stunningly interesting. Ford built the most influential car in the world on the basis of engineering and marketing ideas that could not be disentangled from his personality, his opinions, his prejudices and his economic theory. The car, like the man, contained multitudes. Or, to put it another way, the Model T was the autobiography Ford wrote without the aid of Crowther. Or, to put it yet another way, it was his epic poem.

'No poet,' said the great nature writer John Burroughs, one of his friends and mentors, 'ever expressed himself through his work more completely than Mr. Ford has expressed himself through his car.'

4

Ford had attained this miraculous machine after years of tinkering. He was born in 1863 to a solid farming family of Irish descent in Wayne County, Michigan. 'Certainly they were not rich,' he said of his parents, 'but neither were they poor.'

He was the eldest child of six and his father, William, expected him to take over the farm but Henry wasn't interested. He later said, 'I never had any particular love for the farm—it was the mother on the farm I loved.'

His mother, Mary, died in 1876. He was overcome with grief. It was as if, he later said, 'a great wrong had been done to me'. His mother seems to have given him a rough and ready business plan – 'Life will give you many unpleasant tasks . . . Your duty will be hard and disagreeable and painful to you at times, but you must do it.' He would even attribute the neatness of his factories to the influence of her housekeeping. Finally, she had always said he was a born mechanic.

Farms only interested him to the extent that they provided an occasion for the use of machinery. Four months after his mother's death he experienced 'the biggest event of those early years'. He encountered a steam-powered 'road engine', the first horseless vehicle he had seen. Ford leapt off the wagon he was riding with his father and demanded an explanation of its working from the machine's engineer: 'from the time I saw that road engine as a boy of twelve right forward to to-day, my great interest has been in making a machine that would travel the roads'.

Perhaps his enthusiasm was inspired by his dislike of horses. His feelings were confirmed by several horse-related accidents. In one case a horse threw him, his foot was caught in the stirrup and he was dragged all the way home. Some decades later he wrote triumphantly 'The horse is DONE!' in one of his notebooks.

At the same age he took apart and reassembled a watch he had been given and, subsequently, made some money out of repairing watches around town. At fourteen he took a job as an apprentice machinist in nearby Detroit. He returned to the farm but, again, it wasn't about cows and crops; this time it was about the Westinghouse Farm Engine, a beautiful little steam engine that was towed by horses and which powered threshing machines and sawmills. A neighbour had one of these but it had broken down and the local mechanic was not up to the task.

Ford mastered it in a day and then spent a summer earning money by taking it round from farm to farm. Years later he sought out that machine – serial number 345 – found it in Pennsylvania, restored it and fired it up for his 60th birthday.

Ford never lost his fascination with both his rural past and that of his country. Indeed, he recreated it in 1933 in the form of Greenfield Village, the 'living history' outdoor museum that included not only working farms but also sections entitled Edison at Work and a Model T District.

'Experience firsthand,' says the current website blurb, 'the sights, sounds and sensations of America's fascinating formation, where over 80 acres brim with resourcefulness and ingenuity. Here, 300 years of American perseverance serve as a living reminder that anything is possible.'

Of course, anything is not possible but this sounds cosy and, for the American day-tripper, inspiring. The sub-text, however, is all about the work. Hard work was the sharp edge that emerged from Ford's misty sentimentality.

'In my mind,' he/Crowther writes, 'nothing is more abhorrent than a life of ease. None of us has any right to ease. There is no place in civilization for the idler.'

The moral force of this conviction was to find full expression in the mighty River Rouge complex, completed in 1928, a stupendously scaled temple dedicated to resourcefulness and ingenuity but primarily to hard – very hard – work.

Ford became a local hero for repairing steam engines on farms but his goal was always to create an automobile of some kind. The

Westinghouse had convinced him that steam was not suitable for the kind of light car he intended to make. He was also to reject electricity because of the weight of the batteries. In 1885 he found his solution when, while working at the Eagle Iron Works in Detroit, he repaired an Otto engine – a four-stroke, internal-combustion machine. This was, coincidentally, the year in which Karl Benz built his first Patent-Motorwagen. Subsequently Ford built an Otto engine of his own.

He married Clara Jane Bryant. He had met her at a New Year Ball at Dearborn in 1885. His chat-up line was unique in that company. Clara was in demand and the other boys spoke to her of 'how good the music was and all that sort of thing', whereas Ford told her about a watch he'd fixed. Impressed, she told him on the way home 'how sensible he was, how serious minded'. They married in April 1888.

A well-known story demonstrates the perfection of their partnership. In 1891 he had moved on to the Detroit branch of the Edison Illuminating Company. This had been established by Thomas Edison in 1880 to build generating stations and spread electric lighting across the country. One day Ford brought home the ignition system he had been working on. He clamped it to the kitchen sink and, abandoning the meal she was preparing, Clara agreed to drip gasoline into the engine while he spun the flywheel. It worked – flames and smoke burst forth from the shaking machine. Ford subsequently – and significantly – called Clara 'The Believer'.

They were to have only one child. Edsel Ford was born on 6 November 1893. The birth was easy enough but Clara was later admitted to hospital for, some say, a hysterectomy. This cannot be confirmed because Henry Ford II, Edsel's son, destroyed his grandparents' medical records. Being Henry Ford's only child was to prove an impossible burden for Edsel.

Ford had become chief engineer at Edison, a job that gave him even more time to experiment with petrol engines. He had already, in 1892, made his first car, which he called his 'gasoline buggy'. By the spring of 1893 it was 'running to my partial satisfaction'. He dates that satisfaction to 2 April because the bobolinks – small blackbirds – had come to Dearborn and, he assures us, 'they always come on April 2nd'. This doesn't sound like Crowther; it sounds like Ford, self-mythologising with a touch of rural authenticity.

The car was not, however, to the satisfaction of the people of Detroit. It was noisy, it frightened the horses and it blocked traffic, because every time he stopped a crowd would gather. The car also annoyed the police and he was forced to acquire a special permit from the mayor. He remarks, 'thus for a time [I] enjoyed the distinction of being the only licensed chauffeur in America'. He sold that car for $200 in 1896 and went on to produce more, many more.

Ford by then had met his company boss, the great inventor Thomas Alva Edison. Edison approved of his work on cars. Encouraged by this and by ever-increasing success with his engineering, Ford finally left the Edison company to start his own business – the Detroit Automobile Company – in 1899.

What followed was a largely tedious series of corporate shenanigans in which Ford demonstrated his own messianic self-belief, impatience and perfectionism – and also his ruthlessness. He finally got what he wanted in the form of the Ford Motor Company (FMC) in 1903.

Two curious aspects of these years are worth noting, however. The first is the fate of the Henry Ford Company, founded in 1901. Ford was chief engineer but the primary investors brought in a certain Henry M. Leland as a consultant. Ford left in disgust. In August 1902 the company was dissolved and restructured with the aim of building a car with Leland's engine. Leland was allowed to choose the company name. It was the bicentenary of the founding of Detroit so he chose Cadillac after the city's French founder, Antoine de la Mothe Cadillac. Leland also chose the Cadillac family coat of arms as the company emblem. This became part of General Motors in 1909. It remains the premium marque in the GM range. Ford's walkout had thus helped create cars that were utterly opposed to the puritanism of his first and greatest creation.

The second curious aspect was Ford's discovery of racing as a marketing tool. He seemed to be surprised by the, to him, novel idea that the irrational whims of consumers might have to be taken into account when selling cars. And consumers loved racers: 'It was a curious but natural development—that racing idea. I never thought anything of racing, but the public refused to consider the automobile in any light other than as a fast toy.'

Car races were big events in those days. They were dangerous and unpredictable. The one certainty seemed to be that every race was faster than the last. The outstanding personality in all this excitement was the Scottish-born engineer Alexander Winton, who made a car that won a 50-mile race in Chicago at the astounding average speed of 38 mph in 1900. Winton brought his car to race in Detroit the following year. Rising to the challenge, Ford came up with a 26 hp machine. This was modest – Winton's machine was 40 hp – and he was so confident of winning that he had specified the victory trophy: a cutglass punchbowl that would sit nicely in his dining room at home in Cleveland.

The race at Grosse Point, a suburb of Detroit, was chaotic. With many dropouts and mechanical failures, there were only two starters: the Winton and the Ford, both driven by their makers. Winton took a substantial lead but then the car began to lose power – it was emitting blue smoke. Ford went ahead and stayed there. Ecstatic Clara had a new punchbowl to adorn their house.

The following year Ford produced the 999, an 80 hp racer that looked like an enormous engine to which a driver had been perilously attached as an afterthought. It was named after a train, the *Empire State Express* No. 999, which had set a world speed record of 112.5 mph in 1893. The engine's capacity was 19 litres and it had four bucket-sized cylinders. 'The roar of those cylinders alone was enough to half kill a man,' observed Ford.

Having tried it out for a few laps, it was clear that Ford was too scared of this car to be the driver. Instead, he chose Barney Oldfield, a bicycle racer. The 999 was to be the first car Oldfield had ever driven. But, as Ford remarked, 'The man did not know what fear was.' And, as Oldfield said when he was warned he might get killed, 'I might as well be dead as dead broke.'

Of course he won, beating a Winton yet again. His technique was unusual. He simply floored the accelerator from the start and declined to brake at corners, allowing the car to drift round, a technique later known as four-wheel drift that was perfected by the great racer Tazio Nuvolari, who also disapproved of brakes in cars intended to be quick. Oldfield went on to become a celebrity, the greatest racer of his time. Ford, helped by these sensational races, went on to become the greatest car maker.

5

Before the T the initial response of car makers to the appalling American roads was to pile on more weight and height. Cars, roughly in the Mercedes or, as it was known, French style, were made with increased ground clearance, thicker steel, heavier springs and large-bore engines that yielded more power but also added more weight. This made them slower and more expensive.

There was a pre-T attempt to make lighter cars. These were known as high-wheelers or western buggies. They had high ground clearance thanks to large bicycle-type wheels and they were cheap. Unfortunately, they were also fragile and under-powered, and by 1910 the high-wheelers were dead.

Heaviness was anathema to Ford. Weight to him was little short of evil, a barrier to the possibility of purity and completeness of the final design. Ford's disapproval was technical, aesthetic and moral. Slender himself, fatness was an affront, perhaps a sign of the idleness he so despised. This is the crucial passage in *My Life and Work* – it is, in effect, a verbal blueprint for the T:

> The law of diminishing returns begins to operate at the point where strength becomes weight. Weight may be desirable in a steam roller but nowhere else. Strength has nothing to do with weight. The mentality of the man who does things in the world is agile, light, and strong. The most beautiful things in the world are those from which all excess weight has been eliminated. Strength is never just weight—either in men or things. Whenever any one suggests to me that I might increase weight or add a part, I look into decreasing weight and eliminating a part! The car that I designed was lighter than any car that had yet been made. It would have been lighter if I had known how to make it so.

More brutally but more revealingly he also wrote, 'Fat men cannot run as fast as thin men but we build most of our vehicles as though dead-weight fat increased speed!'

Ford's slimming programme was spectacular. Put at its simplest, a basic Mercedes 35hp weighed 2,646 pounds, a basic T weighed 1,200 pounds. The average American car of the time weighed about 80 pounds per horsepower; the T weighed 60 pounds per horsepower. Vanadium steel helped reduce weight. Ford, in his memoir, said he discovered this at a race in Palm Beach in 1905. After a French car had crashed he picked up a fragment – a 'little valve strip stem' – and noticed it was both light and strong. More likely the idea was picked up by his team from engineering journals and, subsequently, it was a British metallurgist, J. Kent Smith, who demonstrated the material to Ford at his lab in Ohio. This seemingly miraculous material 'disposed of much of the weight'.

Vanadium is a metallic element that rarely occurs in nature. It was first discovered in 1801. It can be found in steel smelter slag or as a by-product of uranium mining. When the T was being built the American Vanadium Company was mining it in Peru. Ford, however, found a steel company in Ohio that could run its furnaces at 3,000 degrees Fahrenheit. This made vanadium production possible. Half the T's components were to be made of vanadium steel.

The first car produced by FMC was the Model A. He then went through the letters of the alphabet – either as concept designs or as manufactured vehicles. He arrived at the letter T in the winter of 1906. It was then that he took Charles Sorensen aside. Sorensen was a woodworker Ford had hired to make three-dimensional models from blueprints. He was led up to the top floor of the FMC building, where he was told to build a room with a big door and a good lock.

The design team that worked here consisted of seven or more people so it would not be strictly true to say Ford 'designed' the T. But, as he supervised every aspect of the process and had specified what the car must be, there can be no doubt that Ford made the T and, in return, the T made Ford.

He sketched out his idea on a blackboard and then the team went to work. Ford's mother's rocking chair was installed in the room on which, according to one of the designers, 'he used to sit for hours and hours at a time, discussing and following out the development of the design'. Ford's basic brief was that the car should be 'capable of carrying its passengers anywhere that a horse-drawn vehicle will go without the driver being afraid of ruining his car'. Few modern cars can achieve this, but the T did.

One immediately visible result of this brief was the car's 10-inch ground clearance and its apparently crazy suspension system. Two lateral leaf springs allowed all four wheels to rise up and radius rods stopped them moving back and forth. The improbable wheel angles you see in silent comedy films are not stunts.

This twisting motion would have destroyed lesser cars. In the T it was controlled by an ingenious system of radius rods and, crucially, a three-point engine mounting. Most cars had four. In Ford's three-point system the single front point was made so as not to transfer any twisting of the car to the engine.

The less invisible innovations were just as remarkable. This was as much to do with manufacturing as it was to do with the car in use. Ford, for example, wanted to make the cylinder block out of a single casting, rather than have separate casting for all four cylinders. Sorensen could not make this work until Ford suggested they simply slice off the top of the block so it could be bolted and unbolted easily. Thus was born the form of millions of ICE engines for years to come.

Then there was the 'planetary transmission', a light gearing system that required the use of all three of the car's pedals – brake, forward and reverse. This was a rarity at the time – sliding gears was the usual system, particularly as the cars became heavier. But sliding gears were hard to manage – one recommendation to the driver was to always 'have a mental picture of just what transpires in the gear box every time he moves the lever or touches the clutch or moves the car'. Get it wrong and there was a hideous grinding noise. The planetary system was always in mesh and no mental pictures were required. Again, this helped with bad roads – by switching rapidly between forward and reverse, for example, the car could be extricated from potholes or ruts.

The final – and most lasting – innovation was the decision to put the steering wheel on the left of the car. Only two other cars had left-hand steering at the time. It is not clear why the decision was made, though a Ford brochure from 1909 offers two justifications. Either it was a thoughtful concession to the lady passengers – they could exit and enter the cars on the kerbside, avoiding traffic and the inevitable mud – or, more rationally, it might have given the driver a better view of oncoming traffic. Either way, thereafter left-hand drive became standard on all cars, except, of course, in countries like the UK where we drive on the left.

Almost everything about the car was original or a careful

refinement of existing technologies and everything was intended to meet Ford's demands for lightness, ease of service and manufacture, durability, and cheapness. When FMC sent specifications of the T out to the dealer network, they were regarded with disbelief mounting to derision. This was combined with anxiety; if the T really was that good, the dealers couldn't see how they would be able to unload their stocks of the preceding Model N.

The first advertisements for the T were not really ads at all in that they offered no dreamy, aspirational possibilities, only rational analysis. In one the only irrational element was the frame of art nouveau columns surmounted by trees. Ford believed that 'if you really have a good thing, it will advertise itself' so all that was really needed was a list of specifications and a low price. The five-seater Touring version was sold as 'A car that possesses at least equal value with any "1909" car announced, and at the same time sells for several hundred dollars less than the lowest of the rest'. Later the wordy blurb announces, 'We make no apology for the price.' The text was littered with numbers – four cylinders, three-bearing crankshaft, 100-inch wheelbase, 1,200 pounds of weight and so on. Even, probably bafflingly to most consumers, the use of vanadium steel was included. Clearly it would be irrational *not* to buy a T. Finally, at the bottom of the ad was a list of Ford branches – New York, Boston, etc., but also Paris, London and Toronto. This was to be a world car from day one.

But the biggest sell of all was not the details of the car but the sheer importance of it as the first car for the masses. The T was to be known as 'the universal car'. This was inscribed beneath a suitably solemn Egyptian hood ornament, a pyramid sprouting two wings. 'The pyramid suggests strength, permanency, stability,' the company blurb explained, 'the conventionalized Sacred Ibis wings typify lightness, grace, speed.'

But the greatest expression of all these values was neither a slogan nor an ornament – it was another momentous race. The Ocean to Ocean Automobile Contest held in 1909 began in New York on 1 June. The winning car crossed the line in Seattle on 23 June. It was a T. Second place went to a Shawmut that arrived 17 hours later and third was another T; no others completed the race. The cars had survived appalling roads, deficient maps, snowdrifts and limited sources of fuel. But the Ts always had the advantage because of their suspension, their lightness and because of the growing network of Ford dealers across the country. In fact, five months later the winning Ford was disqualified because it was found that its engine had been changed in the midst of the race. But by then it didn't matter; the race had established the T as a rugged, all-purpose machine, a truly universal car. As one advertisement put it, 'No Ford owner ever doubts the ability of his car to go wherever he desires to travel.'

Masterminding the transformation of Ford by the T was Norval A. Hawkins, a brilliant if slightly dodgy Michigan man – in 1894 he was imprisoned for embezzling $3,000 from Standard Oil – who took over sales and marketing at Ford in 1907. Lean and severe in appearance, his time at Ford earned him the title of 'The Greatest Salesman in the World'.

He at once made sense of the company's accounts and set up assembly plants outside Detroit. This cut costs by removing the need to ship whole cars. But it was the marketing side of the job that made his name. He was, in a way, a harbinger of the information-driven marketing of today. He set up detailed 'territory reports' of every American town with a population of more than 2,000, which covered everything from the quality of the roads to the personal habits of Ford dealers. By 1913 he had created 7,000 dealerships.

In fact, as he noted, the dealers had an easy job, as 'there was no conflict in the buyer's mind as to what to buy from a Ford dealer' because there was only one car. He said their goal was 'literally baptizing civilization with the Name FORD, and the merits of Ford cars'.

He was the polar opposite of Ford. The first advertisement for the T, in all its perversity and rigour, was as clear an expression of Ford as the car. It was all about the product and its virtues; the approach of his great rival, General Motors, was to be all about the customers and their aspirations.

Hawkins's method anticipated that of GM. He saw selling as 'persuading and creating desire'. The salesman had to appeal to the heart not the mind – 'You do not sell goods but ideas about goods.' So, by some mysterious corporate alchemy, Ford had acquired the best of both worlds – his own practical puritanism and Hawkins's insinuating emotional approach to selling.

Hawkins retired in 1923, the peak year of Model T production, and died, aged 69, in 1936. As T sales began to decline, Edsel Ford was put in charge of a revitalised advertising department. Colour illustrations and fashionable, aspirational imagery began to appear. The T, though now well on its way to jalopydom, was sold as the stylish choice. 'Among those women who are recognized in their communities as arbiters in matters of taste,' ran a magazine ad in 1924, 'the Ford Four-door Sedan enjoys unusually high favor.'

Mass production was, thereafter, to be sustained by the gentler but darker arts of mass marketing.

6

In 1909 it took over 12 hours to build a single Model T; in 1914 it took 93 minutes. Speed is the core value of the assembly line. It is also a core value of America.

This love of speed had been noted by Europeans throughout the nineteenth century. 'The Fast Man must certainly be an American,' remarked a journalist at the Great Exhibition in London in 1851, 'because nobody lives and propagates as fast as he.'

Visitors to the USA noticed, among other things, the speed with which Americans consumed their food – at a Boston hotel in the 1820s it was noted they sat at the table for no more than five to ten minutes. This need for speed was subsequently met by cafeterias, fast-food outlets and supermarkets – all versions of the assembly line.

What Henry Ford saw with typical clarity was the intimate connection between speed, price and profit. There was an almost limitless and largely untapped market for cars so demand would not be a problem as long as the product and the price were right. With the T he had the product; with mass production he had the price.

So, the car was only one half of Ford's masterpiece. Whereas most cars at the time were in effect one-offs, the T could be precisely replicated by his mass-production system. The T is now an amusing, fondly remembered antique; his system, though heavily modified, endures.

But speed needs space and at first Ford had very little. The first T rolled out of the architectural chaos of the small Ford plant in

Detroit's Piquette Avenue in 1908. But in the first month only seven others followed. By 1910, 12,000 had been produced but it was clear Piquette could not cope with many more. There was just not enough room. But how much was enough? The answer to that question was architectural.

Albert Kahn was 11 when his family left Germany for Detroit in 1880. There he became an architect, launching Albert Kahn Associates in 1895. He was fond of reinforced concrete, a technology that, like the car, was created in Europe and brought to a gargantuan climax in America. Concrete, given greater tensile and ductile strength by embedded steel 'rebars', provided better fire-proofing and made much larger spans possible than the wood previously used in industrial buildings.

In 1903 Kahn's 3.5-million-square-foot Packard Automotive plant on Grand Boulevard in East Detroit opened. It was a brilliant and seemingly conclusive expression of the architecture of mass production and it caught the attention of Henry Ford.

And so the company moved to Kahn's Highland Park plant, located a few miles north of downtown Detroit on land that had previously been a racecourse, in 1910. It was a mighty machine – 300 yards long with 50,000 square feet of glass windows – for making Ts. It is hard to overstate the importance of this building, for Kahn, Ford and for the world.

Fine architecture had previously been regarded as the preserve of the rich – houses – and the grandly institutional – civic palaces, churches, temples, museums and monuments. But with this one building, Kahn shifted the focus to industrial design. Highland Park created a new form of grandeur. It brought every function under one roof, creating a temple that glorified functionality and hard work. It made him famous – by 1937 his practice was responsible for 19 per cent of all architect-designed factories in America. But he was not, like many celebrated architects, a design ideologue. He was flexible. His house for Ford's son and his wife in Grosse Point – now a historical landmark known as the Edsel and Eleanor Ford House – is based on vernacular Cotswold design, which had impressed the family on a visit to England.

For Ford, who had played a large part in making Kahn's design work, Highland Park was a cathedral of efficiency, with every space allocated to a specific function so as to smooth the flow from parts to finished cars. The increase in productivity was stupendous, world-changing. By 1913 Highland Park was producing half of all the cars in America. Norval Hawkins could scarcely contain himself; he compared the building to a fairy tale like 'Aladdin and his wonderful lamp'. A pamphlet, published by the company in 1912, said it all: 'Today the home of the Ford Model T stands pre-eminent as the most complete manufacturing establishment in the world, devoted to the production of one motor car—a profoundly impressive monument to the creative and constructive genius of Henry Ford and his associates.'

For the world Highland Park announced a redefinition of the nature and purpose of work and of the organisation of human society. But it was not until 1913 with the introduction of the moving assembly line that Highland Park really came into its own.

This was not, as many have pointed out, Ford's exclusive invention. Almost all the elements of the process had been deployed elsewhere. The moving line, for example, was first seen in 1867 in the Chicago meat-packing factories – carcasses were drawn by a pulley system past workers who could perform a single task. In this case, as pieces were being removed from the carcass, it was, strictly speaking, a disassembly line.

But Ford's genius was expressed in the integration of such innovations into a unified process. He explained this, just as he had explained his craving for lightness in the T design process, in the form of a prejudice. In that case he had been prejudiced against weight; the assembly line was born of a prejudice against walking.

'The undirected worker,' he/Crowther wrote in *My Life and Work*, 'spends more of his time walking about for materials and tools than he does in working; he gets small pay because pedestrianism is not a highly paid line.'

The moving assembly line took the work to the man rather than vice versa and from this emerged two general principles – 'that a man shall never have to take more than one step, if possibly it can be avoided, and that no man need ever stoop over'. So, the oddity of Kahn's vast open spaces was that they were built for machines to move and humans to be still. It was an innovation that has lasting resonance.

The difficulty of implementing this process is that it is intrinsically fragile. The method at Piquette Avenue involved groups of workers swarming around each car – a mistake by one man could be instantly rectified by another. But the moving assembly line where each worker has just one job offers no such flexibility. A mistake or failure can send shock waves down the whole line. The primary defence against this was the high-precision standardisation of parts. The worker did not have to be especially skilled if everything just fitted together properly using a few simple movements.

Again, Ford was not the first to do this. In 1908 Henry Leland took three of his Cadillacs to the Brooklands racing circuit in the UK. Before astounded members of the Royal Automobile Club he had all three fully disassembled and the components of each thoroughly mixed. Engineers then rebuilt them all. The point was that the components were so perfectly standardised that they could be used in any car. Today this is unremarkable; then it was a miracle. 'Nothing, I think,' wrote Alfred P. Sloan, 'ever did more to establish the reputation of American cars.'

But that was play; Highland Park was work. Production of Ts jumped from 69,000 in 1912 to 170,000 in 1913. Peak production was 1.8 million in 1923. Nothing like this had happened before. The assembly line worked, mass production was the future, everybody could have a car and, thanks to this dazzling display of hyper-efficiency, it looked as though very soon everybody could have everything. But only if they obeyed the new rules.

The even mightier River Rouge complex opened in 1928. The great photographer Robert Frank visited and wrote back to his wife, 'Ford is an absolutely fantastic place. This one is God's factory and if there is such a thing – I am sure that the devil gave him a helping hand to build what is called Ford's River Rouge Plant.'

7

Capitalism and communism are both anti- or super-human ideas. The first denies human agency by subjugation to the market; in the second the human agent is drowned in the collective and in the supposedly inevitable tide of history. This means, paradoxically, that it is pointless being either a capitalist or a communist, since the systems are conceived as facts of nature; one might as well be a plantist or an animalist. It is this that explains the eager embrace of Fordism by both the right and the left. The right celebrates the monstrous machinery of mass production in the name of efficiency, the left in the name of sheer production. Both seek a super-human justification for their actions.

Fordism is a global ideology based on the production system of a single car. The name was created in 1934 by the Italian Marxist philosopher Antonio Gramsci to describe the whole structure of mass production and consumption invented in Detroit. It was preceded by scientific management or, as it is more commonly known, Taylorism after its prophet Frederick Winslow Taylor. These two 'isms' had one thing in common – they both aimed to rationalise work and thereby maximise efficiency.

Taylor was an engineer who became the world's first management consultant. He was the leading light of the Efficiency Movement which, in turn, played a part in the Progressive Era in America lasting from the 1890s to the 1920s. The primary themes of the Progressive Era were social and political reform. The secondary themes were Taylorist – increasing efficiency and the reduction of waste.

Taylor was clearly an obsessive-compulsive personality. He developed a device for waking himself up while working and he counted his steps and analysed his movements in pursuit of efficiency. He regarded 'loafing' as a problem to be solved. By inflating this into a supposedly scientific system, he infected the world with a form of his own OCD, a desperate need to tidy things up, to eliminate wasted time.

Unable to go to Harvard to study law, apparently because of failing eyesight, Taylor spent the 1870s working as a labourer and machinist. At Midvale Steel in Philadelphia he noticed that workers were not using their machines efficiently. He analysed what was going wrong. Crucially, his focus was on the actions of humans rather than machines. In 1893 he became a full-time consultant, specialising in 'systematizing shop management and manufacturing costs'. Later, at Bethlehem Steel, he made enough money from a steel process he invented to devote the rest of his life to scientific management consultancy and education. In 2001 his book *The Principles of Scientific Management* was voted the most influential management book of the twentieth century.

'In the past,' wrote Taylor in the introduction, 'the man has been first; in the future the system must be first.' This could be Maoism or Soviet Communism – it was merely a matter of chance that, having been written in America, it was labelled capitalism. Taylor was dismayed – actually disgusted – by the 'awkward, inefficient, or ill-directed movements of men' that caused 'the great loss the whole country is suffering through inefficiency in almost all our daily acts'. Human imperfection at work revolted him. Taylor had seen the future and it suffered from OCD.

This was a precise reversal of the response of earlier romantic critics – William Morris, John Ruskin, William Wordsworth – of industrialisation. They saw a combination of the ruination of nature, the loss of stable and cherished ways of life, and the destruction of the organic link between worker and work. The last became particularly acute in the first age of mass production, because each worker had a single task and little or no contact, physical or emotional, with the finished product. But Taylorism triumphed.

Yet Taylor's vision was narrow when compared to Ford's. He was a nitpicker; Ford was a grand disruptor. Whereas Taylor was primarily focused on the activities of the worker on the production line, Ford saw the entire system – including the world beyond the factory – as a single creation. The most dramatic demonstration of this was his introduction in 1914 of the $5 day wage, more than double what most of his workers had previously been earning. This stunned his competitors.

It was announced to the Detroit press on 5 January as part of a package of reforms which included the reduction of the working day from nine to eight hours – three daily shifts instead of two. The press release made clear Ford's delight in the shocking radicalism of the wage increase: 'The Ford Motor Co., the greatest and most successful automobile manufacturing company in the world, will, on Jan. 12, inaugurate the greatest revolution in the matter of rewards for its workers ever known to the industrial world.' And then the final stunner: 'It is estimated that over $10,000,000 will be thus distributed over and above the regular wages of the men.'

This produced, as intended, sensational headlines – 'Ford Again Staggers The World', 'Ford Factory Has A Heart', 'Crazy Ford They Called Him, Now He's To Give Away Millions'. Most poignantly, in the light of Ford's own background, one cartoon showed a farmer's son saying to his father, 'I want $5 a day for eight hours work or I'll quit right now an' go to Detroit, I will!' Within a month the company received 14,000 letters begging for a job at Ford.

The simplicity of this move concealed, like the T, a complex thought process. The first problem it addressed was staff turnover. Working on the assembly line was gruelling and dull. Staff turnover was astonishing – in 1913 Ford had fewer than 15,000 people on the payroll but he hired 52,000 people. Staff turnover fell after the pay rise from 370 per cent in 1913 to 16 per cent in 1915.

That was the most practical and obvious motive for the pay rise. But the action also had economic, social and moral justifications – all of them arguable but all of them very Ford. Economically the pay rise justified his own virtuous circle theory of capitalism – paying his workers more meant they would buy more cars. In Fordist analysis this became the third leg of the ideology, the other two being standardisation and the assembly line.

In a book published in 1958 Raymond Bruckberger, a French Dominican priest and keen observer of America, concluded that Henry Ford's invention of the $5 and the eight-hour working day combined with the moving-belt assembly line had more impact on the twentieth century than the Russian Revolution. When the Soviet Union was still in the ascendant and was beating America in the space race, this was a bold statement. Now it seems glaringly obvious.

The architecture and systems of production at the Highland Park and River Rouge plants in Detroit dominated twentieth-century working life and crossed ideological boundaries. Lenin and Hitler loved the idea as much as any American capitalist. 'I shall do my best to put his theories into practice in Germany,' said Hitler. The Volkswagen was his version of the Model T.

'American efficiency,' said Stalin, 'is that indomitable force which neither knows nor recognizes obstacles; which continues on a task once started until it is finished, even if it is a minor task; and without which serious constructive work is inconceivable . . . The combination of the Russian revolutionary sweep with American efficiency is the essence of Leninism.'

So keen were the Soviets on Fordist methods that Ford was contracted to create the Gorky Automobile Plant in Russia in 1929. It produced the Ford Model A – the second A, launched in 1927;

the first was in 1903 – and was crucial in the programme of Soviet industrialisation.

For Antonio Gramsci this system of mass production and consumption represented the new ideology of Fordism. Ford had not just made a new car; he had made a new human. As Gramsci put it, 'the biggest collective effort to date to create, with unprecedented speed, and with a consciousness of purpose unmatched in history, a new type of worker and of man'.

The simple project of making cars as efficiently as possible became a world view, a political and ethical truth, potentially a religion. In Aldous Huxley's science-fiction novel *Brave New World*, published in 1932, Fordism became the origin myth of a future dystopia. The years are designated as AF (after Ford) and Henry has become Our Ford, who seems also to have been a prominent psychologist – he was hailed as Our Freud when discussing psychology. At the mention of his greatest creation, the Model T, devotees must make the sign of T on their stomachs.

Huxley's dystopia drew attention to the dark side of Fordism – its suppression of the individual in the name of the collective, the harsh regimentation required to keep the mass-production machine going. All self-expression, all craft skills were eliminated by the assembly line; the worker has to become just another part of the machine.

But at the same time this was funny. Charlie Chaplin picked up the idea that the assembly line could drive workers mad in his 1936 film *Modern Times*. It was, explained the titles, 'A story of industry, of individual enterprise – humanity crusading in the pursuit of happiness.' A clock face dominates the title sequence. This cuts to a herd of sheep and then men pouring into a very Ford-like factory. Inside, the company president of 'Electro Steel' looks remarkably like Ford. He is seen doing a jigsaw, reading a newspaper and swallowing a pill before he turns to his work – barking instructions to speed up the production lines.

Chaplin's job is tightening two bolts but the increasing speed of the line means he cannot even take time off to swat away a fly. The work drives him mad, he goes berserk and is sacked. The modern age, for Chaplin, turns out to be an industrialised hell. He escapes with his girlfriend Paulette Goddard, walking down the open road into a new, free dawn.

8

The workers had to pay for that $5-a-day wage; it came with social and moral strings attached. You had to work at Ford for six months to earn the rate and you had to be morally sound by the standards of the Sociological Department which had been founded in 1913 with Dr Samuel Marquis, an Episcopalian clergyman, at its head. This, surely, was one of the most extraordinary corporate creations – wildly paternalistic, ruthlessly intrusive and yet, at first, successful and apparently well-meaning. The *Detroit Free Press*, perhaps unintentionally, captured the intensity of the authoritarianism and paternalism the department represented: 'Its work will be to guard against an employee's prosperity injuring his efficiency. Employees who cannot remain sober and industrious will be dismissed, but not until an indisposition to become a valuable employee is shown.'

There were 50 investigators, rising to 200, who were sent out to assess the qualities of the employees' lives – their way with money, their drinking and the quality of their marriages. Women didn't qualify unless they were single with children to support and men didn't qualify unless the only work done by their wives was house-work. They even had to ask the company's permission to buy a car; this required the buyer to be married with children.

'A man who is living aright,' wrote Ford/Crowther in *My Life and Work*, 'will do his work aright.' Yet in the same book Ford reversed his position. Having created the most paternalistic system imagin-able, he announced, 'Paternalism has no place in industry. Welfare work that consists in prying into employees' private concerns is out of date.'

Such contradictions are commonplace in the imagination of this 'man so various'. This was often noted by more sophisticated minds. 'He is a remarkable man in one sense, and in another he is not,' said his friend Thomas Alva Edison. 'I would not vote for him for Presi-dent, but as a director of manufacturing or industrial enterprises I'd vote for him – twice.'

'There is something in his face too elusive for either camera or brush,' wrote Reverend Marquis. Marquis also compared this messy elusiveness to the silky perfection of the industrial processes he cre-ated. 'If only,' he cried, 'Henry Ford were properly assembled!'

Yet I doubt that Ford saw any contradictions. He does not seem to have taken the trouble to study his own mind. He was, at heart, a very simple man. His simplicity was a narcissistic circularity – I do what I do and what I do must be right and good because I do it. Such an irrational but self-sustaining credo is not uncommon among people who attain great power; the power provides them with evidence that they are right. With Ford, the complexity and confusion arose when he tried to explain and justify this to himself and the world. He did this through the people he knew, admired and respected.

This could be catastrophic. Ernest Liebold was Ford's secretary and personal financial adviser. He coached Ford in anti-semitism. It was said that 'the door to Ford's mind was always open to anything Liebold wanted to shove in it, and during that time Mr. Ford developed a dislike for the Jews, a dislike which appeared to become stronger and more bitter as time went on'. This was publicly expressed in anti-semitic rants in the *Dearborn Independent*, a newspaper Ford bought in 1919.

The rants in the *Independent* made Ford himself into a mentor to Adolf Hitler. 'Jews,' Hitler wrote in his prison memoir *Mein Kampf*, 'are the regents of the stock exchange power of the American Union. Every year they manage to become increasingly the controlling masters of the labour power of a people of 120,000,000 souls; one great man, Ford, to their exasperation still holds out independently there even now.'

When the rants became a book – *The International Jew* – they infiltrated the minds of all Nazi sympathisers. The chilling testimony of Baldur von Schirach, formerly head of the Hitler Youth, at the Nuremberg trials of the Nazis in 1946 makes this clear: 'The decisive anti-Semitic book which I read at that time, and the book which influenced my comrades . . . was Henry Ford's book, *The International Jew*. I read it and became an anti-Semite. In those days this book made a great impression on my friends and myself because we saw in Henry Ford the representative of success, and also the representative of a progressive social policy.'

Ford even attempted to ban brass in the Model T because it was a 'Jew metal'. Engineers went ahead and used it anyway, painting it black so that he would not notice.

There was something weirdly innocent about Ford's anti-semitism.

He genuinely believed that he was only attacking bad Jews, not good ones. When a rabbi to whom Ford had given a Model T every year returned the gift in 1920 as a result of his rants in the *Independent* he was mystified – 'What's wrong, Dr Franklin? Has something come between us?'

But following a $1 million libel suit, filed in 1925 against Ford for his attacks on Jews, he folded. The trial collapsed but Ford suddenly saw the damage being done by his anti-semitism and he issued an apology to Jews 'asking their forgiveness for the harm that I have unintentionally committed, by retracting so far as lies within my power the offensive charges laid at their door'.

Less catastrophic than his friendship with Liebold was his friendship with Edison, America's greatest inventor. He was certainly one of Ford's closest friends but he was too much the superior partner in the relationship to be relegated to the role of mere mentor. He was, perhaps, a father figure. 'At heart Ford is just a boy,' he said. 'He will never cease to be a boy.'

Ford considered Edison the greatest man in the world: 'He believes that unflinching, unremitting work will accomplish anything. It was this genius for hard work that fired me as a lad and made Mr. Edison my hero.'

Later in life he said, 'We are ahead of all other countries today, simply and solely because we have Mr. Edison.'

More interesting were the people who formed a trio of close advisers or, rather, men whom he felt could give meaning to Ford and elevate him above the daily grind of the company. They were, in descending order, a clergyman, a naturalist and a thug – Marquis was the first, the naturalist John Burroughs was the second and Harry Bennett the third.

In taking on the Sociological Department in 1913 Marquis had felt he was 'to be part of a great experiment in applied Christianity in industry' but he left his job in 1921 as the paternalist phase was ending and, as he put it, the executives who had 'set justice and humanity above profits and production were gone'.

He was a highly intelligent man and a good writer so the book he produced in 1923 – *Henry Ford: An Interpretation* – is incisive. He balanced Ford's qualities with his flaws: 'Henry Ford is an unusual man, a most remarkable man, but not a great man – not yet.' He was impermeable – 'The isolation of Henry Ford's mind is as near perfect as it is possible to make it' – but Marquis detected a need for something more, some transcendent vision: 'As a manufacturer he is naturally immersed in a sea of practical affairs to the surface of which there rises once in a while bubbles of mysticism, haunting suggestions of "The Plan", a shadowy Calvinistic belief in Fate or Foreordination, the serenities of one conscious of being a Child of Destiny.'

The shadowy Calvinism became a more visible puritanism about design: 'Standardization is his hobby. He would have all shoes made on one last, all hats made on one block, and all coats according to one pattern. It would not add to the beauty of life, but it would greatly reduce the cost of living.'

John Burroughs with his immense beard and prophetic manner looked like his hero, the poet Walt Whitman. He was America's leading and most popular naturalist. He had written critically of the impact of industry and he feared that the car would diminish people's appreciation of the natural world. In December 1912, aged 75, he received a letter from Ford, praising his books and offering him a free Model T. He accepted and, after some driving lessons from a relative, he started bounding about his favourite birdwatching hides with the aid of the T's magnificently pliable suspension. Burroughs was converted. Seldom can a corporate gift have been so persuasive. 'Out of that automobile grew our friendship,' wrote Ford/Crowther in *My Life and Work*, 'and it was a fine one. No man could help being the better for knowing John Burroughs.'

They met in Detroit the following year and Burroughs was startled to discover that Ford's knowledge of birds was encyclopaedic – he kept a telescope for birdwatching in his office at the company's Highland Park plant. Later Ford and his wife Clara visited Burroughs in Massachusetts. There he was introduced to the work of a pantheon of American gods – Henry Thoreau, Nathaniel Hawthorne, Louisa May Alcott and, most importantly, Ralph Waldo Emerson.

Emerson, who died in 1882, was the prophet of transcendentalism and 'the infinitude of the private man'. Ford was entranced; he kept Emerson's books about him for the rest of his life. The passages he annotated in the margins make it clear that he had found a thinker who explained his life, the provider of the metaphysics of Henry Ford. 'As there is no screen or ceiling,' ran one approved passage, 'between our heads and the infinite heavens, so there is no bar or wall in the soul where man, the effect, ceases and God, the cause, begins.'

The individual, directly connected to God, strong, impulsive, following his own instincts rather than being tied down by rationalities – this was how, after reading Emerson, Ford saw himself. Thanks to his ensuing mentor, Harry Bennett, this was not going to have a good outcome.

Burroughs died in 1921, his last eight years having been enlivened by a series of wilderness jaunts with Ford, Edison and Harvey Firestone, creator of the Firestone tyre company. They called themselves the 'Four Vagabonds', a comical name for outings that were more like ultra-glamping than camping. Fleets of cars and platoons of underlings and, on later trips, hordes of journalists and photographers accompanied them.

'John Burroughs, Edison, and I with Harvey S. Firestone,' wrote Ford/Crowther, 'made several vagabond trips together. We went in motor caravans and slept under canvas. Once we gypsied through the Adirondacks and again through the Alleghenies, heading southward. The trips were good fun—except that they began to attract too much attention.'

Ford's summary of Burroughs's character was pure Emerson: 'He was not pagan; he was not pantheist; but he did not much divide between nature and human nature, nor between human nature and divine.'

Such high-mindedness could not be ascribed to Harry Bennett, the third Ford mentor. The first thing to be said about Harry was that not only was he not Marquis or Burroughs, he was also not Edsel, Ford's son. Ford's 'greatest failure' was, according to one high-ranking executive, 'the treatment of his only son'. Henry thought his sensitive and thoughtful son was too soft. Edsel admired his father but was temperamentally close to his mother, Clara. He was interested in the arts, a subject of which Ford knew nothing.

He was always interested in cars but he was more of an aesthete than his father. Once, working at the company, he designed a sport version of the Model T but Henry never let him produce it. He was popular at work but as he rose to succeed Henry as company president in 1919 it became clear that Henry was to remain the real boss. Edsel, ever obedient to his father, acquiesced. Decisions were routinely reversed. 'I don't know,' he said, 'what kick Father gets out of humiliating me this way.'

There was a crucial difference between them on company policy. As Model T sales declined in the 1920s, it was clear to Edsel and many others that they needed to come up with a new car. With Alfred Sloan now president of General Motors, the competition, especially from GM's Chevrolet division, was becoming intense. For the first time 'Ford domination,' wrote James C. Young in the *New York Times*, 'has been seriously challenged.'

The battle within the company was long and bitter but, finally, Henry bowed to what by then must have seemed inevitable – he approved the development of a new car. But still father and son fought. Henry continued to act as if he knew what was best for the customers; design-conscious Edsel planned to give the customers what they wanted. Somehow, from this battle, the new Model A appeared in 1927.

But all the while Henry was growing closer to the son he never had, Harry Bennett. 'I sort of raised him,' he said of Bennett. Born in Ann Arbor, Michigan, Bennett joined the navy when he was seventeen. He learned to box, fighting under the name Sailor Reese. Bennett joined the Ford company at service branches in New York and Detroit. He made a name for himself – and caught the eye of Henry – when he evicted some saboteurs and rose to become head of security at the River Rouge plant. He plotted against the Sociological Department, causing the resignation of Ford's previous adviser, Reverend Marquis, in 1921. In the same year he became head of the Service Department which looked after internal security. 'This collection of street fighters,' writes Ford biographer Steven Watts, 'ex-convicts, underworld figures, and athletes numbered about three thousand by the early 1930s.'

Bennett spied on and intimidated everybody, and as unions – notably the United Auto Workers (UAW) – began to form within the motor industry, he fought them off, having become chief labour negotiator. He was near the top of the company, though he remained little known outside.

'In many minds,' said *Forum* magazine, 'he occupies the position Rasputin did in Russia.'

A gangster in appearance – sharp suit, bow tie and fedora – he was a gangster in action. His violent methods came to a climax with the Battle of the Overpass in 1937. While having their photograph taken at a pedestrian overpass by the Rouge, UAW organisers were attacked by Bennett's goons. It was a skirmish rather than a battle – though one of the union men had his back broken – but it made headlines. It was a public display of the transformation of the Ford Motor Company from people's friend to ruthless corporate giant.

Incredibly, Bennett almost rose to the very top. The other, unadopted son, Edsel Ford, died of cancer, aged 49, in 1943. Henry wanted to make Bennett president and he drafted a codicil in his will to that effect. Eleanor, Edsel's widow, and Clara were outraged. Ford backed down and in 1945 Henry Ford II, Edsel's son, became president. Bennett died, aged 86, in 1979.

9

Though surpassed in size by General Motors, the Ford Motor Company endured, along with Chrysler, as one of Detroit's Big Three – as, in effect, just another big car company. But, in truth, it was and will always be *the* big car company and it will be so entirely because of the character of its founder and that character as expressed in the Model T.

Many underestimated Henry Ford but only one man overestimated him – Henry Ford. On the evidence of his success, he believed so much in himself that he came to see his skills as transferable on an epic scale. In the 1920s he began to consider himself as a potential contender for President of the United States, an aspiration that horrified Clara.

She told an assembly of the Daughters of the American Revolution, 'Mr. Ford has enough and more than enough to do to attend to his business in Detroit. The day he runs for President of the United States, I will be on the next boat to England.'

But his greatest and most embarrassing attempt to transfer his skills was the project that came to be known as the 'Peace Ship'. In 1915 he decided to fix the First World War in Europe. He had been convinced that the warring nations so desperately wanted peace that they would accept a neutral mediator. He failed to talk

President Woodrow Wilson into backing the scheme. Undeterred, he announced, 'We're going to try to get the boys out of the trenches before Christmas. I've chartered a ship and some of us are going to Europe.'

The ship was the Scandinavian–American liner *Oscar II*. Ford wanted to fill it with distinguished anti-war politicians and campaigners. At first there was wild enthusiasm for the idea but then doubts began to emerge and the big names started to drop out. Alton Brooks Parker, a Democrat who had run for president in 1904, saw the voyage as potentially shameful: 'If we could only be sure that all other nations would estimate him as we do, as a clown, strutting on the stage for a little time, no harm could come of it. But we have no such assurance. The chances are that his antics will be taken seriously and they will tend to bring us into contempt if not hatred.'

Nevertheless, the *Oscar II* sailed from Hoboken on 4 December 1915, carrying an alarming number of marginals, cranks and eccentrics. Many were violently seasick and the rest formed warring factions about how best to stop the war. Flu swept through the ship, killing one passenger and seriously weakening Ford. The ship was greeted in Norway with little enthusiasm and, on the 23rd, Ford abandoned Bergen and the *Oscar II* and booked a passage home, arriving in Brooklyn on 2 January.

War plainly offended him – it was wasteful. The carnage of the trenches contrasted with the smooth running of his factories. What he perhaps did not realise was that his Detroit was an enclave, an island, an oasis, not a continent. It was the harbinger of a new world, a new way of life, but it did not show how it could – or should – be run.

Indeed, as the American history professor Stefan Link makes clear in his paper 'Rethinking the Ford-Nazi Connection', Ford's political ideas and role have been misunderstood. Merely the fact that he was embraced by the Nazis did not make him a Nazi or a fascist – nor, in fact, did Stalin's praise make him a communist. In the twenties and thirties he merely provided material for 'a whole stratum of illiberal modernizers across the globe'.

At home, having led his people into 'God's great open spaces', he also led them into the factory, the car-made city and the increasing desecration of the wilderness. On the whole they loved him for it.

Believers in progress believed in Henry but so did those who clung on to the old values of the farmer and the small towns of the Midwest, of what some cynics came to call flyover America.

Henry Ford died at 11.40 pm on 7 April 1947 of a massive cerebral haemorrhage apparently brought on when he stooped to untie his shoelaces.

Adolf Hitler with a model of the People's Car

Chapter Three

THE PYRAMIDS OF THE
THIRD REICH

1

On 26 March 1923 Benito Mussolini struck the ground with a pick-axe 41 times – the number was noted by an admiring journalist. He did so in the village of Lainate, 13 miles north-west of Milan, having driven there in his own car. Mussolini had been made Italian prime minister by order of King Victor Emmanuel III five months previously. Lustily swinging the pickaxe and driving his own car were gestures designed to signal the virility and optimism of Italy's new fascist regime. The reason he swung and drove was an invitation to the glories of the fascist future.

After Mussolini had finished, 400 workers swarmed onto the site to begin construction of the Milan–Alpine Lakes motorway that would link the industrial area of Milan to the paradise of the Italian lakes. This is often claimed to be the first motorway in the world, or at least the first in Europe. Neither claim is wholly legitimate.

In America the Long Island Motor Parkway, a 48-mile toll road, opened in 1908. It was a private venture by William Kissam Vanderbilt II, a racing enthusiast. He had seen two spectators killed at his races and he was determined to build a safe road for high-speed traffic. The Parkway was, as a result, a genuine motorway – controlled access, bridges and overpasses instead of intersections, banked turns, guardrails and tarmac surfaces. But it failed as a commercial venture and in 1938 it was taken over by the State of New York to cover back taxes.

In Europe the Milan–Lakes road was preceded by an oddity

known as AVUS. This is the Automobil-Verkehrs und Übungstrasse – automobile traffic training ground – in Berlin, which opened in 1921. It was a dual carriageway but the four ends were linked by hairpin bends to turn the whole thing into a racing circuit. Racing became its most celebrated purpose, though now it is part of the Bundesautobahn 115. The Germans can therefore claim to be, strictly speaking, the first motorway builders in Europe. They now have a popular reputation as the sole inventors of the 'limited [or controlled] access highway' – the technical term for such roads.

Nevertheless, Mussolini was ahead of Hitler in his futurist plans for a network of motorways covering the entire country. The man most often given the credit for this grandiose scheme was Piero Puricelli. He was a stylish engineer – 'never without a starched collar and a sharp suit,' writes journalist Thea Lenarduzzi – and, more importantly, a technocrat. As European empires crumbled after the First World War, old aristocratic forms of governance lost their legitimacy. This created a void that was to be filled, in part, by technocrats – experts possessed, usually, of scientific or technical knowledge. For undemocratic countries like Mussolini's Italy, technocrats became essential to the process of state annexation of large-scale projects and there were no projects larger than road building.

In 1922, the year Mussolini came to power, Puricelli produced a pamphlet. It was first an excoriating attack on the condition of Italian road and rail systems and second a plea to open up the country to the car. 'Industry and modern commerce,' he wrote, 'employ the automobile on the road in the same way that calculating machines are employed in offices. Such are the times . . . The roads for motor vehicles will be real industrial roads and magnificent instruments of work.'

Puricelli regarded with dismay the way 'powerful machines capable of 100 km an hour and your light small cars' only led to disillusionment because these machines were held back by the speed limits and condition of existing roads. 'It becomes a physical martyrdom due to the fatigue of the shaking, the steering, the braking and distress of the dangers, disputes and fights with undisciplined wagons.'

The underlying themes of the pamphlet – rejection of the past, disgust with the present and grandiose plans for the future – would be music to the ears of all good fascists. Fascism was, above all, a futurist project and futurism, the art movement, was Italian. It was launched in Milan with the *Manifesto of Futurism* in 1909 by the poet Filippo Tommaso Marinetti. 'We want no part of it, the past,' he announced. The car, specifically because of its speed, was the emblematic technology of the new age. 'We say that the world's magnificence has been enriched by a new beauty: the beauty of speed. Time and Space died yesterday. We already live in the absolute, because we have created eternal, omnipresent speed.'

Futurism was perhaps the most distasteful and absurd of all art movements. Futurists really liked violence and war, didn't think much of women and despised the old. But in a sense, and for all their sociopathic teenage raving, they were right. The future *was* rushing towards them, bringing the First World War, revolutions and, devastatingly, the collapse of empires – Ottoman, Austro-Hungarian, Russian, German and, ultimately, British. From those ruins would rise fascism, Nazism and communism, political ideologies that genuinely believed in the new ascendancy of the future. Cars, especially moving at speed, were the guiding force of this new age.

But this onrushing dash of the car was only part of what the fascists wanted. By 1922 Marinetti's futurist madness was already part of the automotive past, of the days when only a few rich hobbyists and speed freaks actually owned cars. The new future was a world in which everybody would own a car and would not necessarily want Marinetti's eternal, omnipresent speed. Cars and motorways would, therefore, need to answer to the needs of domesticity, of the ordinary requirements of everyday life.

After all, the fascists – as both Mussolini and Hitler understood all too well – needed the people. So, though Puricelli and Marinetti might have both wanted speed, Mussolini wanted the future and that had to include a happy and biddable citizenry. Of course, he also wanted war – 'War is to man what maternity is to woman' – but he thought this was all part of the ideal domestic life – 'The function of a citizen and a soldier are inseparable.'

Work on the motorway began at once. By 20 September 1923 the first stretch was ready. The first car to use it was a Lancia Trikappa, a coupé de ville – meaning it had an open-topped driving position and a closed passenger compartment. Puricelli was at the wheel and King Victor Emmanuel III was in the rear.

The choice of car was an affront to another Italian car maker, Alfa Romeo, but Alfa later became closely – and ultimately fatally – associated with the great leader, providing him with seven 'parade' cars in 1937. The company also provided his mistress Clara Petacci with an exquisite 1939 Alfa 6c Berlinetta. Together, as the fascist dream fell apart around them, they used this car in an attempt to flee to Switzerland in 1945. They were stopped by communist partisans on 27 April. Both were shot the next day; their bodies were hung from the roof of a petrol station in Milan. The 'lovingly restored' Alfa was sold for £1.4 million in 2015.

Mussolini's grand motorway-building plans fared little better. Whatever its claims to primacy, the Milan–Alpine Lakes road was an awful motorway. It was a single 8-metre-wide carriageway with no centre line and no surface markings. Only motor vehicles were allowed – the one thing that really made it a motorway – and entry was via junctions with tollhouses where tickets were sold, priced according to where the driver intended to leave the road. Tollhouse officers and 'road inspector cyclists' wore military-like uniforms and the road was closed at night. This did not matter much as very few cars used the road, day or night. The one virtue of the motorway was the surface – concrete covered with Mexican bitumen – which made it possible for cars to be driven fast without fear of ruts and potholes. Futurist fans could at least cling on to this.

In spite of its many shortcomings the Milan–Lakes road inspired a frenzy of motorway planning in Italy. Every city seemed to want one. Even Puricelli felt the Italians were getting ahead of themselves – 'motoring is not yet adequately developed here'. But still he went on with his own plans, becoming an international prophet as the world descended on Italy to see the future. The climax of a World Road Association Congress in Milan in 1926 was a convoy of buses taking 1,700 attendees from 53 nations to see the Milan–Lakes motorway. Mussolini presided over the closing ceremony in Rome.

But this was a climax of more than just the congress; it was the high point of Italian motorway mania. Paying for the multiple pro-posals was one problem. Deciding exactly what motorways were for – serving existing wealthy areas or as creators of new growth in poor ones – was another. There were even fears that excluding anything other than motor vehicles from the motorways would eventually mean that cars would be excluded from ordinary roads.

On top of all that, between 1925 and 1927 Mussolini moved to form a dictatorship free of all previous restraints, including that of parliament. He could now only be deposed by the king. The motorway building programme was stalled.

It was not stalled solely by politics; the money also stood in the way. There was the cost of these increasingly mighty road schemes but there were also the disastrous figures from the Milan–Lakes motorway. Annual revenue from its toll was only 4 million lire as opposed to the 7 million promised and only 700 cars a day used the road against the 1,000 promised. If this was the future, it didn't pay and it was sparsely populated.

In the end only 500 kilometres of Italian motorways were completed in the twenties and thirties. It was a sad fraction of the national network of concrete and speed which Puricelli and many others had dreamed of creating. But his idea was to be embraced by another futurist dictator unencumbered by the doubts and divisions of fascist Italy.

2

Tom Hanks once told David Letterman, 'No matter how fast you drive in Germany, someone is driving faster than you.' This is probably true. On some stretches of German autobahns you can take your Bugatti Chiron up to 250 mph without fear of prosecution.

In fact, not only will you not be prosecuted, you will be positively encouraged by the people selling Germany as a holiday destination. Driving on unrestricted autobahns is recommended by the German government as one of 'seven things you must do while in Germany'. They also offer ten guidelines for surviving the experience, including keeping visits to the left – fast – lane brief because 'It's a dog-eat-dog world out there!'

For eager holidaymakers, a German car-rental company – Motion Drive – offers a tourist package entitled 'German Autobahn Experience'. You can terrify yourself for a day in a Ferrari 488 GTB – top speed 400 kph – overseen by an instructor for €799. Of course, you must be careful. The government also helpfully suggests you keep a safe distance at high speed. This is half your speed in metres – around 200 metres in the case of the maxed-out Chiron.

Unrestricted public roads have become a proud, national asset. Katrin Bennhold in the *New York Times* compared this German oddity with whaling in Japan and gun ownership in America – a 'quasi-religious' obsession incomprehensible to other nations.

Adolf Hitler is responsible for this state of affairs but his legacy is ambiguous. He was, first, against speed limits. In 1934 the Nazis' Highway Code abolished all speed restrictions, even in built-up areas. This was done on the assumption that all good Germans would drive cautiously and courteously. They did not do so. German roads quickly became the most dangerous in Europe. This made Adolf angry. He said the drivers who were causing thousands of deaths were 'a plague on the people'. He then became a big fan of speed limits – imposing 60 kilometres per hour (kph) in built-up areas and 90 kph on open roads. He cut them even further when the war began and petrol needed to be conserved. After the war and the partition of the country, East Germany persisted with the Nazi regulations but West Germany wouldn't touch them.

This was an odd gesture, since Hitler had first supported limitless roads before imposing limits. There was nothing that was especially Nazi about either choice. Nevertheless, in spite of oil crises and environmental campaigns, the Germans clung to their derestricted roads throughout the post-war period. It was, perhaps, a gesture of freedom from the strictures of bourgeois life – the car as private space and provider of limitless freedom.

Nevertheless, Hitler might have been right about the cautious, courteous *volk*. At 3.7 annual traffic fatalities per 100,000 inhabitants, German roads are now safer than those of France, Belgium and Italy, but more dangerous than the United Kingdom – in other words, better than average in Europe. The number in the United States is 12.4. The relative safety of German roads may be due to the thoroughness of their driving tests. These are intense, involve attending special driving schools and taking multiple examinations.

3

Autobahn, historian Thomas Zeller points out, is, like *Kindergarten*, *Blitzkrieg* and *Angst*, one of the few German words now commonly used in English. In part this is because of pop cultural references such as Kraftwerk's rather dismal song 'Autobahn', the German TV cop show *Alarm für Cobra II – Die Autobahnenpolizei* and a variety of computer games with autobahn settings. It is also a word that is easy for English speakers to pronounce correctly.

But mainly it is because the word has acquired a historical resonance denied to motorways, highways, autoroutes or even autostrada. That resonance is twofold. It derives, first, from the autobahns' pre-1939 role as concrete glorifications of the Nazi regime, both its power and its spiritual roots in the German landscape. The roads were seen, like other building projects, as 'Pyramids of the Third Reich' – to the humans of the deep future their ruins, like the pyramids of ancient Egypt, would signify the greatness of the National Socialist ideal. They are now, in contrast, seen as emblems of the post-1945 mythology of German efficiency, modernity, economic success and, of course, speed. The 'economic miracle' that rose from the ruins of the war would flash by at terrifying speed on superbly constructed roads.

But neither Nazism nor democratic efficiency quite capture the strange cultural and political assumptions and the magical thinking that gave birth to the autobahn. This was all distilled in the personality of Alwin Seifert.

He possessed, it is said, a 'calcium aura'. His body reacted to calcium-rich soil with rheumatic pain. In a moving train he claimed to be able to sense the geology below. He was sleepless because his house in Munich was built on a gravel plain. He was certain that subterranean water affected people's health. If a large number of accidents occurred on a stretch of new autobahn, he brought in a dowser to check the ground beneath these Pyramids of the Third Reich. Seifert's enthusiasm for dowsing was shared by Fritz Todt, the engineer who became a leading Nazi prior to his death – possibly an assassination – in a plane crash in 1942. Todt once called in a dowser, Professor Wimmer, when one autobahn was struck by lightning in 1936.

Seifert was born in Munich in 1890. His imagination was formed by the Wandervogel (wandering bird) movement. This was a hiking club with attitude – members disdained urban comforts in favour of rural authenticity and they defended untouched nature against the encroachment of industry. Nature, they thought, was the only way of finding one's true self. The Wandervogels were greens who happened to be precursors of the Nazis in their faith in the unique values embodied in the German landscape, especially the forests.

Seifert self-trained as a landscape architect and garden designer. None of which sounds much like a qualification for building autobahns but, in the strange world of Nazi ideology, it was. In the First World War he was an army railway engineer. Near the city of Metz he constructed a line that meandered up a mountain through forests – 'A true work of art,' he called it. More precisely, it was a combination of the comparatively modern technology of the railway with the sanctity of the woodland. The meandering line anticipated his thoughts on autobahn design.

He was, apart from being a proto-green, an ethnocentrist and an anti-semite. He was also anti-rationalist; he rejected mechanistic thinking of any kind in favour of feeling and intuition. He was a Nazi futurist in his belief in the dawning of a new age.

'A revaluation of all values is at hand,' he wrote, echoing Nietzsche. 'The countable and the measurable, which was yesterday still the absolute, the unalterable, has become today very relative; now only the unprovable is absolute, imperative.'

In 1919 he met Rudolf Hess, later Hitler's deputy, who subsequently funded his work, as did Fritz Todt. As a result of such contacts, in 1934 he was assigned to Todt's department of road construction. In the ensuing years he made contacts with more leading Nazis and rose to become the central figure in the landscaping of the autobahn system. In the process Seifert's greenery and anti-rationalist thinking had somehow been transformed into a justification for building Hitler's highways. The German land – like 'God's great open spaces' evoked by Henry Ford – would be invaded by concrete and steel but the roads would be curvaceous, sinuous and they would be lined with trees and plants.

Fritz Todt agreed in principle. Straight roads evoked not the future but the mechanistic past of the railways.

'The railway is a medium for mass transit . . . The roadway is a medium for individual transport. The train is usually a foreign body in the landscape. The motor roadway is and remains a road, and the road is part and parcel of the landscape. The German landscape is full of character. The motor roadway, too, must be given a German character.'

In reality, the pursuit of curves and trees did not really succeed. Todt was unconvinced by Seifert's meanderings. The ensuing debate on the apparently simple matter of road design became psychological and anthropological. Straight roads made people tired and bored but curved roads decreased visibility and might cause accidents. Todt became a straightist: 'After all, the motor vehicle is not a rabbit or a deer that jumps around the terrain in winding and twisting lines, but is a technological artifact that was created by man and demands a suitable driving surface.'

The point of both Seifert and Todt was that they had tapped into the magical thinking that lay at the heart of Nazism. These roads were not just roads nor even autostrada; they were expressions of the ancient Teutonic land newly created for the modern world. This was made clear in May 1935 when 600,000 people turned up to a ceremony to mark the first stretch of autobahn between Darmstadt and Frankfurt. Todt described them as 'Adolf Hitler's roads' and 'symbols of the new Germany' and, crucially, 'a mediator between man and landscape'. This was obviously ideological madness but it demonstrates the way cars had by the thirties begun to dominate forms of political thinking other than the capitalist/Fordist forms of America. They were populist in intent. It has been said the autobahns were military projects. In truth, they were genuinely designed for people in cars.

4

Glorious as the concrete Pyramids of the Third Reich might have seemed, they were doomed to failure because the people they were meant to serve did not have cars. There were eight cars per 1,000 inhabitants in Germany in 1932; in the United States there were 183. In 1929 a team from General Motors visited Germany and concluded the Germans were 18 years behind the Americans.

When he first came into power in 1933 Adolf Hitler put Todt in charge of road building and, by 1936, almost 1,000 kilometres of autobahn were being constructed annually. The goal, says Thomas Zeller, 'was to symbolize power and the conquest of space by means of a large-scale technological system and to stabilize the dictatorship'. Also in 1933 Hitler announced he would develop a people's

car, a *volkswagen*. The genre had been created by the Model T and
the Führer had already professed his admiration for Henry Ford.

But there were German antecedents, notably the Hanomag 2/10
built between 1925 and 1928. This looked a little like the Beetle and,
like the Beetle, it had a rear engine. It was known as the Kommisbrot,
a small loaf of bread usually eaten by soldiers. It was the cheapest
car available at the time and it could do 40 mph and travel 60 miles
on a gallon of fuel. But only 16,000 were sold. Then there was the
Standard Superior, which, again, looked a little like a Beetle – especially from the rear – and, in fact, it was briefly called a Volkswagen.
It had a mid-mounted engine – in front of rather than behind or on
top of the rear axle. It was released in the same year Hitler made his
announcement. Bizarrely, the Czechs almost produced a near-Beetle
in the form of the Tatra V570, though this never got beyond a couple
of prototypes – the second in 1933, a fateful year for cars and the
world. It had an air-cooled rear engine and a very Beetleish profile.

Clearly there was some collective central European pressure,
some Jungian archetype, driving designers and engineers towards
the Beetle. And it was not just the designers. The Small Car Club of
Germany was founded in 1927 in a suburb of Berlin. The founders
were ambitious; they campaigned 'in the interest of civilisation's
progress' and to 'raise the social levels of the German people'. A
magazine – *Mein Kleinauto* – was launched. But, like the pre-Beetle
cars, the club soon faded from view.

Meanwhile, the German car industry was in trouble. There had
been 86 car makers in the twenties but only 12 survived the Great
Depression and four of those merged into one company – Auto
Union, later Audi. Some genius was needed to cut through all this
and complete the project. His name was Ferdinand Porsche to whom
Hitler awarded the contract to build his *volkswagen* in 1934.

In fact, there is some dispute about whether Porsche really was
the first to pluck the true people's car from the cloud of predecessors
drifting above central Europe. Béla Barényi was a brilliant inventor,
born, like Porsche, into the Austro-Hungarian Empire. When he
retired in 1972 he had 2,000 patents to his name, twice as many as
Edison. A technical drawing from 1925 seems to confirm that he had
come up with a fully fledged Beetle design before Porsche. In 1953
he was able to prove in court that some of Porsche's patents should
have been his and Mercedes-Benz, for whom he was then a designer,

supported him. The State Patent Office in Mannheim agreed and Barényi accepted compensation of a single Deutsche Mark. He also successfully sued Volkswagen for copyright infringement so that he was legally acknowledged as a creator of the Beetle.

But Porsche was Hitler's man. He was born in 1875 in Bohemia. Aged 13 he was something of a freak in his neighbourhood when he became obsessed with a building lit by electricity. He prompted fears locally that he was somehow possessed. His father, Anton, wanted him to go into his own trade of panel beating but his son's obsession could not be cured. With the compliance of his mother, he created a secret laboratory on the top floor of their house. His father discovered it and in his anger he stamped on the equipment causing a spillage of battery acid that burned through the soles of his boots. Still the boy persisted, acquiring little formal education, because, at heart, he was an autodidact.

In 1898 in Vienna he worked for a coachmaker that was planning to produce cars. Their first was the C2 Phaeton; all the primary components were stamped P1 by Porsche to claim the car as his own design. It would subsequently become known as the Porsche P1. The car was electrically powered with a 50-mile range at a speed of 9 mph. He followed up with one of the first hybrid cars – the Lohner-Porsche Mixte Hybrid in 1901 – though Henri Pieper in Belgium might have beaten him by a few months. Porsche himself drove it at the Exelberg Rally in 1901 and won.

He became chief designer of Austro-Daimler in 1906. There he designed the beautiful Porsche 27/80, known as the Prince Henry Car, as it was made for Prince Henry of Prussia. He also became linked with the Jellinek family; he built a car for Mercédès Jellinek's younger sister, André Maja. His career soared thereafter and in 1931 he founded the Porsche company that is still with us. In 1934 he won the contract for Hitler's people's car. By then Porsche was clearly a Bauhaus modernist, a believer that form followed function without the intervention of any aesthetic nonsense. 'Design must be functional,' he said, 'and functionality must be translated into visual aesthetics, without any reliance on gimmicks that have to be explained.'

He became known as 'The Great German Engineer'. To make this true he had to renounce the Czech citizenship he had embraced in 1918 after the collapse of the Austro-Hungarian Empire. As Hitler regarded Czechs as subhuman, Porsche was swiftly turned into a German. He was to remain a faithful German patriot, joining the Nazi Party in 1937 and becoming an SS-Oberführer, perhaps one of the most tainted ranks in military history, in 1942. He built tanks and other weaponry for the war effort. That he was an engineer of genius is beyond doubt, as is the fact that he was an enthusiastic Nazi.

The Porsche 356 was launched in 1948. It was the first car bearing the company name, the forerunner of the celebrated 911 and, in a sense, all of Porsche's post-war cars. Some might reasonably argue that, aesthetically and mechanically, it was Ferdinand's masterpiece. They would be wrong. His masterpiece was the first true successor to the Model T, the Volkswagen Type 1 – known in German as the Käfer, meaning beetle.

5

It was the best of cars; it was the worst of cars. Spawned in one of the foulest of human imaginations, the Volkswagen Beetle went on to become an emblem of peace, freedom, hope and resistance to the automotive empire of Detroit. What it signally failed to do was make sense of the autobahn system and its attendant theologies. This was because it never went into mass production under Hitler.

A state organisation in 1936 took over the project. It was called Kraft durch Freude – Strength Through Joy. This was, basically, all about tourism and making the masses happy, a programme that included making them a nice car. This would, according to Hitler's specifications, carry two adults and three children at speeds of up to 100 kph without using more than 7 litres of fuel per 100 kilometres. The Führer also favoured an air-cooled engine. It was to cost no more than 990 Reichsmarks, a very low figure indeed – the Hanomag mentioned above cost 2,000 RM. Production of the KdF-Wagen, as it was originally known, was to be financed by regular down pay-ments made by potential buyers – they would put little red stamps marking their 5 RM-a-week contributions in their KdF *Sparkarte* (savings booklet). Between 1938 and 1939 about 270,000 people had opened one of these accounts. This canny move, obviously a way of pre-financing production, was disguised as a worker benefit: 'In

Germany, there is not supposed to be anything the German worker cannot partake of.' Anything except peace and a decent car.

On 26 May 1938 Hitler laid the foundation of the factory that would build the car in a forest clearing – a symbolic setting given the concerns of Todt and Seifert – near Fallersleben in Lower Saxony. He said the car was 'a symbol of the National Socialist people's community'. He had presented a Beetle prototype at the Berlin Auto Show in February, promising, 'This model will open up the automobile to millions of new customers on low incomes.' A deluge of international public relations ensued. A reporter in the *New York Times* speculated about a future in which the autobahns would be filled with 'thousands and thousands of shiny little beetles'.

Hitler was right to be enthusiastic about the car. The Volkswagen Type 1 was to be in production around the world until 20 July 2003 when the last one rolled off the line at the Puebla plant in Mexico. Over 21.5 million had been produced. The Beetle had outstripped the Model T in longevity – the T had been produced for only 19 years – and in numbers – a mere 15 million Ts had been produced.

It shared with the T a fierce single-mindedness in design. In fact, it was fiercer; whereas the T had looked like an assembly of parts, the streamlined Beetle looked like a single finished object that anticipated the look of post-war cars. It had to be pared down because of Hitler's preferred selling price but this suited Porsche's functionalist minimalism. Its engine was a four-cylinder, 1-litre 'boxer', meaning the cylinders were opposed horizontally and moved outward like a punching boxer, that produced 23 hp. Being air-cooled the car could be left out in winter without any danger of freezing. The engineering was simple, making the car easy to manufacture and service. It was certainly small – 4.5 metres long, 1.54 metres wide and 1.55 metres high – for Hitler's specified passenger capacity but it was comfortable enough.

The smooth flow of the body was created in-house by Erwin Kommenda on the aerodynamic principles developed by the Hungarian pioneer of streamlining Paul Jaray. But, though functional, the look was friendly, even cute, a factor that was to be crucial in the car's post-war success and which was to become a design theme in much of the Volkswagen range. This theme was, crucially, the opposite of the more baroque extravagances of Detroit in the fifties and sixties.

The output targets for the Fallersleben plant were 150,000 in 1939 rising to 450,000 within five years and thereafter to a peak of 1.5 million annually. This would have been the largest car plant in Europe and the ultimate goal was to exceed in scale and productivity Ford's River Rouge complex. A model city was planned on the site to house between 30,000 and 60,000 people.

None of which went according to plan. By the time the Third Reich collapsed in 1945 only 630 cars had been produced, most of which were given to Nazi leaders. This failure points to what is most remarkable about the Beetle. It was effectively never delivered before or during the war. As a result, the entire automotive and cultural significance of the Beetle is based on its popular presence in the post-war era. It appeared in children's films, and on hippie road trips, and its now loveable shape – though nothing else – was approximately resurrected in the new Beetle produced by Volkswagen between 2011 and 2019. All the loyal Germans who had assiduously collected the red stamps to put in their *Spartkarten* were never rewarded with a car.

The problem was that Hitler's ambitions were, to say the least, in conflict; a family car for the people would hardly stay high on his agenda once he had launched the Second World War by invading Poland on 3 September 1939. The war was to become the only consumer of Porsche's car. The Beetle was given higher ground clearance, a wider wheelbase, better transmission, broader tyres and a lightweight body with a canvas roof. It became the Kübelwagen – bucket car – a machine that anticipated the Jeep and the Land Rover. But the Beetle itself went into hibernation when the tanks rolled into Warsaw, only to be woken in 1945 by a car-crazy British soldier.

6

On 11 April 1945 American troops arrived in Fallersleben. The conditions of the 7,700 slaves they found there were unspeakable. Among other horrors, women had been forced to give up their new-borns; about 300 of the 350 babies died as a result of the conditions in the building to which they were removed.

In May Fallersleben was renamed Wolfsburg after the local castle and with the final defeat of Germany the country was broken up – the Russians took the east and the west was divided into French,

American and British zones. The VW plant fell into the hands of the British and was to be administered by Colonel Charles Radclyffe and Major Ivan Hirst. The plan was to use part of the plant for servicing army vehicles and to dismantle and ship out the machinery to the UK where it would be given to UK car makers. But the British car bosses turned down the machinery as useless and, having looked sneeringly at the car they were intended to produce, concluded, 'the vehicle does not meet the fundamental technical requirement of a motor-car . . . it is quite unattractive to the average buyer . . . To build the car commercially would be a completely uneconomic enterprise.' But for that ludicrous misjudgement the Beetle would have been a British car.

The British Army had more sense – it would have been difficult to have less – and, having seen a demonstration of the vehicles, they ordered 20,000. Hirst managed to make 2,490 cars by the end of the year, often cannibalising parts from Kübelwagens. The following year production rose to 1,000 cars a month. Hirst was a car fanatic and a brilliant organiser. He even made improvements to the Beetle and started a sales and service network. He also had a conscience; throughout Hirst was committed to handing the plant back to the Germans. He did, however, allow himself and his boss the luxury of their own special cars. The Radclyffe Roadster, a two-seater, was made for the colonel and a four-seater convertible for Hirst.

The Beetle had yet another freakish slice of good luck. In 1947 Radclyffe set out to recruit a German manager to take over the plant. He stumbled upon Heinrich Nordhoff, a 48-year-old banker's son with a degree in mechanical engineering. He had joined car maker Opel in 1929 just after it had been taken over by General Motors. It was to become the largest producer of passenger cars during the Third Reich – as such Opel tried to put a stop to the plans for a people's car. Nordhoff travelled to America several times. He was a negotiator and in the late thirties the company sent him to Berlin to win contracts from the Nazi government.

After the war he wanted to stay on at Opel but in spite of support from Detroit he lost his Opel/GM job as part of the denazification process. The German jurors had approved him but the American military government had the power of veto. Nordhoff had never joined the party but his problem was that the Nazis had honoured him as 'a leader of the war economy'. Nevertheless, after a compulsory period of unemployment he was able to take the job of general director at Wolfsburg on 1 January 1948. In his first year he doubled production to almost 20,000 cars and by 1961 the figure had risen to 1 million. He was to prove one of the greatest automotive managers of the post-war period and the true founder of what is still one of the biggest car companies in the world. He died in April 1968, a few months before his retirement date.

7

The greatest oddity of this story of autobahns and Beetles is Adolf Hitler. He had always been keen on cars. In his early years in Vienna he studied art and he read motoring journals, becoming something of an expert. In the twenties, when he emerged as the leading figure in what was to be known as the Nazi Party, he was constantly to be found in a Daimler-Benz showroom near the party's headquarters. There he met a salesman, Jakob Werlin, who became his motor mentor for the next 20 years.

Werlin joined the party and the SS in 1923, the year of the Munich Beer Hall Putsch, a failed Nazi coup attempt. One account suggests he was picked up by Hitler in 1924 when he was released from jail – he had been found guilty of treason following the Putsch. Werlin rose to a directorship at Daimler-Benz and simultaneously became, in 1942, 'General Inspector for the Führer in all manner of automobiles'. This put him at a very high level for a mere car dealer; he was alongside the likes of Fritz Todt and Hitler's architect Albert Speer.

'The German automobile industry can count itself lucky,' Werlin once said, 'that the Führer himself was an enthusiastic and experienced driver.' This was not true. Hitler never had a driving licence. He was driven everywhere, though he did make a point of sitting next to the driver rather than on a back seat. His automotive enthusiasm was all about engineering and appearance and nothing to do with the experience of driving. The people's car obsessed him for political reasons, but also just because it was a car. His admiration of Henry Ford – 'I regard Henry Ford as my inspiration' – was because he showed his automotive obsession could be turned into new forms of organisation and control.

His drivers became unusually important figures. His most lasting, from 1932, was Erich Kempka. He became a member of Hitler's personal eight-man SS protection squad and was put in charge of his fleet of cars. He was present in the Führerbunker in Berlin in April 1945 when Hitler and Eva Braun, his wife of the last 40 hours, killed themselves. Kempka provided the petrol to burn their bodies.

Hitler's first car was an apple-green Selve 6.20, a neat enough machine from a company that was to be destroyed by the Great Depression. But, a year later, rich friends and Werlin enabled him to buy his first Mercedes. Thereafter the man and the marque were inseparable. At his peak he was being driven around in the G4, a monstrous six-wheeler.

He was proud of his safety record; he told his drivers to moderate their speed. He explained, 'If a child walks on the road and gets hit it is not the child's fault because the child doesn't think. The driver has to think.' He was also proud of the part he claimed to play in the design of Mercedes cars. 'I can claim credit for the things that make the Mercedes cars so beautiful today! In drawings and designs, I tried hard—year after year—to perfect that shape to the utmost.'

After the war many of Hitler's cars were used and abused by Allied armies – most probably ended up as scrap. The Russians simply dragged anything of value back home. Several 770Ks – full name Grosser Offener Tourenwagen – which Hitler often used as parade cars, have appeared at auctions, one selling for as much as £13.3 million. Anything, however mundane, touched by a movie star or great artist acquires value. So, apparently, do some things touched by evil.

Harley Earl in his Buick Y-Job

Chapter Four

DESIRE

1

With a few exceptions, I dislike driving American cars. They rarely handle well and often corner horribly. The worst handler and cornerer was a Chrysler Sebring, a convertible, which I rented in 2008. It was, I concluded, the worst car in the world. Coincidentally, a few days after I returned from that trip, Jeremy Clarkson reviewed the Sebring in the *Sunday Times*. He called it 'almost certainly the worst car in the entire world'. I felt vindicated but saddened because I love the *idea* of American cars.

I love the extravagant poetry of their names – Eldorado, Mustang, Charger, Impala, Bel Air, Toronado, LaCrosse, LeSabre, Cherokee, Imperial – and the touching majesty of their bizarre heraldry. To this day the Cadillac badge is the coat of arms of Antoine de la Mothe Cadillac. There is also a poignancy about the brand names – Dodge and Oldsmobile both commemorate early car creators; Chevrolet, a heroic French racer; Cadillac, an explorer; Lincoln, a great president. But most poignant of all there is Buick.

Perhaps it's just the hard, slightly awkward sound. That sound is, I am sure, what inspired Bob Dylan to call one of his best songs 'From a Buick 6' – it is certainly not about a car – and Stephen King to write a novel entitled *From a Buick 8*. Karl Shapiro, American Poet Laureate in 1946, wrote an erotic poem simply entitled 'Buick' about making love to his car – 'Flouncing your skirts, you blueness of joy, you flirt of politeness . . .'

Buick cars are still produced but the brand now has an old-fashioned feel. It is seen as an old people's car in America and it is often said to have stolid values of sturdiness and sound construction. 'Built like a Buick' is said of large, strong men.

Yet Buick was once at the pinnacle of automotive style. It had an intoxicating effect on the Chinese; Buicks arrived in China in 1911. The following year Sun Yat-sen, the first president of the republic, was photographed in a Buick in Shanghai. The last emperor, Puyi, who had abdicated as a child, bought one in 1926. In 1929 a Buick sales office was opened in Shanghai and the next year an advertisement claimed that one in every six cars in China was a Buick and that 'Buick owners are the leading men in China'. Zhou Enlai, Mao Zedong's prime minister, owned a 1941 Buick. Well into the 2000s the marque remained a big seller in China.

Back in the USA, the Buick Y-Job of 1938 was a concept car. Designed by General Motors stylist Harley Earl, it was his most extravagant display of lavish excess. He drove it as his own car until 1951. From its aggressively swollen front end to its tapering tail, it was Earl at his best and his most brazen. In case anybody missed the point he even gave the Y a gunsight hood ornament.

David Dunbar Buick was born in Arbroath in 1854; the family moved to Detroit when he was two. His father died when he was five and his mother worked in a candy factory to support the boy. At 11 he started work on a farm and, aged 15, he started work at the Alexander Manufacturing Company, a plumbing supplier. He was a foreman when the company went bust in 1882 and with a school friend he bought what remained. He renamed it Buick and Sherwood. Luckily for Buick, who had a disastrous business sense, William Sherwood, vice-president, looked after sales and the money.

Buick was a gifted inventor, creating, among many other things, a new toilet-flushing mechanism. But his true love was internal combustion and he began working on stationary and marine engines. This irritated Sherwood, who thought plumbing was in their best interests, so Buick sold him his stake and went off to found Buick Auto-Vim and Power. In 1902 this was renamed Buick Manufacturing and he started working on cars.

In the process he invented the OHV (overhead valve) engine design. Only Oldsmobile was making money out of cars at the time and bankers were suspicious of the whole business, though almost everybody else was by then convinced they were the future. But

Buick did eventually find finance from the Briscoe brothers, sheet-metal suppliers to Oldsmobile. They ruthlessly fixed the company's structure and renamed it Buick Motor. This left hapless Buick with only $300 of the $100,000 capitalisation; the Briscoes also landed him in debt by giving him a personal loan of $3,500. He had six months to pay it back, in which case he would receive 100 per cent of the company; if not, he would lose it all.

A few days before the payback date the Briscoes sold the company and Buick found himself an employee of Flint Wagon Works. The new owners were not much better at car making than the Briscoes and the company was then sold again. Buick had become little more than a spectator to all this. The new buyer was none other than William 'Billy' Durant – much more of him later. He took one ride in the Buick Model B – a peach of a car thanks to Buick's OHV engine – and he was sold. On 1 November 1904 he took over the running of Buick Motor. Durant became the founder of General Motors in 1908. So perhaps David Buick's most lasting legacy was not a car but the mightiest industrial enterprise of the first half of the age of cars.

Durant, to his credit, kept Buick on, but the survival of his name was threatened. Everybody said the new name should be Durant and Billy himself worried about the pronunciation: 'Wonder if they'd call it Boo-ick.' But, apparently out of a sense of engineering justice, he stuck with Buick. He took the Model B to the 1905 New York Automobile Show and sold 1,108, an impressive feat for a virtually unknown car when there were only a few thousand cars on American roads. It was also impressive because only 40 of the Bs had actually been built and there were no plans for scaling up production.

Undeterred, Durant indulged in what came to be known in the car industry as 'whipsawing' – basically bullying local towns and states into competing for car plants with subsidies. He ended up back in Flint, Michigan. He also set up a national network of dealerships and by the start of 1908 Buick was the biggest car maker in the USA. A couple of years later 30,000 Buicks were being produced annually.

Buick the man, however, in the words of automotive historian William Pelfrey, 'never found another dream to chase'. In 1905 he was broke and all he owned was one share in Buick. Two years later Durant bought that share for $100,000. Buick lost it all in a series of awful investments. He took a series of menial jobs in Detroit and died of cancer on 5 March 1929, a year in which Buick sold 196,000 cars.

In 1937 Ralph Pew, a styling researcher for GM, was scanning *Burke's Heraldry* when he found an entry that read, 'Gu. A bend chequy, ar. and az. betw. a Buck's head erazed in chief, and a cross couped and pierced, or, in base.' It was the Buick's family coat of arms. This was roughly interpreted as a shield with a chequered diagonal band, a stag's head and a cross. Americans being suckers for anything vaguely medieval, this became the radiator insignia for 1937 Buicks. In 1959 this was modernised to become three shields in red, white and blue arranged diagonally. The seventies, being the seventies, saw the logo changed to a very trashy hawk image, but, in the eighties, the 'tri-shield' returned in silver without the colours and it is still there.

A plaque on Green Street, Arbroath, reads, 'David Dunbar Buick – September 17, 1854 – March 5, 1929. American motoring pioneer and founder of the Buick Motor Company of America. David Dunbar Buick was born at 26 Green Street, Arbroath which lay approximately 90 metres north of this, the only remaining building to show the line of the original street. Sponsored by the Buick Motor Division of the General Motors Corporation of America.'

The current Buick models are indistinguishable from the models of every other car maker. But for the badge.

2

Ford bears the name of a man, General Motors of an idea. Henry Ford was a unifier; he drew all things to himself. Alfred P. Sloan Jr, for 33 years the presiding genius of GM, was a divider. He said that the way to run a great industrial company was 'to divide into as many parts as consistently can be done'. The parts – Buick, Chevrolet, Cadillac, etc. – may bear the names of men, but they all were – and remain – aspects of the man whose name was never emblazoned on a car.

For Ford the car was everything; for Sloan it was a product. Read Ford and – his dreadful politics aside – every word, every idea, feeds into the ruling idea of the car, usually the Model T. Read Sloan and everything feeds into the dominant idea of the corporation. In his 1941 memoir *Adventures of a White Collar Man* (ghosted by Boyden Sparkes) individual cars are seldom mentioned and towards the end the memoir concept is simply abandoned in favour of a treatise outlining his philosophy of 'scientific' management.

Ford had little time for mere money; for Sloan there was nothing mere about it. Explaining the failure of his Detroit Motor Company – it lasted from 1899 to 1901 – Ford blamed his backers as 'a group of men of speculative turn of mind'. He added that 'being without authority other than my engineering position gave me, I found that the new company was not a vehicle for realizing my ideas but a money-making concern'. In stark contrast, in a 1921 paper entitled 'Future Manufacturing Lines of General Motors Corporation', Sloan announced, 'The primary object of the General Motors Corporation, therefore, is to make money, not just to make motor cars.'

They were, in short, singularly opposed businessmen, but they were the most successful industrialists of the first half of the twentieth century. This proves, if nothing else, that there is no one right way to run a big company.

Timing was important. Ford was twelve years older than Sloan and he had the position and the company he needed by 1903. Sloan's ascendancy at GM did not begin until 1923. Those twenty years made all the difference. Ford's job was to create the car market; Sloan's was to beat Ford by expanding the market into every aspect of the lives and imaginations of his customers. The ending of Model T production in 1927 was the start of a new automotive era, one dominated by marketing. It was, in fact, the year that the consumer society was born. Ford had been pregnant with the idea; Sloan delivered the baby. The car was parked at the summit of consumer desire and it is only now beginning to be dislodged.

Ford was all about utility; Sloan was all about desire. This may seem odd, in that Sloan was a good deal more cold-blooded than Ford, but the truth is they were both practical men, they just had two opposing ideas about how to sell cars. Ford sold them by making them useful and filling people's minds with ideas about how they could be used, Sloan by making them desirable. 'Humanity,' the latter wrote, 'had never wanted any machine as much as it desired this one.'

Often quoted in the context of both men's lives is a line from the philosopher Ralph Waldo Emerson: 'an institution is the lengthening shadow of one man'. This is seldom true but in these two cases it was. Both men generously praised their teams of managers and executives but I don't sense that either quite meant it.

They were both puritans. The puritanism of Henry Ford was inward facing. He looked solely at the product and himself. In these he saw all that needed to be known; build what I tell you to build, he assumed, and they will come. The money was a welcome side effect. The dry, rational puritanism of Alfred Sloan was outward facing. He looked solely at the market; know your customer, get him in debt, consume him with envy of his neighbour and the profits will flow. From 1927 until his death in 1966 Sloan's customer-facing, management-theory approach was to dominate and define the world car market. His fiercely rationalist ideas about management endure to this day.

And so from this dry man with his single-minded commitment to corporate efficiency emerged the most extravagant, absurd, inefficient, flashy, often dangerous and occasionally glorious cars ever built.

3

In 1905 Cadillac produced a very strange car. It was taller than it was long and it looked like a sedan chair to which wheels had been, rather capriciously, attached. It was called the Osceola Coupe. Osceola was a Seminole Indian chief who led the resistance to government attempts to remove the Seminoles from their tribal lands in Florida. Why Henry M. Leland, who conceived this car, alighted on this name is unclear. Leland was the man who had been brought in as a consultant by the Henry Ford Company in 1901 and thereby caused Ford to walk out in disgust. The Osceola, even before the Model T had been produced, was an omen, a sign of the forces that would arise to topple Ford from his place as the supreme car maker.

It was a kind of concept car. Leland wanted to try out 'closed body' construction – cars at the time were primarily open-topped, some with a fabric 'convertible' roof. The man who built the Osceola was Fred Fisher, one of seven sons of an Ohio family. The father

had a carriage-building shop in Norwalk. In 1908, having moved to Detroit, the brothers formed the Fisher Body Company. By 1913 they were producing 100,000 bodies a year for all the major car makers. In 1919 General Motors bought 60 per cent of the company and Fisher became a full subsidiary of GM in 1926. Buying that stake in 1919 was a huge strategic leap for GM. By the end of that year GM was capitalised at $1 billion.

The closed body was the future, as was GM. Ford resisted change and stuck for far too long with T-only production. Sloan seemed to be baffled as to why Ford allowed himself to be overtaken by GM – 'the old master had failed to master change. Don't ask me why.' But that vital stake in Fisher Body was not bought by Sloan. It was bought by his predecessor and the founder of General Motors, William Crapo Durant.

4

Billy Durant emerged, as did Sloan and Ford, from the automotive rush that hit Detroit at the start of the twentieth century. The gold rushes and the oil frenzies of the nineteenth century had been followed by the car craze. As the idea of 'automobilism' dawned first on speculators and then on the public, Detroit became Motor City. The population soared from 120,000 in 1880 to 1 million in 1920. Cowboys were replaced by cowboy mechanics as mythic heroes. Sloan again: 'In those years the American mechanic was a restless wanderer.' The frontier was now industrial: this wasn't the Wild West; it was the Wild Mid-West. The poor mechanics had no choice but to ride the new range as car and parts companies were being born and dying at a phenomenal rate. Everybody had something to sell and everybody wanted to buy. The place was giddy with growth. Sloan's first big company, Hyatt Roller Bearing, held annual Christmas parties and every year they were bigger. The largely teetotal Sloan recalled cocktails being pumped from 50-gallon oil drums.

The Ponchartrain Hotel, opened in 1907, was where they all met, the 'very heart' of the industry. If you hung about in the bar for long enough, it was said, you could meet everybody in the motor trade. In the dining room the tablecloths were buried beneath engineers' sketches.

The automotive industry was being born. In 1895, with the ink barely dry on the breathless reports of the Duryeas' first drive, two automotive magazines were launched: *The Motorcycle* (*Automobile*) – 'motorcycle' was then a popular word for car – and *The Horseless Age* – 'A monthly journal devoted to the interests of the motor vehicle industry.' The latter survives today as *Automotive Industries*. In the same year there were 500 applications for car-related patents.

The problem was that as yet nobody knew what cars would be like so any and every idea represented a golden investment opportunity to the geniuses and suckers that flooded into Detroit. Clarity was a long time coming. In 1899 American companies produced 2,500 vehicles, most of them steam or electric. But all was clear by 1910 when 458,500 vehicles were registered, electric and steam were dying, and the USA had become, as Rudi Volti puts it, 'the world's leading car culture'. In the midst of this frenzied climate was the most frenzied man of all, Billy Durant. In his memoir it is clear that Sloan really liked Durant, but so effusive is his praise one can't help noticing that this is a hatchet job. Their methods, he noted, were 'entirely different'; utterly opposed would have been more accurate. Durant – in his prime a fit, boisterous-looking man with none of the corporate desiccation of Sloan – was a high-roller. His assets once amounted to $120 million. When he filed for bankruptcy in 1936 he had $250 worth of clothing. Nothing like that could ever have happened to Sloan. Durant dropped out of school to become a dreamer and a risk-taker. Sloan was a cool engineer and organisation man. Durant's fate was sealed when he got it all wrong just at the moment when Sloan was getting it all right. Crucially, Sloan saw that GM's growth was being paid for by stock issues and on the back of Durant's personal charm, a combination that was bound to fail. In the history of the car, and therefore the world, Billy Durant goes down as an energetic, loveable, wildly over-optimistic but very lengthy footnote. He did, after all, create the greatest industrial concern of the age.

He was born in Boston, Massachusetts, in 1861. His father was a drunken chancer – 'a schemer and a dreamer' – and his mother came from a grand, wealthy family. They finally separated when Durant was still a child and she settled in Flint, Michigan, the home of Henry Howland Crapo, Durant's maternal grandfather. At 16 he decided he'd had enough of education and went to work at Crapo

Lumberyard run by his grandfather. It was a dull labouring job but while moonlighting he discovered a talent for selling, first patent medicines and then cigars. He was so successful with the cigars that his reputation spread. It was later said he could sell sand to the Arabs and then sieves to sift it. He was deluged with offers. He was even asked to fix the financial problems of the local waterworks, which he did in a few brilliant months. He also started an insurance agency and aged 22 he was able to buy his own house. He, now the most eligible bachelor in town, married Clara Miller Pitt, one of the most desirable girls. His father did not turn up for the ceremony, his name by then having been more or less erased from family memory.

And then one day in 1886 – the details of this may have been somewhat enhanced in the retelling – he was walking to a waterworks board meeting when a friend, John Alger, appeared driving a peculiar horse-drawn cart with two large wheels and a very fragile-looking axle and suspension arrangement. Alger offered Durant a ride. He was reluctant at first, considering the machine dangerous. Finally, he boarded the cart and discovered it was a little masterpiece of ingenuity. The next day he was on a train to Coldwater to meet the makers. He offered to buy a share of their company; they, to his surprise, sold him the whole thing and threw in the patent on the suspension system.

His selling genius ran ahead of his nascent production talent. But the latter soon caught up. He achieved what Henry Ford was to achieve on a much larger scale more than two decades later. He created an integrated company – it made all its own parts – and the world's first vehicle assembly line. The success of his Durant-Dort company transformed the city of Flint. Once, there had been a few small carriage makers; by 1900 there were more than 30 and Flint had become known as 'Vehicle City' – two arches across Saginaw Street marking the fact were erected in 1905. The company itself became the largest vehicle maker in the country.

In spite of the city's success, it was by then clear to many, if not most, people that the days of the horse-drawn vehicle were numbered. It was not yet, however, clear to Durant. In 1902 Durant's daughter Margery told her father she had taken a ride in a car – a yellow Panhard with red leather upholstery that belonged to the father of a schoolfriend. The ride was pretty typical for the time; the car terrified a few horses and stalled as onlookers gathered, shouting, 'Get a horse!' Durant was furious: 'Margery, how could you be so foolish as to risk your life in one of those things!' But his scepticism and fear of cars melted away almost as quickly as his doubts about John Alger's cart. By 1904 he was ready to make his move – the acquisition of Buick – into what was surely the business opportunity of the twentieth century.

Durant turned Buick around with the same speed and intelligence with which he had saved the waterworks. The company was all but ruined when he took over: it had produced only 37 cars in 1904; in 1908 it produced 8,800 – half of them Model 10s, direct competitors to the Model T – and had become, albeit briefly, the biggest car maker in America, ahead of Ford, Cadillac and Oldsmobile.

Three themes seemed to provide the foundations of Durant's success. The first was corporate acquisitiveness at a time when it was the right thing to do. This was how, after establishing General Motors in 1908, he turned it into a consolidation of 13 car companies and ten parts makers. The second was the fierce directness of his decision making. Sloan told the story of a visit to the Oldsmobile plant – the company had been acquired by GM in 1908. Durant had driven there in a Buick Model 10. Oldsmobile had no plans for a new model so Durant ordered workmen to remove the wooden body from his Buick and cut it into four quarters. He then moved the four quarters a few inches apart, making the car wider and longer, thus turning the Buick into the new Oldsmobile. The third theme was charm. Nobody seems to have been immune from this. Even Walter Chrysler, who had little sympathy for Durant's methods and resigned as president of Buick in 1919 to form his own company, could not help succumbing to the man's winning ways. 'I cannot hope,' he said, 'to find words to express the charm of the man.'

In his 1941 memoir Sloan was even more effusive but also damning. He went out of his way to praise the Weston-Mott axle company, a subsidiary of Buick. In particular he spoke warmly of Charles Mott in ways that clearly indicated that this man was the opposite of Durant and a lot like Sloan himself. His praise of Mott concluded with a clear sideswipe at Durant. He said he had no time for people who worked on hunches and who liked to be called geniuses. Durant was routinely referred to as a genius. Sloan had the wisdom of hindsight. Durant's methods led to failure. He was a fatally optimistic man and this drove him to believe too much in his own passion for acquisition while ignoring consolidation.

Between 1908 and 1910 he bought control of at least one car or parts maker every 30 days. One deal done, he had to move on to the next. He bought Cadillac and he even tried to buy Ford. Henry Ford, possibly because he was crippled by back pain, agreed to an offer of $8 million in cash – 'And tell him I'll throw in my lumbago!' – but Durant couldn't raise the funds and moved on.

It was, obviously, an unsustainable business plan. Ford by this time was selling just one car – the T; Durant was selling 21 different ones, all from a series of independent manufacturers, each with its own manufacturing and administrative costs. In 1910 there was a downturn in large car sales and GM started running up massive debts. Durant toured the banks but none would lend. Finally, a syndicate of banks did lend on crushing terms that involved sidelining Durant. He pulled out, privately vowing to return, which he did.

In fact, the crisis in the car market faded within weeks, convincing the bankers that they had done the right thing and further entrenching Durant's self-belief. His route back into GM was via a large Swiss-Frenchman with an enormous moustache. Louis Chevrolet was born in 1878 and he moved to America in his early 20s. He was a self-taught mechanic and then a racing driver. He was good; he beat Ford's risk-hungry racer Barney Oldfield three times. His brother Arthur joined him in the USA and he too took to racing. Together they arrived in Flint, attracted by the ascendancy of Buick, and turned up unannounced in Durant's office. Arthur, the slightly slower driver, was hired to be Durant's chauffeur and Louis joined the Buick racing team. Louis was a terrifying driver, taking appalling risks on the track. But he won repeatedly, though he killed four mechanics in the process – in those days the mechanics rode with the drivers.

In 1909 Durant decided to back Chevrolet's plan to build a small car. After his departure from GM, Durant created four new car companies, one of which was Chevrolet Motor Company. Unfortunately, Louis never came up with a design that suited Durant's plans and they parted company in 1915. Louis survives as a name, rather than a man, on cars and on a gravestone in Indianapolis.

Durant, however, used Chevrolet to do what he did best – buy stock. In April 1917 the United States entered the First World War, having been up to then defiantly non-interventionist. Strangely, President Woodrow Wilson explained that the USA was 'too proud to fight', a virtue that did not survive the sinking of seven merchant ships by German submarines. Car sales held up in spite of the announcement of war but car company shares slumped. In January GM shares stood at around $200; by October they were selling at $75.

Durant saw his way back in, buying GM shares riskily on margin – should they fall below his purchase price, he could be ruined. And, of course, they fell. He was bailed out with $1 million from the GM board, a backhanded deal that was not made public. Durant's position was weakened and then weakened further by a huge investment in GM by the chemical company E.I. du Pont de Nemours. Nevertheless, bringing Chevrolet with him, he was back on board at GM.

With the end of the war business began to boom and Durant started spending, helped by a massive recapitalisation that made GM a $1 billion company, the second biggest company in America behind US Steel. By the end of 1919 Durant was presiding over an unwieldy portfolio that included 70 factories in 40 cities in the USA. Sloan saw the dangers in this madcap expansion, as did the chairman Pierre du Pont, who commissioned a report that pointed out the obvious – the company was a chaos of uncoordinated operations. Durant accepted the report but did little about it. Now his time was running out. The great reckoning of Billy Durant was at hand.

His last spending spree was desperately ill-timed. Beginning in January 1920 the USA and other countries plunged into a depression that lasted until July 1921. This was combined with the Spanish flu epidemic that began in 1918 and kept returning in waves until 1920. It killed 675,000 Americans. General Motors was perhaps the worst hit company. Ford was all in Henry Ford's hands and he did not finance himself by simply issuing stock. He was able to lower his Model T prices in response to the breathtaking swing from boom to bust. Durant had no such flexibility and GM's debt soared as Ford's actually fell. Having been $420, GM shares fell to $20 in July. Du Pont subsequently blamed Durant for the whole thing. This was not entirely fair; Durant had warned about some excessive spending but there is no doubt that his inability or refusal to impose a structure on the company was disastrous.

Incredibly, bafflingly and in direct defiance of an agreement with the banks, Durant continued to buy stock on his own account in an attempt to support the share price. Again it was on margin and again he was wiped out. It was his last throw of the dice at GM. On 1 December 1920, a week before his 59th birthday, the 'soul of General Motors' turned up at the office for the last time. It was not his lucky day.

He went on to play the stock market with the usual disastrous results. He opened a bowling alley and a fast-food joint in Flint and a cinnabar mine in Nevada. He had a stroke and moved to his final home, a flat in New York, with his second wife Catherine. He was supported by $2,500 cheques sent every three months by a group of four led by Sloan. Gamely, irrepressibly, he predicted an economic boom at the end of the Second World War. His last investment was in a hair tonic. He died on 18 March 1947.

Durant never really escaped from the car-crazy days of the early 1900s. He had no understanding – as did both Ford and Sloan – of the significance of scale in the motor industry. All he saw were quick-hit investment opportunities and all he felt was the thrill of the deal and the market. Cars were to him the most glorious punt of all. Certainly by 1920 he was an outdated figure but, curiously, he now seems contemporary – a neophile, a thrill-seeking market manipulator of a type that now seems to run entire economies. But Billy was, at least, loveable.

5

Alfred Pritchard Sloan Jr – the manner of the man somehow demands the full name – was nowhere near as much fun as Billy Durant. He was known as the motor industry's first 'gray man', though, judging by the various online videos of his performances, even grey seems too definite a colour. He did not want to be known other than as a manager and he largely succeeded. At the time of writing the main body of the Wikipedia entry for this supreme industrialist, the most successful of all automotive managers, barely reaches 3,000 words – the entry for Henry Ford runs to 9,400. Even the General Motors archive, according to William Pelfrey, seems to have been pared down to the bare minimum. One wonders what, exactly, he had to hide.

Clearly, he wanted to be seen, in public, as a man with a single attribute and achievement – General Motors. The quotation 'The business of business is business' is usually credited to the economist Milton Friedman; in fact, Sloan used it first. It effectively strips away all other possible functions of the corporation – and the man – to this single project of sustaining itself.

He started as he meant to go on. He was born in New Haven, Connecticut, on 23 May 1875, the son of a machinist turned coffee and tea importer and Katherine Mead Sloan, the daughter of a Methodist Minister. He was the eldest of their five children. The family moved to Brooklyn when he was ten. At school he was a prodigy and he acquired a degree in electrical engineering from the Massachusetts Institute of Technology at the age of 20. He married Irene Jackson in 1898 – he mentions getting married in his book as he would a decision to buy a suit. But she was not a suit; he was devoted to her and to the preservation of her privacy. In Sloan's obituary in the *New York Times* on 18 February 1966 it was noted that his office 'was always brightened by fresh flowers and it contained a portrait of his wife, the former Irene Jackson, whom he married in 1898. She died in 1956. They had no children.'

He took a draughtsman's job at the Hyatt Roller Bearing Company in Newark, New Jersey. It was not much of a company – a shabby, broken-down place. A man of his talents would have had no problem becoming, a year later, president at the age of 24. It was, in effect, his first car-related job – roller bearings were to become crucial to the engineering of cars. But he left Hyatt in 1897. The company had limited prospects at the time and he needed money to marry. Sloan moved to Hygienic Refrigerator, a company also ahead of its time, but with the wrong product. Later, a company bought by Durant and renamed Frigidaire had the right product and it became a highly successful part of General Motors.

In 1899 he returned to Hyatt, the company having been bought by his father and a fellow investor. Sloan was given six months to turn the company round. He succeeded and later that year the future unfolded before him in the form of a letter from one Elwood Haynes of Kokomo, Indiana. Haynes was making a few cars a year so any order would have been insignificant but according to Sloan it was a revelation. If he could sell axles to one car maker, why not to all of them? The following year there was a sample order for 120 bearings for the rear axles from the Olds Motor Works, which was on the verge of making the Curved Dash Oldsmobile, the first car produced at volume in the USA.

Hyatt, now a major company, was merged into United Motors, which was, in turn, absorbed into General Motors in 1916, a move that brought Sloan into the company he would stay with until his death 50 years later. With the fall of Durant and the withdrawal of Pierre du Pont, he became president of GM in 1923.

6

There are many things that can be – and have been – said about Sloan's reign at General Motors. Most are about corporate organisation, industrial relations and management theory. But these now seem outdated subjects. Bill Gates, also a creator of a new type of business, might have said that Sloan's *My Years with General Motors* 'is probably the best book to read if you want to read only one book about business' but I doubt that he would have learned many lessons from it.

What I think is most important for the history of the car in the world is Sloan's emphasis on the customer. He wanted, above all, to turn the car into an object of desire and to this end he provided financing for car purchases, he introduced planned obsolescence via the annual model change and, most importantly, he put stylists, rather than engineers, at the heart of the production process.

There are arcane arguments about when consumerism and/or the consumer society began; the arguments become even more arcane when people attempt to explain why it began. Generally, it is said to have started in the seventeenth or eighteenth centuries and to have been caused either by the growth of the middle class, the unloading of colonial booty or by the need to sell the surpluses generated by the Industrial Revolution. What lies beyond dispute is the explosion of consumerism into a world-transforming force in the twentieth century. Equally beyond dispute is Sloan's part in that process.

Two things made this possible – mass production to reduce prices and elaborate marketing techniques to persuade people not just to buy but to buy much and often. Henry Ford created the former; Alfred Sloan the latter.

Sloan might have been an engineer and a brilliant industrial organiser and strategist but he did little or nothing to market himself. His own account of his career – the aforementioned *My Years with General Motors* – did not appear until 1963 and was bewilderingly impersonal. What he did do, however, was identify the end of the age of the Model T and the start of a new age in which simple utility was not enough. It was now necessary to engage the emotions.

Sloan was not alone in thinking this. In the twenties Edward Bernays, nephew of Sigmund Freud, effectively founded the public-relations industry and transformed advertising by arguing for ignoring the consumer's rational mind and targeting the unspoken and irrational motives. 'Men,' he said, 'are very largely actuated by motives which they conceal from themselves.'

'Man has been called the reasoning animal,' said the psychologist Walter D. Scott, also in the twenties, 'but he could with greater truthfulness be called the creature of suggestion. He is reasonable, but he is to a greater extent suggestible.'

The idea that people could be persuaded by accessing irrational, subconscious or simply non-utilitarian emotions was in the air when Sloan became GM president. But it is unlikely he would have found that out by reading Bernays or Scott. As ever, he would have arrived at the strategy by examining the state of GM and of the marketplace. He needed to develop a plan to stimulate growth in what was fast becoming a saturated market. The first part of the strategy was to exploit a division created by Durant called the General Motors Acceptance Corporation (GMAC). It was in effect a bank that provided finance to dealers and customers. This went far beyond Ford's simple price cuts as a way of expanding the market. The customer would have to part with very little at first in order to possess a car.

The second part involved annual design changes to the cars. This promoted customer dissatisfaction, in that they became aware that their car was out of date after a year. The practice was christened 'planned obsolescence' in 1932 in a pamphlet by Bernard London, a real-estate broker. He saw it as a way out of the Great Depression. The government should, London argued, impose a legal obligation to impose obsolescence on consumer articles to promote a consumption-led recovery. The term was popularised in the fifties

by an industrial designer named Brooks Stevens, who defined it as 'instilling in the buyer a desire to own something a little newer, a little better, a little sooner than is necessary'. Planned obsolescence characterises our age even more than it did Sloan's. We are, as he intended, in a permanent state of enervation as each new product declines in our estimation to the point where it must be replaced by a newer one.

This sounds depressing, which it is, but Sloan – aided by Boyden Sparkes – found a more inspiring and very well-rounded way of defining and defending his annual model changes. It is a sublime piece of sugar-coated hard selling. He justified the changes as a way of making the latest technology available to the consumer. Not only that, the buyers were also being, 'perhaps unconsciously', patriotic Americans because their old cars would be passed on at a lower price, making them available to poorer people. An irrational, enervating consumer impulse – buying a new car just because it's new – was translated by the magic of management-speak into a philanthropic act. As with Ford, so with Sloan: sometimes one can only watch and wonder.

There is one final piece in Sloan's motivational jigsaw. On 8 July 1926 he wrote to H.H. Bassett, general manager of Buick. He spoke of the first Cadillac he had owned and how he had bought specially small wheels to 'get the car down nearer to the ground'. Lowering the body, he argued, improves the appearance of the car and appearance is the new way to sell cars. For one thing – Sloan did not say this – it means annual changes can be trivially cosmetic but visible enough to make buyers upgrade. And so, in 1927, Sloan created the Art & Colour section of General Motors.

7

First, note the spelling – 'colour', not 'color'. The English spelling was yet another symptom of Detroit's surprising Europhilia. It was seen as a sign of a certain classiness, as was the word 'art'. Europe was still seen as a more sophisticated continent and a flick of European style was an aspect of the new, consumer-driven age.

In spite of American dominance of the auto industry, US car

makers have long been afflicted by a strange Francophilia. The word 'automobile' derives from the French as does the word 'chauffeur'. The great motor city Detroit was named by the French *le détroit de la Érié* – the Lake Erie Strait. It was a French explorer who settled the place in 1701, Antoine de la Mothe Cadillac. A couple of centuries later the Cadillac badge was bestowed on the most upmarket GM cars, often with added French flourishes – the Cadillac de Ville, the Brougham d'Elegance. Another luxury GM marque in the early days was LaSalle, named after another French explorer, René-Robert Cavelier, Sieur de la Salle. Then there was Chevrolet, a downmarket GM brand, named after Billy Durant's Swiss-French pal, Louis Chevrolet. There was, finally, a fire-engine company called American La France which also made a few cars, notably the Speedster of 1916.

On top of that, French names, slightly adjusted, were used as car categories – limousine, coupe, cabriolet – or for parts of cars – tonneau, chassis. Germany, the other birthplace of the car, was also annexed by Detroit. Landau, the name of a city and then a horse-drawn carriage, became the name given to a type of convertible car. Landau was also celebrated in the form of Landau bars or irons – S-shaped hinges originally seen on carriages that later became functionless decorations on some luxury US cars.

Then there was the GM LeSabre – admittedly sabre is both an English and a French term, but the 'Le' is clearly there to make it excitingly French. It began as a concept/show car in 1951. It looks, to the jaded contemporary eye, completely ridiculous. There was a weird oval at the front and circle at the rear, evidently designed to evoke the intake and the exhaust of a jet aircraft. Monumental fins at the rear were matched by two bumpers suggesting a comedy moustache at the front. It was a car out of *Thunderbirds* or *The Jetsons*. The LeSabre name was later used by Buick. One Buick LeSabre sticks in my memory as one of the few decent American cars I have ever driven. I am told there are others.

There are two sides to this Europhilia. The first makes some practical sense. A typology of vehicles was plainly necessary, so the importation of existing carriage names seemed reasonable. The second is purely marketing, a desire to make the customer feel he has made a 'classy' decision. It was another age, an age when Europeans could still cause a cultural cringe in Americans.

8

Four very closely linked things happened in 1927: Ford discontinued production of the Model T, Charles Lindbergh became the first man to fly solo across the Atlantic, General Motors released the strikingly handsome LaSalle and Sloan created his Art & Colour department.

The Atlantic flight was comparable to Neil Armstrong's first step on the moon. A total of 4 million people are said to have turned out to see Lindbergh on the day he returned to New York. He became the first *Time* magazine Man of the Year and was awarded the Medal of Honor by Congress. But it wasn't just the heroism. Suddenly everybody thought they could fly just as the Model T made them realise they could own a car. Investors struggled to pour money into any plane maker they could find. More than that, it was a general celebration of American innovation and of what was rapidly becoming, in the words of Karl T. Compton, president of the Massachusetts Institute of Technology, 'the most vigorous and productive era in American history'.

Meanwhile, back on the ground, there was Harley Earl, the first director of Art & Colour. Described by Stephen Bayley as 'big, sharp-suited and bullying', he was an aesthete with the appearance and manner of a boxer. He was utterly unlike the dry, analytical Sloan. Earl was born, appropriately, in Hollywood, where his father had a coachbuilding company. Coachbuilding involved constructing bodies for carriages and later cars which were simply bolted on to an undercarriage or chassis made by the manufacturer. Ironically, the son was to destroy his father's craft by establishing the in-house unification of bodywork and chassis. Abandoning his studies at Stanford, Earl worked for his father's company, often building cars for the stars – Tom Mix and Roscoe 'Fatty' Arbuckle were among them. Then, in 1919, a local Cadillac dealer, Don Lee, bought Earl's Automobile Works. This led to Earl's work being seen by a Cadillac executive who commissioned him to design a car which turned out to be the LaSalle.

At first glance, to the contemporary eye, the LaSalle looks like just another two-box car of the period – bulging headlamps between massive mudguards, running boards, squared-off windows, etc. At second glance you notice the roof line seems lower than usual and the parts of the car seem sculpted into a smooth, rhythmic whole. In fact, it was sculpted; Earl was to introduce the use of modelling clay to car design. The flow of running boards and mudguards and the general lowering of the car gave a sleeker, faster look that was unprecedented – in America at least. 'If you go by a school and the kids don't whistle, back to the drawing board,' Earl once said. At the LaSalle they whistled.

In fact, the look of the car was borrowed from a European car. Earl had brazenly plundered the styling of the Spanish-built Hispano-Suiza H6, itself a summit of pre-war car design.

(The one car the LaSalle did not outclass was the Bugatti Royale, also launched in 1927. This, however, could not be regarded as a car so much as an object to be driven straight into a museum. It was 4.3 metres long and weighed 3,200 kilograms. The engine was a 12.7-litre straight eight that was later used to power locomotives. Its looks were implausibly, undriveably perfect. But it didn't sell and only seven were ever produced. I doubt that Earl, had he seen one in 1927, would have felt threatened.)

The LaSalle was the first production car that gave primacy to styling – previously the coachbuilder, not the car maker, had been responsible for the look of the finished product. It was also Earl's first car for GM and it was a huge success, proving to mass car makers that looks mattered. He went on to be responsible for the appearance of 50 million GM vehicles between 1927 and 1959. By any conceivable metric he was the most influential designer of the twentieth century. Except that he wasn't exactly a designer – he seldom had much contact with a drawing board – but he was the cause of design in others and he knew exactly what he wanted visually. That, in the end, was all that mattered.

9

Earl had visions; Sloan had worksheets. He also had a problem to which the LaSalle was the solution. GM's Cadillacs had been dominating the luxury end of the car market but by 1925 Packard was beginning to catch up. In particular the Packard Six was both better-looking and $600 cheaper than the Cadillac rival. There was also a big gap between the price of the Cadillac and GM's own Buick

Master Six. The price of the Buick two-door sedan was $1,195; the next Cadillac up was $2,995. (The average income at that time was $1,380.)

The gap was an irritation to Sloan. Ever the finicky categoriser, he was particularly finicky about market segmentation. He wanted 'a car for every purse and purpose'. This meant a model range that covered every price band smoothly and without interruption, an ambition he realised through the lugubriously titled GM Companion Make Program. His idea was that consumers should be lured into gradually trading up from Chevrolet through Oldsmobile to Cadillac. But there was this yawning price gap between Cadillac and the second-place Buick.

Sloan had first announced this pricing policy in that momentous paper in 1921 – 'Future Manufacturing Lines of General Motors Corporation'. This outlined a plan to cover 'the market for all grades of automobiles that can be produced and sold in large quantities'. GM, he argued, would thus be able to out-compete other car makers 'even if General Motors cars in the respective grades are no better than the best competing automobiles of the same grade'. He suggested six price bands rising from $450 to $2,500. At the lowest level Sloan said they should not try to compete with Ford on price but to produce a better car that was near enough to the price of the Model T so 'that demand will be drawn from the Ford grade and lifted to the slightly higher price in preference to putting up with the Ford deficiencies'. Like Apple with its iPhones, Sloan's aim was to lock customers into a GM 'eco-system'.

In the event the LaSalle came in at $2,295, significantly cutting the leap from the Buick. This time, however, the vision trumped the worksheet. Visually it outclassed everything else by General Motors. Earl and his many imitators went on to change the shape of the American car, making it ever lower and ever wider. A few resisted this process. Kaufman Thuma Keller was president and then chairman of Chrysler between 1935 and 1956. Nominated by *Fortune* magazine as one of 'history's ten worst auto chiefs', Keller is fondly remembered as the boss who thought drivers should be able to sit upright in a car wearing a hat. He also said he wanted comfortable cars 'to sit in, not piss over'. This explains – though does not justify – the curiously elevated roofline of the Plymouth Cranbrook, a car that was put out of its misery, aged two, in 1953.

Earl's team, in contrast, came up with the fin, the peacock's tail of car design – mad, absurd, functionally unjustifiable but also, for some reason, the climax of the process which started with Sloan's decision to have smaller wheels on his first Cadillac. Nothing in consumer history compares to the folly of the fin.

10

The Lockheed P38 Lightning, introduced in 1939, was an improbably beautiful American air-force plane. Its double booms extended elegantly backwards from its twin engines to a suave tailplane with two ovoid rudder assemblies. The pilot sat in a central nacelle that tapered to a point at the centre of the trailing edges of the wings. As sculpture it was magnificent and, surprisingly for something so obviously designed to be beautiful, it was also an effective war plane. The Germans called it the 'fork-tongued devil'.

Before it had even fired a shot or dropped a bomb, the P38 caught the attention of car designers. The thirteenth P38 to be manufactured was sitting on Michigan's Selfridge Field when a team from GM – Frank Hershey, Bill Mitchell and Harley Earl – turned up. They were allowed in because a GM division had made the plane's engines. But they weren't interested in the engines; they were looking for lessons to be learned for car design. Even though they were only allowed to go no nearer than 30 feet from the machine, they were thrilled. The twin booms suggested the possibility of a car designed with an unbroken, flowing line from the front to the rear. The booms ending with the rudders were to inspire the tail fins that in the fifties and beyond infected just about every American car maker and many others around the world.

Car design had yet fully to emerge from the two-box style of the Model T. There had been attempts to move on driven by the obvious shortcoming of the T – it had the aerodynamic efficiency of a brick wall. Streamlining became more necessary as speeds increased, so aircraft design was the obvious place to start. In the 1920s an Austrian aircraft designer, Paul Jaray, produced peculiar prototype cars which looked like, according to one critic, an airship with a greenhouse on top. They would have been faster and more fuel efficient than any cars then on the road, but 'the public rejected these futurist cars'.

Equally unnerving was the 40/60 Castagna, a cigar on wheels made by ALFA, the company that later became Alfa Romeo. It was commissioned by an Italian count in 1913. In the thirties, there was Buckminster Fuller's Dymaxion car, which abandoned all automotive design principles and had an alarming tendency to take off. The Rumpler Trumpfwagen, first revealed at the 1921 Berlin car show, was the first streamlined production car. It was aerodynamically efficient and as ugly as sin. If the Trumpfwagen was the answer, then clearly the question had to be reframed. In the thirties, the question became: how do we combine at least the pretence of aerodynamics with marketability? The answer was streamline moderne, a stripped-down variation of art deco, which emerged in the thirties.

This meant design needed to be extravagantly moderne rather than austerely modernist. For modernism the motto was the Porsche one of 'form follows function' – every element had to be justified as functional and the object would thereby become beautiful. This was faith rather than technology but the designers found it consoling. The modernes also offered justifications but they were absurdly tenuous. Streamlining was the default claim but in reality these designers just liked the look of ocean liners, fast trains and aircraft. In effect, moderne was baroque after modernism's classicism.

Fabulous extravagances emerged – the Chrysler New Yorker, the Cord 812 or the staggering, curvaceous, bulbous, magnesium-bodied, and not especially aerodynamic, Bugatti Aérolithe. Nevertheless, the roads were still jammed by variations of the jalopy. But now the direction of travel in car design was clear. Equally clear was who would lead the way. With the end of Model T production and Ford's subsequent decline relative to the more clear-sighted consumer-centredness of General Motors, the search for new styling devices became ever more urgent.

11

The *Spirit of St Louis*, the plane in which Lindbergh flew across the Atlantic, looked streamlined and purposeful; though it was not beautiful, it was no jalopy. But its impact was not stylistic, it was cultural. The heroic gesture of the 3,600-mile flight signified the arrival of the aircraft as a glamorous, aspirational emblem of modernity. At

Selfridge Field, Michigan, looking at the P38, this was exactly what dawned on Frank Hershey, Bill Mitchell and Harley Earl.

The war, however, stalled their ambitions when it came to transferring moderne to mass-market cars. This delay was fortuitous to the extent that it allowed the appearance of a new styling vocabulary – that of jet aircraft and rockets.

But first the memory of the P38 was modestly marked in 1948 by the third generation of the Cadillac Series 62. Certainly this had Mitchell's flowing line but, most importantly, it was interrupted by a tentative homage to the P38's rudders. Rising above three purely decorative chrome bands were two absurd little bumps at the rear encompassing the tail lights. Unlike the rudders, however, the bumps performed no meaningful purpose. In fact, they looked slightly comical. But the joke had hardly got started. When the sixth generation of the Series 62 appeared in 1958 the bumps had turned into preposterously giant fins that ended in two lethally sharp chrome chevrons from the centre of each of which projected two phallic tail lights. In fact, the red ends of these twin phalluses were supposed to suggest the afterburners of jet aircraft.

By that time the tail fin had undergone a process not unlike the runaway sexual selection that produced the peacock's tail. Desirability, having fastened on one superfluous feature, had created a monstrosity. And what drove desirability was GM's greatest innovation – planned obsolescence. What could be more glaringly humiliating than having last year's fin when your neighbour had this year's?

But the fins did not simply grow larger; they spread across the world. In Britain the humble Ford Anglia had fins; in Czechoslovakia the Skoda Octavia had a vestigial pair. Even the Germans succumbed with the Mercedes Fintail, produced from 1959, though here a spurious justification was provided – they were said to be parking aids which helped the driver see the end of the car. Meanwhile, Plymouth, a division of Chrysler, called their fins – just as preposterous as the Cadillac's – 'stabilisers'. These would, apparently, 'reduce by 20% the needs for steering correction in a cross wind'. We need not believe this because it is not true.

Chrysler as a whole seemed obsessed with justifying the functionality of fins. Their advertising line for the 1956 models asked, 'How is a Chrysler-built car similar to a jet fighter, a Gold Cup racing boat, and a big-time race car?' The answer 'to this riddle lies in the silhouette — namely the wedge shape'. Well yes, but so what?

Two further cars need to be mentioned as representing a crazed climax to this flaunting peacockery. Both came out in 1959, the year of peak fin. The first is the downright satirical Dodge Coronet. This had huge fins but they contained no tail lights – they did not contain anything. Indeed, the chrome strip around the base signalled they were nothing to do with the structure of the car, they were merely bolted on. These absurd superfluities may be seen as the death throes of the fin.

But they weren't. The second car was a collection – the '59 Chevrolets Impala, Biscayne and Bel Air, all of which had two ruthlessly horizontal chrome lines running from the head to the teardrop tail lights above which rose two vastly elongated fins which sprang from the centre point of the car's rear and curved outwards until they became parallel with the road surface. From the rear they look like lethal eyebrows over the narrowed, threatening gaze of the tail lights. These cars had become alien objects in the landscape. They were intruders in the wilderness. They were urban, or rather suburban, spaceships and jet planes. Or, as the interstates spread across America, they were continental cruisers, floating, finned and gleaming, from city to city.

But around 1960 something changed. Excess started to become tasteless, ugly. Thereafter, it was all downhill for the fin. On the Cadillac 62 series they gradually shrank, though other models continued to be finned until 1966. By 1961 the Chevrolet Impala's outward-swooping fins had slumped into the bodywork and by 1964 they had vanished entirely. Buick had weened itself off the fin by 1963 and they disappeared from Ford's Mercury marque in 1964. Even faux-function-obsessed Chrysler had abandoned the fin by 1961 but for the one continuing extravagance of the '61 Imperial. All the peacocks had died at once.

One startling theory is that the fins disappeared because of the Soviet Union's launch of the Sputnik satellite in 1957. The communists had, shockingly, reached space before the capitalists. The fake imagery of rocketry and jet planes suddenly seemed pathetic when the Soviets had beaten America to the real thing. Charlie Ascher in *Hemmings Motor News* suggested that the humiliation of Sputnik forced American buyers to turn away from finned fantasies and embrace the tougher realities of the sixties. Ascher acknowledges that the deaths of the two most manic fin designers – Harley Earl at General Motors and Virgil Exner at Chrysler – in 1958 and 1962 might have also had an effect. As indeed might many other things. But there is, undoubtedly, much truth in the idea that the revelation of Soviet technical competence had a chastening effect on American culture. The fin could indeed have been a casualty of that change of mood.

It survives, vestigially, in a few odd cars. The 1999 Cadillac de Ville had near-fins in the form of a tail-light tower and even Toyota has succumbed with a strange, jagged fin-like structure on the rear of its Prius from 2016 onwards. Even the East German Trabant, generally regarded as the worst car ever made by anyone anywhere, was resurrected as a concept car in 2009 with a suspiciously fin-like tail-light cluster. But, undoubtedly, the glory days are gone.

The fin was an expression of the capriciousness of car design – indeed, of almost all consumer design. It was also an expression of the way the car, more than any other consumer good, can absorb and inflate the imagery of the culture as well as the meanings of that imagery. Specifically, it expressed the imagery and meanings of the consumer boom in 1950s America and of its accompanying technology; the fin's appearance in other countries was feeble in comparison. This context was replete with the idea of a new world of wealth, consumption and ease of movement combined with all the trappings of a family-centred, morally and politically stable society that had left the horrors of the first half of the twentieth century behind. It was, as the sixties were to reveal, a fragile combination. Still, what survived of the tail-fin moment was the absolute centrality of the car and its imperious dominance of landscapes and ways of life.

12

One final oddity of the Earl era is worth mentioning. There was a gap in all this GM marketing. Men might buy a car with phallic tail lights, but what would women buy? In 1958 Earl decided to find out. As he pointed out in a press release, women had the final vote in three out of four car purchases, families were beginning to buy second cars and women were often doing the driving. He formed a group of nine women whom he called his 'Damsels in Design'. Publicity photographs of bruiser Earl surrounded by women excited speculation, but one, Suzanne Vanderbilt, stepped forward to defend him. She said he was a gentleman and a father figure.

He put on a show – the 'Feminine Show' – in the General Motors Styling Dome. The Damsels were given the chance to redesign GM cars. The results were, among others: the Corvette Fancy Free with a different set of seat covers for each season; the child-friendly Olds-mobile Fiesta Carousel with toy storage and a magnetic game board in the back; and the Chevrolet Impala Martinique with built-in cos-metic box and a huge mirror for the front-seat passenger. Visitors were asked to vote on their favourite – the Fiesta Carousel, a colossal station wagon, was the winner.

It was Earl's last hurrah. That same year he retired to be replaced by Bill Mitchell, who showed little interest in the fripperies of for-the-ladies design. Earl died in 1969, aged 76.

13

The Austrian-born management consultant Peter Drucker arrived in America in 1937. In 1942 he published his book *The Future of Industrial Man*. This made him famous and a year later he was invit-ed in to study and make recommendations about the functioning of General Motors. It was described as a 'political audit'. He spent two years at the company. His report and the ensuing book – *Concept of the Corporation* – were full of praise for GM but it incensed Sloan, who insisted for the rest of his life that Drucker had got it 'dead wrong'. His own was written to set the record straight.

Drucker was ahead of his time. He later admitted that he was 'at least ten years premature with every one of my forecasts'. In other words, he saw signs of decay within GM as early as the mid forties but the flaws did not come home to roost until the mid fifties and later.

The truth is that Sloan should never have let him in. Drucker was precisely the wrong man for the job. Sloan was a 'realist', a term Drucker used to define the aggressive, hard-headed leaders who were the exact opposite of the 'values-based' leaders he admired.

Realism, he argued, simply doesn't work and 'there is no alternative to values-based leadership'.

What Drucker had said, in essence, was that GM was not ready for the future, a future which included global competition, new social values, automation, a knowledge-based economy and greater consumer demands for quality. What Sloan called his 'scientific' approach to management with its emphasis on measuring and controlling 'facts' was inadequate and obsolete. As Drucker put it in 1972, 'what is needed is not facts but an ability to see facts as others see them'. Or, as he also said, 'management is not a science, but an art'.

There is some uncertainty about whether Drucker and Sloan remained on good terms. But Sloan's book does not mention Drucker, even though it was written as a refutation. Drucker did, however, write an introduction to the 1990 edition entitled 'Why My Years with General Motors is Must Reading'. In this he revealed that Sloan was only once angry with him. This was about a review he had written of My Years in which he described the book as 'enjoyable'. Sloan regarded the word as misleading. He did not want his book to be enjoyable. He just wanted to define a new profession, that of professional manager.

In this unenjoyable role he succeeded. He did indeed invent a new profession and he did prove to his own satisfaction that the business of business was business. He also presided over what was the very enjoyable – in retrospect at least – unleashing of a menagerie of extravagant automotive creations.

The General Motors he created became a global business, the world's leading car maker and the pre-eminent industrial concern. The weaknesses detected by Drucker weren't in fact ten years ahead of their time. They were more like twenty years; it was then that the Japanese invasion of America began to undermine the pre-eminence of Detroit.

Sloan himself maintained his steely, rationalist manner to the end. He had, after all, been vindicated by the company that did not bear his name. But he could seem inhuman. His rejection of the word 'enjoyable' is revealing, as are comments like 'Bedside manners are no substitute for the right diagnosis.' He did not want to let in a single chink of light, any awareness of the importance of human passions other than the passion to consume. But he was himself afflicted by one very human passion – hubris. During a sit-in strike at GM in the thirties he confronted Frances Perkins, Roosevelt's Labor Secretary: 'You can't talk like that to me! You can't talk like that to me! I'm worth 70 million dollars and I made it all myself. You can't talk like that to me! I'm Alfred Sloan.'

His cars were seldom as good as they might have been because of the prevalence of style over engineering. Japanese quality exposed this shortcoming. He could also be cavalier about safety. In 1929 du Pont offered him safety glass developed by his company. Sloan declined the offer, fearing such safety measures could 'materially offset our profits'. It was safety concerns which, along with the Japanese invasion, all but brought GM to its knees in the sixties and seventies.

In the end he remains as opaque as he would wish to have been. If he was intent on hiding something, he has succeeded. With Ford almost everything is known; with Sloan almost everything is not. But if Ford's true biography is a car, then Sloan's is General Motors. He died in 1966, the year the first Toyota Corolla was launched and the year after Ralph Nader published *Unsafe at Any Speed: The Designed-In Dangers of the American Automobile*.

Taiichi Ohno

Chapter Five

THE EAST WIND PREVAILS
OVER THE WEST WIND

1

At the beginning of John Updike's novel *Rabbit Is Rich*, the hero, Harry 'Rabbit' Angstrom, revels in his own wealth and in the decline of America. It is 1979 and he runs a Toyota dealership. His cars are selling because the oil price is rising and Detroit is unable to produce a decent small, fuel-efficient car. The year before, Ford had recalled the Pinto, the smallest car it had made since 1907. It was said to be lethal and even if it wasn't both *Forbes* and *Time* magazines had said it was one of the worst cars of all time. Detroit is on the run. In July America's first space station, Skylab, plunges into the Indian Ocean, its orbit having terminally 'decayed'.

This sense of American decay had been growing since the debacle of Vietnam, the corruption of Watergate and the launch of Sputnik in 1957. The automotive irony of this technological triumph was that the launch happened on 4 October. Exactly one month earlier on 4 September the Ford Edsel had been launched. This was the car named after Henry Ford's son. Its most noted feature was the 'horse-collar' grille. Critics suggested it looked more like a toilet seat or a vagina. It also had a weird button at the centre of the steering wheel which changed gears. Drivers found themselves changing gears when they tried to sound the horn. Mechanically the Edsel was horrible; it was, along with the Pinto, one of the worst cars Ford ever made. The advertising line read, 'They'll know you've *arrived* when you drive up in an Edsel'. They certainly would. The Edsel's failure cost the company $300 million.

Whichever way you looked, America had problems. So, when Ralph Nader published *Unsafe at Any Speed* in 1965, the American public was primed to believe his condemnation of Detroit as a monstrous producer of dangerous machines. A year later Toyota launched the Corolla, which, in various incarnations, was to become the bestselling marque of all time.

In the sixties, among a generation born after the war, Japan was becoming fashionable. Japanese art and culture were being admired by the smart sets while hippies were writing haikus and speaking in Zen koans. A similar wave of Japanophilia had hit the West in the early 1900s, but this one was different. Whereas previously the interest had been almost entirely aesthetic, this time it was also consumerist and technical. Japanese products were seen as well made; American products were regarded as shoddy.

In 1970 Detroit had a near monopoly in the US car market. People just assumed they were buying the best in the world. By 1990 millions of Americans were buying Japanese cars because they knew they were good value and much better made. The transfer of industrial power across the Pacific was astoundingly quick. Between 1950 and 1990 Japan increased its productivity at twice the rate of America. In 1970 Japan produced a little over 10 per cent of cars in the world; by 1980 it accounted for a quarter of the US market. In that same year Chrysler needed a $1.5 billion government bailout to save it from bankruptcy.

Rabbit Is Rich was published in the midst of this process in 1981. Its topicality was brutal. Ford, like Chrysler the year before, was in deep trouble, losing both money and market share. The following year even the government grew edgy. Raymond Donovan, Secretary of Labor, said America was 'experiencing an extended period of absolute decline in our production efficiency'. And Secretary of Commerce Robert Dederick said that 200,000 automotive jobs in the auto industry would vanish in the next decade.

This was not a merely cyclical downturn that would in time correct itself. Detroit was being defeated by Rabbit's Toyotas and an alarming assortment of other Japanese cars. A way of life defined by Detroit metal was fading. Also in 1982, a team of Ford executives and union bosses travelled to the Mazda complex in Hiroshima. Ford had bought 24 per cent of Mazda in 1979, a company which had suffered its own crisis in 1974. It recovered by transforming the

Hiroshima plant with the introduction of the Toyota Production System (TPS). This was renamed for American consumption as Lean Production in 1988 by John Krafcik, now head of Alphabet's self-driving car project.

The Ford team discovered that a Mazda 323 could be built with 40 per cent less effort than a Ford Escort. New models were developed more quickly, they were produced with fewer errors and the supply chain ran faultlessly. TPS was the future.

2

TPS was a victory of meticulousness over industrial brute force. It was, in essence, a way of turning a customer order into cash as quickly as possible. This was achieved, paradoxically, by slowing things down. The system would only work, said Taiichi Ohno, the TPS mastermind, when all the workers became tortoises.

This was not a rejection of the Ford-Sloan system. In fact, it was, at heart, a development of American mass production. But it was a refutation of what Ford-Sloan had become. Ohno always acknowledged not just the Fordian roots of the system he developed but also its connection with the 'scientific management' of Frederick Taylor.

But the Japanese differences were crucial. Ohno's version of Taylorism was both more humane and more realistic. He understood that the Taylorist insistence that the fastest worker should determine the speed of the line was destructive. In TPS the speed of the line was set by the rate which the average worker could maintain in a day.

Furthermore, chasing speed in the American way was, Ohno realised, counterproductive – it produced more errors, which, if the line could not be stopped, would result in costly corrections in house or, even worse, dealers loaded with defective stock. In TPS workers were allowed to stop the entire line if they found a fault.

Crucially, Ohno saw that the Americans had sacrificed key parts of Henry Ford's original idea. Ford wanted to keep costly inventories low but by the forties and fifties in Detroit this had become secondary to the speed of the line and high productivity. Ohno had raw experience of where this could go wrong. In the five years after the war he had massively raised productivity of trucks. The company

could turn out 1,000 a month but demand collapsed and the company found itself with an enormous number of costly unsold trucks.
Raising productivity was no cure-all.

Developed by Ohno with the support of Kiichiro Toyoda, son of
Sakichi, the company's founder, and also a brilliant engineer, TPS
was 20 years in the making and it is still with us. Just as once the
ideas of Taylor and Ford were celebrated as the last word in capitalist success, so Lean Production, as it came to be known in the West,
is now hailed as the *ne plus ultra* of industrial thinking. Books with
titles like *The Machine that Changed the World*, *The Toyota Way*
and *The Birth of Lean* provided the liturgy of the new faith for eager
Western adopters.

Ohno was a rationalist but he often played along with the visionary, quasi-religious, mysteriously oriental aura that Western minds
detected in his system. He liked to deploy Zen-like paradoxes –
'Having no problem is the biggest problem of all', 'We are doomed
to failure without a daily destruction of our various preconceptions'
and, most importantly, 'Ask "why" five times about every matter'.
This was all a long way from the dry precepts of Sloan and the
homely strictures of Ford. But it wasn't really.

3

After the war, Ohno frequently visited Detroit. This was not unusual.
From the completion of Ford's River Rouge plant in 1928, executives
and managers from all over the world had travelled to Detroit to
marvel, look at and learn from the mighty mass-production machine
– generally regarded as the future – in action. Before the war,
European corporate pilgrims like André Citroën, Louis Renault,
Giovanni Agnelli, Herbert Austin and William Morris had visited
the Highland Park plant. This, they thought, was the modern world;
this is what we must do in our countries.

Ohno, an engineer with the Toyota Motor Company, looked but
he did not marvel. First, he estimated that the productivity of the
American car industry might be ten times that of the Japanese.
Second, he saw that, even so, the American system was desperately
inefficient. All he saw in those temples of industry was *muda*.

The most striking thing about Toyota is the continuity of its founder's obsessions. Sakichi Toyoda, born in 1867, founded the Toyoda Automatic Loom Works in 1926. He had watched his mother working with a manual loom and he had seen what Ohno saw in Detroit – *muda*. In 1890 he created a 50 per cent more efficient hand loom. In 1896 he made Japan's first power loom. And then in 1924, with his son Kiichiro, he created the world's first non-stop loom, the Model G. Previously if a thread snapped a good deal of material was wasted. But the Model G automatically stopped if a thread broke. This meant each machine did not need to be continuously tended by an operator. Now an operator could watch over 30 machines. Much *muda* had been removed in the name of *jidoka*.

To explain: *muda* is the Japanese word for waste, futility, uselessness. There are two other linked words that were to obsess the Toyoda family: *mura* – unevenness, irregularity – and *muri* – unreasonable, too difficult, immoderate. The entire Toyota Production System was designed to suppress all three and, in principle, its key elements were all present in Sakichi's Model G loom. The auto-stopping function, for example, became in the TPS the ability of each worker to stop the entire production line if a fault is detected.

Jidoka roughly means intelligent automation but in the TPS it specifically denotes the ability to stop the line. This would have sounded like madness to Henry Ford, who believed in the speed and continuity of the production line. But Ohno saw that the American companies were forced to add separate sections to their plants to correct faults. This, if the line worked properly, should not be necessary. Ohno was also interested in speed – not that of the line but the speed with which an order for a car is turned into cash for the company – and *jidoka* actually accelerated this process.

Sakichi's travels for the loom business, especially to America, had convinced him that cars were the future. In 1929 he sold the patent for the Model G loom to the British company Platt Brothers. He died a year later, having given Kiichiro his blessing to make cars. This was even mentioned in his will – Kiichiro was 'to serve the country with automobiles'.

Cars began as a division of the loom company and later it became independent as the Toyota Motor Company. The 'T' in the company name had replaced the 'D' in the family name. Toyota is easier on Western ears but there seems to have been two other reasons. First, in Japanese Toyota could be written in eight brush strokes and eight is a lucky number; second, Toyoda could mean 'abundant rice field', which sounded a little antique.

Success was slow in coming. By 1950 Toyota had produced just 2,685 vehicles; at the time, Ford's River Rouge plant was producing 7,000 a day. Then things began to improve and, even before it conquered America, Toyota became more than just another company. On 1 January 1959 the city of Koromo in Aichi Prefecture was renamed Toyota in honour of its biggest employer.

Armed with the obsessions of the family, Ohno's trips to Detroit convinced him that Ford-Sloan mass-production systems were wasteful and inefficient. He set about creating something better. It took him – aided initially by Kiichiro, who died in 1952 – 20 years to do enough to beat Detroit. But, in reality, eliminating *muda* should take forever.

There is no end to the process because it involves the pursuit of the unattainable. Ohno's Toyota Production System has been defined and redefined in many ways but at the heart of it is the idea that perfection is unattainable. Perfection is a necessity, a quasi-religious dream, that you want to be true even though you know it can never be in this world.

Perfection involved a redefinition of the word 'problem'. In Fordist mass production an error was a random incident that produced little more than a shoulder shrug. In contrast Ohno's system required every error to be traced back to its first cause. This was where Ohno's 'five whys' came in; you keep asking why until there is nothing more to be asked and then the first cause is fixed so that it cannot occur again.

This endless pilgrimage to perfection with its overtones of religious revelation is entertaining but faintly absurd in that it is an *ex post facto* justification of a simple but relentless process of eliminating production problems. Neither Ohno nor anybody else spent years in silent, Zen-like contemplation to arrive at TPS; they simply had problems to fix, most of which stemmed from the Japanese government's outburst of protectionism in 1936. This closed down American production in Japan. Ford had dominated the Japanese market with cars assembled locally. Now companies like Nissan and Toyota would have to fend for themselves.

Some elements of Lean Production started appearing, usually with foreign precedents. Japanese aircraft companies embraced the

German concept of *Taktzeit*. Each workstation on an assembly line was given a fixed time to complete its tasks. At the end of that time, the plane was pushed forward on to the next station. Then, in the Japanese version, the national flag was raised before they returned to the next cycle of work. It was a way of inserting a level of precision into the assembly line process that could not be matched by the Ford-Sloan obsession with speed.

After the war, the statistical control systems, as taught by Bell Telephone Laboratories to students at the Japanese Union of Science and Engineering, were embraced. Also, two Toyota executives noticed the employee suggestion system at Ford's River Rouge plant in 1950. This was massively expanded to become one of the key pillars of TPS. It is defined in one of Ohno's Ten Precepts that have been used by management coaches around the world – 'The workplace is a teacher. You can find answers only in the workplace.'

A further vital element was derived from something Toyota executives noticed about the production of Hotpoint fridges. Several different models could emerge from a single assembly line. American car makers could only make one model per line. The Japanese managed to make several models by massively reducing the time needed for retooling.

So Lean Production emerged not from a programme of abstract contemplation but from decades of learning, fixing and engineering ingenuity. The TPS was not the only system to emerge from this – Toyota's focus was on costs, Nissan adapted the Sloanist principle of multi-model ranges and Honda emphasised product innovation. But historian David E. Nye lists the four attributes that all shared: several models per production line, less capital tied up in parts because of just-in-time delivery, lower wages paid by suppliers in Japan and the subordination of speed to quality in assembly line processes. With these in place, Japan had defeated Detroit by 1980.

4

At this point a kind of cultural and philosophical comedy emerges. The glaringly obvious question to ask about Japanese success is: why didn't Detroit simply copy the superior production methods of Japan?

Some serious intellectual armour can be deployed here. Economic and social sciences can be brought in with their idea of 'path dependence' – people and companies are too hopelessly dependent on past decisions and practices to accept the necessity of change. Then in comes the philosophy of science with much the same point. There was Thomas Kuhn's idea of the paradigm shift. Just as Einstein's physics was not simply a development of Newton's, but a whole new way of doing things, so Lean Production was a whole new way of making cars. People on the wrong side of a paradigm shift tend to be losers.

But the most obviously absurd explanation was the cultural one. In 1946 Ruth Benedict, an American anthropologist, published *The Chrysanthemum and the Sword*, a book written at the invitation of the Office of War Information. It was intended to predict the behaviour of the Japanese based on their traditional culture. The book was variously interpreted but the big takeaway for anybody trying to defend Detroit was that the Japanese were just too damned different. They were locked in a kind of feudal system in which the relationship between workers and employers was like peasants and lords. Also, there was strong group loyalty as opposed to American individualism.

This became the standard defence of the failing American way of making cars. It completely ignores the facts that, first, Lean Production emerged from a multiplicity of sources, many of them American, and, second, when the Japanese car companies established factories overseas, Lean worked just as well there as it did in Japan. With surprising clarity I remember thinking that the Nissan Sunderland plant in the UK, established in 1984, would certainly fail. After two decades of decline and union intransigence, British workers would never adapt to such alien methods. But they did and it was a huge success.

Perhaps the key to this transferability was that the system was not particularly Japanese at all. Rather, it was successful because it answered the universal human desire for recognition and involvement. This was natural in a craft-based system of production but the mass-production system of Ford and Sloan had destroyed the craft car-making industry. The worker in mass production becomes a machine, endlessly repeating a task and utterly alienated from either the finished product or the processes in which he is involved.

The final twist in this comedy of ideas is that the Americans might have thought they resisted the Japanese way because they were too heroically individualistic but, in fact, they resisted because they weren't individualistic enough. They stuck to their Chaplinesque assembly line while TPS gave the worker the power to stop the line. Individualism in the American way did not extend much below the highest ranks of management and, most of the time, hardly at all below Henry Ford and Alfred P. Sloan.

One last point needs to be made about Lean Production – it is potentially very fragile. The most obvious fragility is the just-in-time delivery of parts. A car needs every part so if one batch of parts does not arrive, then production stops. For Ohno this was a virtue because it forced every person in the production chain to concentrate and to anticipate failures. There were no safety nets.

But if internal fragility can be managed, external fragilities cannot. The Covid-19 pandemic exposed the fragility of all global systems, notably supply chains. Lean survived that disaster but will its intrinsic fragility survive the next one?

All business ideas are strictly time limited. Lean is only different to the extent that it seems to celebrate its own fragility as a workplace incentive. But that fragility – notably in just-in-time delivery – guarantees its failure. As Nassim Nicholas Taleb has pointed out, it is simply foolish to remove the buffers against inevitable disaster that high levels of inventory would provide. Far better to accept lower profits than inevitable extinction.

5

TPS was a world view and a way of life. It was a version of industrial reality attuned far more closely to the conditions of the second half of the twentieth century than anything in the Detroit playbook. But if they were to succeed, Japanese car makers had to invade America. This was, to say the least, tricky. To the post-war car bosses of Detroit, it was obviously eccentricity bordering on madness or pure snobbery to own a foreign car. Even when these alien vehicles became a serious threat, they continued to call them 'shitboxes', a very Trumpian trope.

In January 1949 Detroit felt the first drops of rain warning of the storm to follow. A Volkswagen Beetle was shipped to New York. Precisely two were sold in that first year but the figures rose steadily, though it always remained a specialised product. In 1950 330 were sold out of total new car sales of 6.6 million. Then 20,000 were sold in 1955 and 177,000 in 1961. This was, of course, still peanuts in a year when GM sold 142,000 of just one of its premium marques – the wallowing, chrome-heavy but profitable and expensive Cadillacs.

The low numbers made the bosses miss the point. The issue was not the Beetle itself; it was what it represented. Foreignness in cars was not a simple marketing segment; it was a cultural realignment, a generational change. John DeLorean, head of Chevrolet from 1969, commented on the 'mystique' of the Beetle: 'The foreign car buyer has an image of craftsmen in the Black Forest, building cars by hand.' The high ideal of foreign craftsmanship had returned in opposition to Detroit's brute force.

One way of dealing with this was to copy the Europeans, as Chevrolet did with the launch of the Vega in 1971. It was a sub-compact that looked like a Fiat; one motoring writer suggested Chevrolet should pay a fee for the styling to the Italian master Pininfarina. Even the name, Vega, sounded Italian. Unfortunately, the Vega had rust and engineering problems and was discontinued in 1977. The Beetle endured; it was everything Detroit's cars were not – small, clever, cheap to run, reliable and alternative, in the most radical meaning of the word. In the sixties it came to symbolise the key aspiration of youth culture – sticking it to 'The Man', the capitalist oppressor, who in this case lived in Detroit. The message of the Beetle was simply that cars could be done differently.

But Detroit's eyes were not on Germany nor on Japan; they were on Britain. In 1932 the UK overtook France as the world's largest car maker and in 1950 she overtook America as the world's largest car exporter.

In that year British companies produced 522,000 vehicles, twice as many as France. America had the Big Three – Ford, GM and Chrysler – Britain had the Big Six – Austin, Morris, Rootes, Standard and the two American subsidiaries Ford and Vauxhall (GM). These six companies made 90 per cent of British cars. The rest were made by an assortment of mostly high-end producers – Rolls-Royce, Jaguar, Aston Martin – and a few cheaper sports cars. This proliferation might look like a rosy picture of capitalist health. But it wasn't. The first problem was that the British companies had failed to update their manufacturing processes to American production standards. In the mass market how you make cars, as the Japanese would soon demonstrate, is at least as important as what cars you make. Second, as the Americans had discovered, in the car industry size matters.

Nevertheless, in 1950 anybody betting on which nation would be the first to break into the US car market would have put their money on Britain. The British had a good automotive image in the USA thanks to a reputation for the best luxury cars – notably Rolls-Royce – and for very driveable sports cars from Triumph, MG, Jaguar and Austin-Healey that actually handled pretty well, certainly better than anything made by Detroit.

Those sports cars persist in the American automotive imagination. On Jalopnik.com – a votive site for intelligent and funny car worshippers – there is a video review of a 1970 Triumph GT6 which toys sceptically with the idea of Englishness and the poor reputation of British cars – 'unreliable, slow, maintenance nightmares' – before concluding that the car is, in fact, 'bloody brilliant'.

Britain's pre-war place in the US market persisted after the war. A very small niche market of specialist cars somehow made their way to America. There was the MG TC, a smart two-seater, and at the highest end there was the Aston Martin DB2, a very successful racer as well as a road car. Most spectacular of all, there was the Jaguar XK120, which was for a time the fastest car in the world. Its beauty alone was enough to inspire Chevrolet to produce the first Corvette sports car in 1953, a pretty rather than beautiful roadster that could do 0–60 mph in 11.2 seconds and reach 108 mph. It was, according to L.J.K. Setright, 'pathetically primitive' compared with the Mercedes 300SL – a beauty with gull-wing doors launched in 1954 – but it was at least a step away from the 'big standard domestic sedan'.

But British industry was too insular, complacent and self-regarding to break into America on any scale. They would send out cars like the Hillman Minx, which, on the face of it and ignoring the oddity of naming a car as a flirtatious or wanton woman, should have been a contender. It had an engine at the front, a proper trunk/boot, four doors and, though it was the same length as a Beetle, it had more room inside. It wasn't as alien to US eyes as the VW. In both Mark III and Mark V forms it looked vaguely like a pre- or immediately post-war American car.

On the other hand, the Minx wasn't as well finished as the VW. To mention this shortcoming is to send a shudder down the spines of British car owners above a certain age. For decades the British-owned mass car industry was to prove incapable of producing a well-finished car. Take the Princess, an ugly 'family' car produced by the death-spiral conglomerate known as British Leyland between 1975 and 1981. I remember being shown a new Princess by a dis-consolate salesman in south-east London. There was a prominent glue smear on the plastic fabric of the roof. The salesman shrugged: 'Comes as standard.' The Brits weren't alone in their casual incom-petence. A survey in 1972 found that the Detroit Big Three plus American Motors delivered cars to their dealers with an average of 24 defects, some safety related.

But Detroit survived, whereas, to general rejoicing, British Leyland finally succumbed in 1986. By then the British-owned car industry was expiring under the weight of terrible management and extraordinarily unpleasant union bosses. Most prominently there was Red Robbo – aka Derek Robinson – who organised a series of crippling strikes that brought BL to its knees in the seventies. His one saving grace, however, was that in March 2000 he succeeded in making me laugh outright with a single-sentence commentary on his career: 'The pressures were immense but were it not for the ideological understanding that I had, I could very well have ended up with a nervous breakdown.'

Anyway, the Minx did not handle as well as the Beetle and, worst of all, it came without any realistic service back-up, as did the Austins, Fiats and Renaults that were also trying to break into America. There were few mechanics that could do anything with these machines and parts were scarce – if one was needed that was not on American soil, customers had to wait for them to be sent by boat from Europe.

At VW, Heinrich Nordhoff did not make the same mistake. Nordhoff sought dealers willing to take on a few Beetles. Notably he discovered Max Hoffman, who ran a foreign car supermarket in Manhattan. Hoffman was an automotive aesthete; he wasn't initial-ly interested in the Beetle but he was interested in the Porsche 356, a cute, efficient and fast sports car. Nordhoff gave him the Porsche as long as he agreed to carry the Beetle. He became the exclusive VW importer for the East Coast. Nordhoff then gave him the West Coast as well. But Hoffman's heart wasn't in the Beetle; it was in higher things – cars like, in 1954, that 300SL and the BMW 507 Roadster.

Nordhoff did not renew his contract. Not that Hoffman would have cared much. Having commissioned Frank Lloyd Wright to build his Jaguar showroom in Park Avenue in 1954, he then asked him to build an exquisite house in Rye, New York. In 2019 the fashion designer Marc Jacobs bought it for $9.2 million.

Leaving Hoffman aside, Nordhoff's Beetles were backed up by expert mechanics and readily available parts. From 1954 this network was massively improved by an ex-Luftwaffe pilot named Will van de Kamp. He was a ferocious organiser but with marketing blind spots which made him sound like a comedy German. Seeing models surrounding VWs at an auto show, he exclaimed, 'Girls? What for do I want girls? Engineers in white coats, ja, not girls!' He eventually allowed girls in uniforms but only after they had been trained for two weeks in driving the car.

In spite of all of which, the problem for European makers attempting to crack the post-war American car market was the iron grip of Detroit. Until 1965 this was the golden age of the Big Three – Ford, Chrysler and General Motors. They, in John Jerome's words, re-arranged 'the very social and moral structure of the nation'. Detroit dominated the economy of the fifties and sixties in the same way that Silicon Valley now dominates the twenty-first-century economy. And, like the tech companies, they were convinced that they and only they knew what their customers wanted and they and only they were able to make it. These delusions were to be their undoing but not at the hands of any European maker.

Surveying the post-war period, Herman Kahn, the Cold War strategist and futurologist, asked us to imagine a Rip Van Winkle falling asleep and waking in 1980. Kahn said he would assume that Japan had won the war.

6

Nevertheless, the Japanese automotive invasion did not start well. The shortcomings of the Toyopet Crown, launched by Toyota in 1955, only really became apparent when Toyota tried to sell it in America. The Crowns were highly regarded in Japan as sturdy and reliable city cars, many of which were taxis. They also looked quite nice – lots of chrome, a high roof for men with hats and a slightly muscley haunch. Like the Hillman Minx, this was a car obviously influenced by American cars of the forties, but on a much smaller scale.

Plans were laid to introduce the Crown to what in theory would be eager buyers in the USA. In 1956 Shotaro Kamiya, Toyota Motor Sales president, sent a three-man team over to the USA and armed with their report he attempted to persuade the reluctant main board to export to America. They were reluctant because they didn't think their cars were ready and they wanted to wait another five years. Kamiya responded by pointing to the success of the VW Beetle – over 50,000 were to be sold in 1957, a drop in the ocean of US car sales but a significant one nonetheless. He added that this success might cause a restriction on foreign imports – higher tariffs perhaps. At the time the American tariff on car imports was 7 per cent, the lowest in the world. So Kamiya was basically making an offer the board could not refuse – export now or be shut out forever.

The board was persuaded and in August 1957 the freighter *Toyota Maru* left Yokohama for Long Beach, California. On board were two Crowns, one white and one black. I doubt that Kyoko Otani – Miss Japan 1957 – was on the freighter but she was on the dockside at Long Beach carrying a large bouquet. This she placed on the first car to be unloaded.

Meanwhile, Seisi Kato, the executive in charge of the launch, had established his base in a Los Angeles hotel. Both he and Kamiya were encouraged by the initially positive reception of the two cars, which Americans had taken to calling 'baby Cadillacs'. Kamiya was so thrilled that he wired Tokyo to say he expected to sell 10,000 cars in the first year.

The team was further encouraged by the number of West Coast dealers who applied for a franchise. But these dealers were the first problem of what would become a lengthening list. They would have seen the Crown as very much a second-choice import. To the continuing bafflement of the Big Three in Detroit, the VW Beetle was the only import Americans seemed to want. The dealers chasing the Crown would have been the ones who had failed German vetting.

Then there was the name. Toy? Pet? American cars at the time had names like Bel Air, Thunderbird and Imperial. Oddly, a couple of years later Nissan, which was also trying to break into the US market, made the same naming mistake with a car called Cedric. This was, it is said, named after the lead character in Frances Hodgson Burnett's novel *Little Lord Fauntleroy*, a book of which the Nissan CEO Katsuji Kawamata was inordinately fond. Also, Nissan had been a partner of Austin for most of the fifties, building almost 22,000 Somersets and Cambridges under licence, so Cedric was a kind of fraternal tribute.

But the really serious problem with the Toyopet was the car itself. Soon after the cars landed they were taken to a vehicle-testing station where they were declared unfit – poor rearview mirror and defective lights. It was also expensive – $600 more than a Beetle. It plainly wasn't a quality car, nor a large one. Worse still it was designed for urban use and in California cars were routinely used to drive long distances at high speed. Kato noted this problem in his memoir, written 25 years later. When the Crown was launched onto a freeway at 80 mph 'loud noises soon erupted and power dropped sharply'.

The Toyopet, for all its faults, was tough; it had to be because Japanese roads were not smooth. Floaty American cars exported to Japan had resulted in head injuries to drivers because of their inability to handle potholes. In this context perhaps the car's greatest triumph came when two journalists drove a Toyopet from London to Tokyo, a journey of 31,000 miles. But it was not built for high-speed, long-distance cruising.

The Toyopet struggled on. Its US sales peaked at 1,028 in 1958. Toyota was selling them alongside its Land Cruiser, a four-wheel-drive car inspired by the American Jeep. But it was not enough and in December 1960 the export of cars to the USA was halted. The Toyopet adventure had failed, a failure that confirmed prevailing American views of the Japanese. This was partly the remains of post-war resentments and partly because of entrenched racism. Many simply did not believe the Japanese were capable of producing better cars than Detroit.

Nevertheless, in 2008 Toyota passed General Motors as the largest car maker in the world. Japan now has 30 per cent of the US car market and Detroit has less than 1 per cent of the Japanese. General Motors sold just 700 cars in Japan in 2018. Harry 'Rabbit' Angstrom was not just rich, he was right.

7

Misleadingly, the Toyopet Crown seemed to be the harbinger of precisely nothing and so by 1965 Detroit executives were oozing confidence and complacency. They sold a record 9.3 million cars and, they told themselves, they had seen off the threat of foreign imports. In 1962 only 399,000 imports were sold with the Beetle accounting for 57 per cent of those. By 1965 there had been a slight foreign improvement. Sure, the VW Beetle then sold nearly 400,000 but that was a car for oddballs and, OK, British MGs and Triumphs were selling a few but not enough to disturb the deep dream of peace that had settled on Motor City. And who cared about the Japanese? The 18,000 Datsuns and 6,400 Toyotas sold in that year were more of a rounding error than a threat.

In fact, there was a lot more to celebrate in 1965, notably the amazing fact that Chevrolet had conquered the cosmos. A writer in *Car and Driver* reported the findings of a Yale physicist – Chevrolet offered a choice of 46 models, 32 engines, 20 transmissions, 21 colours (with nine two-tone combinations) and 400 accessories and options. As a result, the number of cars potentially available exceeded the number of atoms in the universe. In response John Jerome pointed out that not only were Chevrolet beating Ford, they were also ahead of God.

In the same year Ford launched the Mustang. It was a beautiful if rather ordinary machine that created a new market segment now known to *Top Gear* aficionados as 'pony cars'. It was basically a cosmetically altered version of Ford's very successful Falcons and Fairlanes – primarily the cab had been moved backwards to create a longer bonnet. But its performance and handling simply drew attention to the fact that all Big Three cars were pretty much the same. A reviewer in *Road & Track* suggested if all Detroit's cars were lined up and tested by a blindfolded driver, he would be unable to tell them apart. The Mustang, the reviewer concluded, was no different from at least half a dozen other cars.

Never mind, in the marketplace it worked. The Mustang sold well on the basis of its long-nosed beauty. But, in fact, even before the Japanese wave hit the beach, the success, as far as Ford was concerned, was largely illusory. Despite the company's two other successes – the

Falcon and the Fairlane – it had still lost market share – 'So what the hell did we prove?' asked an executive.

What Detroit thought it had proved was that there was a gullible youth market out there and that these young folk did not want their parents' big blousy sedans. So, they came up with so-called super-cars – Pontiac GTO, Plymouth Road Runner, Dodge Charger and the Oldsmobile 442, all higher-powered machines. They provided some increase in straight-line acceleration and a degree of glamour but with Ralph Nader and the Japanese closing in on them they did little to slow the onrush of the Big Three's declining years.

Crucially for Detroit's inflated self-image in 1965, the move into small or not so small 'compact' cars to thwart the European import threat seemed to have proved unnecessary. The people still wanted their big cars. This was a great relief to the executives because, as one executive put it, GM could make more profit from a single loaded – i.e., stuffed with extras – full-sized Chevrolet Bel Air than it could from five compact stripped-down Corvairs. No doubt about it, in 1965 Motor City was cruising along one of the new interstates without a care in the world.

It was all, of course, about to go horribly wrong. That year Ralph Nader published *Unsafe at Any Speed*, a book that effectively accused the Big Three car makers of murder. The unfortunate Corvair and its maker General Motors were first in the dock. I shall return to that in a later chapter. But more damaging than any of this was the discovery that the trickle of Japanese cars in 1965 was to turn into a tsunami that would overwhelm Detroit's complacency and, most shockingly, its reputation for industrial competence.

8

Though the first American adventure had failed, Toyota's Japanese base was booming. At a plant at Motomachi, opened in 1959, it could make 10,000 vehicles a month and the company was on its way to becoming the biggest car maker in Japan. But they had not given up on the USA. In 1961 they attempted to export the Tiara, known as the Corona, but that too failed. They also attempted to make a deal with Ford which would hand over US sales of the Publica, a sedan of amiable appearance, but Ford suddenly pulled out in a way that to Eiji Toyoda, cousin to Kiichiro, suggested 'bla-tant disrespect'. The company also managed to export a few of its Stout trucks but that too failed and the Stouts were withdrawn in 1967. Only the Land Cruisers continued to sell.

Meanwhile, they had been working on the Corona and with the third iteration in 1964 they seemed to have a potential winner – an elegant, sharp-looking, 'shovel-nosed' sedan with, for the US market, a 1,900 cc, 90 hp engine. It was to be the car that broke America.

In fact, this didn't start well either. At the launch party in 1965 there was not a single Corona – the cars had been shipped to Port-land rather than Los Angeles. Unfazed this time, Toyota embarked on a primarily West Coast advertising and PR campaign.

The reviews were good. Consumer reports said the Corona had 'special virtues for long-distance driving'. *Popular Mechanics* came up with some quotes that should have alarmed Detroit – the Corona was 'a civilized-looking car', it was 'modern and functional with more than a passing Italian influence' and, this was the killer, it was an 'Eastern import with Western values'. One ordinary punter so liked his car that he shot a film of it, saying, 'Once you get your hands on one, you never want to let it go.' The company slogan then became, 'Get your hands on a Toyota and you'll never let it go!' US sales jumped from 6,404 to 20,908 and kept on rising.

But if the Corona was the car that broke America, the Corolla was the car that ate America. It first appeared in Japan in 1966 and a slightly more powerful version was launched in the USA in 1968. Everybody seemed to agree that it was as good as the Corona but for the fact that its engine delivered 30 per cent less horsepower. Also, reviewers found the brakes a little dubious and noted a tendency for its wheels to lift off the road surface during high-speed cornering. But the really big improvements over the Corona were its looks – tilting the engine slightly had allowed for a lower, sleeker front end – and the price: $1,660, $200 less than the Beetle and even slightly cheaper than its direct competitor, the Datsun 510.

It was enough. American customers couldn't get enough Corol-las. 'Move Over World', cried the cover of the August 1968 edition of *Car Life Magazine*, 'Here Come the Japanese'. The car seemed to sell to all age groups, including the politically active young. They had been buying Beetles but Corollas passed the VW as the largest-selling imported car in 1973. By then it accounted for half of all

Toyota's sales in the USA. And, the final affront, Toyota produced the Celica to compete with the Ford Mustang.

But something much more important for the car industry also happened in 1973. In October of that year Arab oil producers announced an embargo on sales to countries regarded as supporters of Israel in the Yom Kippur War. By March oil prices had risen 300 per cent. The average price of petrol in 1973 was 37 cents a gallon; it had been falling in real terms for a decade. After 1973 it began to rise. The full measure of the 'oil shock' was felt in American gas stations.

Sales of US cars had raced up from 7.1 million in 1970 to 9.7 million in 1973, but in 1974 they slipped back to 7.4 million. If fuel prices had continued to fall, as they had done until 1973, Detroit might have survived the Japanese invasion more or less intact. But it never happened.

Sales of Japanese cars in America had already leapt from 70,000 in 1967 to 704,000 in 1972. By 1985, aided by US-based factories, Honda, Mazda, Toyota and Nissan had claimed 30 per cent of the entire US market of the 10 million units sold that year.

9

The Japanese businessman – intensely conservative in his dress and manner, hedged about by customs and rituals and unlikely ever to divulge gossip or off-message insights – does not grip the western imagination. Such stereotypes are, of course, never quite right but it is certainly true that the great figures of post-war Japanese capitalism either lacked or appeared to lack the star qualities of their western counterparts.

Except for Soichiro Honda. American executives who struggled to understand their Japanese counterparts had no trouble with Honda. There was no oriental mystique about the man; he was, according to one journalist, 'a passionate man of almost Latin propensities'. He was also an engineer of genius, a drinker and compulsive womaniser. Around 1945 he capriciously took a year off, spent a huge sum on a large drum of medical alcohol and used it to make his own whisky to fuel incessant parties.

But he was never distracted from piston rings, motorbikes and, finally, cars. Like Henry Ford, with whom he is often compared, he was an engineering obsessive. In his early years of tinkering he became hermit-like when trying to solve a problem. Day and night he could only be found in his workshop; even his wife Sachi had to turn up there, often to cut his hair. No wonder the Americans understood him; he embodied their romantic idea of the maverick, the outsider, the lonely driven genius.

Born in 1906, even as a toddler he was thrilled by cars. He trembled when he first saw one – a Ford Model T – and chased it down the road. He had little time for school. 'A diploma,' he said, 'is less useful than a ticket to a movie.' So, he cheated. Pupils had to take their grade reports home to their parents who would then stamp them with their family seal. Honda made his own stamp so that his parents wouldn't see his presumably abysmal grades. He was found out when he created stamps for other children – a fatal mistake. He had not known that the stamps were mirror reversed; his own family name wasn't affected since, printed vertically, it was symmetrical.

He was the son of a blacksmith and bicycle repairer in a rural village. He became an apprentice to an auto repairer in his teens and then set up his own company which, among other things, produced piston rings, some of which he sold to Toyota. He also raced – for a while. In 1936 he drove in the All-Japan Speed Rally using a supercharged Ford engine which he had tilted to the left. The race ran counterclockwise so this, he reasoned, would help with cornering, a typically Hondaish thought, crazy and possibly right. He set a speed record of 75 mph but approaching the finishing line he crashed into another car. He was horribly injured, spent three months in hospital and would never race again.

When his company Tokai Sekei was taken under government control during the war, he started mass-producing wooden aeroplane propellers. He could turn out four an hour – previously they had been hand-carved and each one took a week.

But his production facilities seemed to be cursed. One was destroyed in an air raid in 1944 and another by the Mikawa earthquake the following year. Honda sold the remains of the company to Toyota and used the money to found the Honda Technical Research Institute. Knowing that in the ruins of war the Japanese couldn't afford cars, Honda decided to produce a small engine that could be attached to a bicycle. A proper motorcycle – the Type-D – followed in 1949. To this, somehow, the name Dream was attached. It was a startling and stylish machine that, of course, did not look quite like any other motorcycle. Ten years later Honda was the biggest motorcycle manufacturer in the world and about to break into the American market with his much more powerful C-series Dreams.

As with the Toyopet, his machines struggled with long hard driving on American roads and in any case a bike that sounded like a lawnmower was hardly in a position to compete with the thunderous Harleys and Indians favoured by Americans. So, Honda created the Super Cub and spent $5 million on the creation of a new corporate image. 'You meet the nicest people on a Honda' was the oddly winsome advertising line. There was no attempt at the usual macho-sell of motorcycles. Instead, the TV ads sold the machines as sweet, stylish, cheap domestic accessories, especially desirable for women – the 'underbone' or 'step-through' design made skirt-wearing less problematic. There was even an anti-car theme in some of the ads – you could, after all, glide through traffic jams on a Honda.

But then Soichiro Honda had to take on the mighty MITI – the Ministry of International Trade and Industry. MITI existed to promote and protect Japanese industries. The ferocity with which it fulfilled its brief was extraordinary. In 1955, when domestic cars could not compete with imports, MITI ruled that any foreign car could only be purchased in Japan once it had been in the country for a year, it must be two years old and it had to be sold by an American who had not done such a deal for at least three years.

Honda had a problem with MITI's interventionist frenzy. It was clear the plan was to rationalise Japanese car production so that by 1968 there would be just two or three big companies – Toyota and Nissan obviously. In 1961 he had announced, 'I will make the best cars in Japan. To do that, I must make the best cars in the world.'

Fearing the MITI strategy would cut him out of the car business, in 1962 Honda rushed out the S360, a roadster with a vaguely British appearance – it resembled the MG Midget that had been released the year before. This was also an implicit challenge because MITI had demanded that the car companies should come up with a 'People's Car', meaning a cheap four-seater with a top speed of 60 mph.

The next year came another slightly more powerful roadster – 'a motorcycle disguised as a car', comments historian Wanda James. This was followed by the S-600 and the L-700 estate. But then came

the N series – the 360 and the 600, both small two-box 'city' cars –
and Honda became a serious contender.

The N-600 was sold with the same chirpy domestic tone as the
Super Cub. TV ads were cheerily practical, emphasising low fuel
consumption and small size. Clearly, they were aiming for the same
market as the motorcycle. It worked, as did the similarly shaped but
slightly larger Civic which arrived in the USA in 1973. The timing –
it was the year of the oil shock – could not have been better. It was,
in fact, a great car. The reviews were ecstatic: 'the most brilliant
small car in automotive history', one of the 'twelve best cars to own
in an energy crisis' and so on. Honda had achieved what Detroit
had so signally failed to achieve – a popular and sellable small car.
The company was to become – and remains – the third big Japanese
maker after Toyota and Nissan.

Honda's production methods were not unlike the TPS but they
were adapted to conform to Soichiro's personality. He had no time
for the corporate conformity of his competitors. He told his assembly line workers that they were working first for themselves and only
secondly for the company. Like Ohno, he saw imperfection as the
road to improvement – success only happened 1 per cent of the time
and was made possible by the 99 per cent of time spent failing.

In 1990 Honda launched the car that remains, to engineers and
petrol heads everywhere, the company's greatest achievement. It sold
thousands, not millions; as far as the mass market was concerned, it
was meaningless. But it did once again demonstrate that Honda was
pre-eminently an engineer-led company.

In 1984 Honda embarked on a project then known as the HP-X,
the Honda Pininfarina eXperimental concept, a mid-engined sports
car powered by a 3-litre V6 engine. Pininfarina is an Italian family-
run car-design company that designed most post-war Ferraris. And
that was the point; HP-X targeted the Ferrari cars of the 1980s,
notably the 328 and the 348. It was intended to match or exceed
their performance and to undercut them on price and reliability. The
great racing driver Ayrton Senna was brought in as an adviser. He
drove the car, told Honda to make it stiffer and so they did. The
project evolved into the NSX – new sportscar eXperimental – and
it appeared at the Chicago Auto Show in 1989 and went on sale in
Japan in 1990. It was sold in America as the Acura NSX – Acura
being the premium brand Honda had launched in the USA in 1986.

It did indeed match the Ferraris on speed and beat them on price and reliability. It also beat them on design – the cabin was inspired by that of an F-16 fighter jet and provided levels of all-round visibility unprecedented in a mid-engine sports car. And, finally, it beat them on engineering.

Gordon Murray, one of the greatest fast-car designers in the world (more of him later), was in the eighties pursuing a thought process that would in 1992 lead to the McLaren F1, then the fastest road car ever built and for most critics the best. He visited Ayrton Senna at Honda's Tochigi Research Centre – McLaren's Formula 1 cars were then using Honda engines. He spotted a prototype of the NSX and they let him drive it.

Until then his 'benchmark' cars – i.e., cars his had to be better than – for the design of the F1 had been Ferraris, Porsches and Lamborghinis. After the drive there was only one benchmark – the NSX.

'The moment I drove the NSX,' he tells me, 'all the benchmark cars . . . I had been using as references in the development of my car vanished from my mind. Of course, the car we would create, the McLaren F1, needed to be faster than the NSX, but the NSX's ride quality and handling would become our new design target.'

He did, in fact, tell Honda that the NSX chassis was good enough to take a much more powerful engine than the 270 hp V6 but though they did increase the power in later iterations, they did not go on to build a true supercar. He also thought the public were not ready to pay such a high price – $58,000 in 1990 – for a Japanese car and that it could have looked sharper: 'With just a slightly lower price, or possibly selling it with a different brand name and a different badge, or perhaps endowing it with a touch flashier and more aggressive styling and additional power, there is no question the NSX would have reigned as a cult star of the supercars.'

Soichiro Honda once said, 'I'd sooner die than imitate other people.' In this too he succeeded. He died, aged 84, in August 1991; Sachi, with nobody's hair to cut, survived him by 22 years.

10

James David Power III was born in Massachusetts in 1931. He became an officer on a Coast Guard icebreaker before earning an

MBA in finance. He went on to work in finance and marketing for, among others, Ford and General Motors. Then, in 1968, he had his big idea.

He noticed the rate at which Toyota was gaining market share. He was at the time working from his kitchen table but, by devious means, he gained access to a Toyota executive who agreed that he should conduct a survey into how customers felt about their new Corollas, etc. On the back of this, he launched J.D. Power and Associates – at the time the 'associates' were his wife and children. Power later admitted he used child labour. His children Scotch-taped a quarter, face up, to the surveys as they were sent out – an extra incentive to respond. It worked; the response rate was close to 50 per cent – 'Because,' he explained, 'people wanted to talk about their cars.' As the TPS included relations with customers – a particular strength of Toyota's dealers – the survey came out well. Other Japanese companies noticed and started carrying out their own surveys. Detroit was at first unconcerned.

Power's wife Julia also played a part. In 1972 she identified a flaw in the rotary engine then being used by Mazda – an O-ring in the cooling system was failing after 30,000 miles. The whole engine would have to be removed to fix this. The survey results were confidential at this point but this one was leaked to the *Wall Street Journal* by one of Power's subscribers. Power was convinced it was leaked by one of Detroit's Big Three. He issued a press release explaining the context of the finding and the next day it hit the front pages. J.D. Power Associates was suddenly famous and its surveys went public.

For decades Japanese cars rated higher than any others on reliability and customer satisfaction. In 2018 Cheatsheet.com published a list of twenty cars that since 2010 had been rated highest on reliability in consumer reports. Every one was Japanese. This has latterly changed as Korean and US makers have caught up. Dodge and Kia scored highest in 'overall initial quality' in 2020, though Toyota, notably its Lexus brand, was still up there in reliability.

11

The grand historical narrative of the decline of America, the defeat of Detroit, of the rise of Lean, of just-in-time and the pursuit of perfection, of philosopher bosses and Soichiro Honda, of *muda* and MITI always seems to omit a whole buoyant category of Japanese cars that may, in fact, play a bigger part in the future than any management theory, midsized sedan, roadster or sport-utility vehicle (SUV). It is a category that sometimes seems to cause embarrassment and which has at times been deliberately suppressed. I have a supposedly complete history of Japanese cars, published in 1985, that carries no mention of this category. You will almost never see these cars reviewed in the mainstream motor magazines but you can catch up with them on websites like Jalopnik.com and you can even buy them at Ukkeicars.com and Andrewsjapanesecars.com. Nevertheless, these cars account for a third of all used car sales in Japan; in 2013 the figure was 40 per cent.

MITI was, after the war, very keen on the idea of a people's car. In the event, this category somehow morphed into something called a city car, an ultramini or, in Japan, a *kei* car. *Kei* is short for *keijidosha*, meaning light car; the category was created by the government in 1949. This stipulated that these cars were to be no more than 2.8 metres long and 1 metre wide with a maximum displacement of 150 cc for a four-stroke engine and 100 cc for a two-stroke. These figures changed progressively, reaching 3.4 metres, 1.48 metres and 660 cc in 1998. *Kei* cars had special number plates – black on yellow for private use and yellow on black for commercial vehicles. Owners paid less tax, registration and insurance. The idea was to promote car ownership.

It worked; the Japanese couldn't get enough of these *kei* cars and trucks. As a result, Japanese roads are still full of tiny vehicles seen nowhere else in the world. In some rural regions between 75 and 100 per cent of households own a *kei*. But, in fact, it almost worked too well. In the seventies, probably to defend the more profitable and exportable cars then being produced, the government started reducing the tax advantages and imposing stricter emission regulations. Honda and Mazda pulled out of *kei* production for a while. But in the end *kei* makers' protests forced the government to climb down and permitted engine sizes were increased.

In 2014 the government once again cut back on the incentives to buy *kei*s. 'We need to rebalance our priorities,' said Yoshitaka Shindo, the minister for internal affairs. The car companies were devoting too much time to researching and developing *kei*s solely for the home market. That money was thought to be wasted. But also the production of *kei*s meant that the companies could not achieve the economies of scale necessary to survive in the international market. As one automotive analyst put it, 'For years, the *kei* was the people's car in Japan. But now its role is over. The distinction no longer makes sense.'

Unfortunately for the government it makes a good deal of sense for *kei* owners and users. Somehow they still survive and thrive and the designs are proving very amenable to electrification.

All of which is exotic and mysteriously oriental enough but nothing like as weird as the design culture that developed around the *kei* format. Very small cars usually excite derision. Few British people above a certain age will have forgotten the Sinclair C5, a sub-*kei* sized electric 'car' which, when all else failed, as it often did, could be pedal-powered. It was created by Sir Clive Sinclair, who had successfully produced calculators and home computers in the seventies and eighties. But cars are different, not least because you can be seen driving them, and nobody wanted to be seen driving a C5. It flopped and only survives among a few crazed hobbyists and as a warning against alternative automotive technologies.

But Japan did not suffer a C5 trauma. It did, however, suffer a defeat in war. There was a need to reconstruct the country. *Kei* cars were part of the solution. In spite of tough size and power restrictions car makers came up with a menagerie of brilliantly useful and often absurdly cute little cars.

At the useful end of the scale, the Suzuki Wagon R, for example, has been produced since 1993 and has been the bestselling *kei* car in Japan since 1993. Like many *kei*s, notably the commercial ones, it is a tall box – the government restrictions do not specify a height limit. In 2011 another very similar car was produced by Honda. This too is a tall box and, *kei*s having become in the interim a cult, Honda celebrates this oddity by calling it an N-Box. Since 2019 1.7 million N-Boxes have been sold, making it another of Japan's bestselling cars. This transition from legally mandated product to design cult has led, first, to a move beyond mere practicality and, second, it has recreated both an official and informal export market for *kei*s.

The fun side of the *kei* reflects – as did Honda's promotion of its motorcycles – a Japanese acceptance and celebration of more domestic, friendly, cute and often toy-like automotive styling and promotion. So, the Daihatsu TAFT is a Jeep-like car that looks vaguely like a Tonka toy and its name is said to stand for 'Tough & Almighty Fun Too'. More extreme forms of fun are offered by *kei*s with sports or even supercar styling. The Honda S660 looks like a baby McLaren and the Autozam A-1 with its optional rear wing looks like a stubby first-generation Honda NSX.

Government resistance to the *kei* may be short-sighted. Rather than a relic of post-war reconstruction *kei*s should be seen as harbingers of the automotive future, especially in urban areas. Small cars are the next step. The SUVS that block city streets will soon be forgotten like the giant-finned and chromed carnival floats that drifted out of Detroit in the fifties and sixties.

With its *kei*-like Ami Citroën might have started the shift to small city cars. It has a top speed of 28 mph and in France it can be driven by 14-year-olds so it is a car that could replace motor scooters or even bikes.

But the automotive future might not be decided in Europe, America or Japan, but in China.

12

Mao Zedong, unlike his fellow mass murderer Adolf Hitler, did not believe in a car for the people. He regarded private car ownership as corrupt bourgeois consumerism. And so, from 1949 onwards, taxi companies died and private car ownership in the big cities plummeted. Of course, high-ranking and state officials retained their access to cars. In 1993 96 per cent of all vehicle sales were to government departments or state-owned businesses.

For more than 50 years the Chinese car industry lay dormant. In 1978 only 2,640 cars were produced. But by 1984 the authorities were beginning to think private car ownership was not corrupt, bourgeois, etc. To make the point they planted an upbeat news story about the first peasant to own a car. Sun Guiying had bought a Toyota Publica, a tiny sub-compact, with the earnings from her chicken farm. This was a great success. Sun and her family were photographed posing by the car. 'The family,' as a newspaper report explained, 'is the first to have ever purchased a car in the suburbs of Beijing. This year she sold 32,000 kilograms of eggs to the state. But having got rich herself, she never forgot the collective . . .' and so on.

Mark King, a journalist from the *Sydney Morning Herald*, then discovered that the Toyota was old; it had been used by the Japanese Embassy and sold to Sun via the only used-car agency in Beijing. Moreover, Sun did not have a licence and could not drive. Her husband demonstrated the car, which had a large plastic chicken on the dashboard, and reversed it into the corner of the family house. He explained that he worked for the National People's Political Consultative Conference. He insisted, 'I'm not a capitalist, they exploit people. I prefer to be called an entrepreneur.'

Chinese car buyers probably only heard the first part of this story and it gave them automotive aspirations. Sales started increasing and then, in 2000, the tenth Five-Year Plan announced that 'letting passenger cars into the family is to be encouraged'. Suddenly the Chinese were allowed to be middle class and they had to have cars. The pent-up demand caused explosive growth in the industry. In 2010 Chinese car production passed that of the USA. In 2012 10.8 million cars were produced; in 2018 the figure was 20.53 million. China has become the biggest car maker in the world.

The first oddity about the Chinese car market as it began to grow was a weird affection for the boot/trunk. This was because of a lingering admiration for the shape of the cars driven by the governing elites. These were big, black sedans which provided an aspirational image for the rising middle classes. As a result, car makers exporting to China decided to perform bizarre cosmetic surgery on their models, adding boots to hatchbacks. Everybody wanted three-box sedans so Audi, BMW and Infiniti – Nissan's luxury brand – stretched their wheelbases to give a more 'official' look. US cars were symbols of freedom; in China they are more to do with status. This resulted in bizarre prejudices. Mercedes were for rich people as were BMWs but the latter were associated with the tasteless and irresponsible nouveau riche. Mini Coopers and Beetles were said to be for mistresses.

The most important official cars – 'representative sedans' – that had formed consumer taste emerged from the state-owned FAW (First Automobile Works) Group. Previously a truck producer, FAW was ordered in 1957 to make a car for the nation's leaders. In 1958 they came up with the Dongfeng CA71. Dongfeng – meaning east wind – was a homage to a speech Mao made in Moscow which included the line, 'The east wind prevails over the west wind.' It was later used as the name for a series of Chinese missiles, including the Dongfeng CA41, a multiple warhead monster with the longest range of any ICBM – almost 10,000 miles. The Dongfeng – the car – was not entirely original; it was reverse engineered, a polite term for copied, from the Simca Vedette and the Mercedes 190. From the Vedette it acquired a very American appearance and from the 190 it acquired an engine.

The CA71 was taken to Beijing to be presented outside Mao's residence. The prime minister, Zhou Enlai, opened the bonnet and remarked, 'I hear this engine is copied from Mercedes-Benz Model 190, right?' He advised copying more cleverly, notably, in this case, by changing the shape of the valve-chamber cover. One did not mess with Zhou.

The Beijing reveal of the CA71 established the idea of an official car and thereafter FAW served Mao directly. The Great Leader's personal Dongfeng had silk brocade seats, velvet ceilings, wool carpets, lacquered control panels, carved ivory switches and cloisonné smoking utensils. But, sadly, the CA71 was a terrible car that broke down repeatedly. The reverse engineering had been in vain.

And so as Mao's 'Great Leap Forward' starved somewhere between 18 and 45 million of his people to death, FAW embarked on a new, better machine, the Hongqi (Red Banner) CA72. This was based on a 1955 Chrysler Imperial that FAW had bought from the Yugoslav Embassy. It had a challenging V8 engine. The Soviets told them not to try and reverse engineer this as even they could not manage an eight-cylinder engine at the time. This drove the Chinese to a frenzy of work on 100 engine blanks from which the best three were chosen to produce a prototype. In August 1958, after just 33 days, the first car emerged. Two months later a convertible was produced for the tenth National Day military parade.

They then spent a year upgrading the design of the car under the influence of the Cadillac Fleetwood and the Lincoln Continental. Unsurprisingly, it looked like an American car, though quite a handsome one and a little more restrained than the originals, perhaps because it also looked like a Bentley. But, again, things went wrong. Only 206 were produced because Mao's new murderfest, the 'Cultural Revolution' – perhaps 2 million dead – somehow interfered with production. And so it went on all the way down to Xi Jinping's

Hongqi CA7600J L5 parade car which, bizarrely, was reviewed by Jeremy Clarkson in 2018. He concluded it was heavy, slow and uncomfortable but, 'It is the meanest, baddest-looking son of a bitch the world has seen.'

The parade-car culture also inspired the automotive wedding fleets which replaced the old fleets of sedan chairs and horses. These new fleets emerged in Guangzhou in the 1980s. They usually consist of four to six cars. They are called flower cars because of the elaborate decorations attached – heart-shaped rose arrangements, ribbons, more flowers, and toys like teddy bears and cartoon figures. Blessings written on paper are also attached. The most expensive cars go first and the whole thing will be filmed, usually by a cameraman in a hatchback with a sunroof. Jun Zhang, author of *Driving Toward Modernity: Cars and the Lives of the Middle Class in Contemporary China*, says he has seen fleets consisting of a single type of car – 7 series BMWs and Mini Coopers.

The car industry in China now consists of four big state-owned companies and half a dozen smaller makers. There are several joint ventures with foreign companies, notably the Volkswagen Group China, Mercedes-Benz and General Motors. Volvo, meanwhile, is entirely owned by Geely, China's biggest private car maker. Most cars are sold in China and exports largely go to emerging economies. China has become the fourth big car-making region alongside Europe, America and Japan. This sounds like the profile of the next global automotive superpower.

So does this. In September 2020 Xi Jinping spoke to the UN General Assembly. 'We aim,' he said, 'to have CO_2 emissions peak before 2030 and achieve carbon neutrality before 2060. Humankind can no longer afford to ignore the repeated warnings of nature.'

The man who is likely to lead this process is Wan Gang, China's Elon Musk. Having been exiled to the countryside during the Cultural Revolution, Wan taught himself engineering in a very Henry Ford way by taking apart and reassembling a tractor. He earned his PhD in Germany, worked for Audi and then returned to China. In 2000 he produced a paper entitled 'Regarding Development of Automobile New Clean Energy as the Starting-Line for Leap-Forward of China's Automobile Industry'.

Among many other incentives to buy one of the more than 100 EV cars now made in China is the avoidance of the lottery system in the crowded and traffic-clogged megacities. To get a licence for an oil-powered car you must accept odds of 907 to 1 and then pay a very high fee. Buy an EV and you might have to wait but you will get your licence and there will be no fee. In 2019 nearly 1 million EVs were sold, 4 per cent of China's new car sales and more than half of all the EVs sold in the world.

Meanwhile, three Chinese companies – Nio, Xpeng and Li Auto – are competing with Tesla to be the world's leading premium electric car maker.

If the future of the car is not to be a car, then whatever it is it might well be Chinese. The east wind will have prevailed.

PART TWO

BREAKERS

Forton Motorway Service Station under construction, 1964

Chapter Six

THE HITHER EDGE
OF FREE LAND

1

A car can go anywhere as long as there is a road and now there usually is. An off-roader, sport utility vehicle or a truck can go even further. As a direct result of this imperious extension of human mobility less than a quarter of the world's land is now wilderness and that figure is declining rapidly – 10 per cent of wilderness has been lost since the early 1990s.

The car has given us freedom but are we 'free' to do this? This is not, as it is usually framed, merely a scientific issue involving the potential threat to human survival posed by wilderness loss. This is also a value-laden imaginative issue. It is a treacherous rhetorical device to say we should not harm the wilderness because to do so is bad for humans; it implies the untouched land has no intrinsic value independent of human concerns. If it does have such intrinsic value, then the road is not endless – it cannot lead you everywhere.

The word 'wilderness' is often loosely used to mean a wasteland or a garden run wild. Or it is an officially endorsed space – a national park for example – that humans should treat with care. But the word is at its strongest when it signifies a place utterly untouched by humans. Such places, we feel, ought to exist to remind us of our place in the living and geological world. But, paradoxically, we cannot go there to be reminded without breaking the spell.

There's a further paradox – the wilderness can be claustrophobic, nightmarish. I once spoke to the actor and screenwriter Tracy Letts about the wilderness. 'I'm from the plains in Colorado,' he said, 'and I understand you can have these beautiful, huge horizons and yet feel very claustrophobic because there's nothing nearby and there's nowhere to go.'

This suggests we cannot cope with the wilderness so perhaps we should be content with just knowing that the wilderness is out there somewhere. But the car destroys such contentment.

The concept of the wilderness, the untouched land, calls into question not only our stewardship of nature, but also our concept of freedom. Are we free to roam wherever we like or should the wilderness be free of our presence? Is our automotive-assisted freedom limitless or is it bound by the freedom of other creatures, other landscapes?

2

In 1890 the bulletin of the superintendent of the US census included two sentences that were both casual in expression and momentous in content: 'Up to and including 1880 the country had a frontier of settlement, but at present the unsettled area has been so broken into by isolated bodies of settlement that there can hardly be said to be a frontier line. In the discussion of its extent, its westward movement, etc., it cannot, therefore, any longer have a place in the census reports.'

America began in the east and spread, slowly, to the west. Founded in 1776, the country only attained its full, transcontinental extent in 1912 when Arizona became the 48th state, thereby completing what is officially known as the Conterminous United States. So, for more than half of its existence America had a frontier, not in the sense of a border but in the sense of a line moving ever forward into the wilderness. But, as that census bulletin noted, in the 1890s the frontier line had fallen apart; in 1912 it officially vanished as the United States was made whole.

The great theorist of this process was a historian, Frederick Jackson Turner, who delivered a paper explaining his frontier thesis to the American Historical Association in 1893. His case was that the American character was formed by the frontier. Movement in the European past always ended with a border between one settled country and another. Americans encountered no such borders in their progress westward. 'The American frontier,' said Turner, 'is sharply distinguished from the European frontier—a fortified boundary line running through dense populations. The most significant thing about the American frontier is that it lies at the hither edge of free land.'

Of course, Native Americans will and should disagree about how free that land was. But this is about the significant mythology of a new world built on the conquest of a people and of a vast wilderness. The message most people took away from Turner's thesis was that the frontier was now closed. Replacing the frontier was the car, a new form of movement that would, in the twentieth century, combine with the idea of the frontier to reinvent the American character and imagination.

In the same year that Turner delivered his paper the Duryea brothers demonstrated the first petrol-powered car in America, the Motor Wagon, on Taylor Street in Springfield, Massachusetts. Also, six motor vehicles were on display at the 1893 Columbian Exhibition in Chicago. The history of America, the frontier, the wilderness, the car and, therefore, the modern world are tightly bound together in time.

3

The Great Divide, less grandly known as the Continental Divide, runs from the Bering Sea in the north to Tierra del Fuego in the south. In the United States it forms, among other things, the Rocky Mountains. It is a hydrological divide: to the east water flows towards the Atlantic; to the west it flows towards the Pacific.

But it is also poetry. There's a song by The Band called 'Across the Great Divide'; there's a Red Dirt music group called The Great Divide; there's a fashion label with the same name; countless political commentators routinely use the phrase; in Flint, Michigan, there's the Great Divide shopping centre. The phrase is always in demand as an erotic or romantic metaphor. Most importantly, the Great Divide is the barrier that first prevented and then permitted America to become whole.

Knowing the United States, as we do now, as an infinitely accessible continent, it is hard to imagine what it looked like when, with the Louisiana Purchase in 1803, the United States bought huge tracts of land in the Mid-West from France, thereby uniting the country from coast to coast. Soon after the purchase President Thomas Jefferson commissioned the Corps of Discovery Expedition – now better known as the Lewis and Clark Expedition – to cross the continent and thereby establish sovereignty over the Native American lands and the West Coast before the French or the British could beat them to it. Captain Meriwether Lewis and Lieutenant William Clark staked the claim with the establishment of Fort Clatsop in Oregon between 1805 and 1806. In 1848 the Mexican Cession – the handing over of much of the west – completed the continental United States.

The Great Divide of the Rockies had been crossed if not entirely bridged but there remained a vast and dangerous wilderness between the populated East and the still largely unexplored West. On horseback and in caravans of covered wagons and with the ruthless genocide of the native tribes, the West was painfully, bloodily conquered. The process and the bloodshed were accelerated by the 1848 California Gold Rush in which 300,000 new settlers rushed to the West Coast. In 1869 the 1,912-mile Pacific Railroad from Iowa to San Francisco completed a mechanical transcontinental connection. The Great Divide no longer divided; the West had been won. But not quite. One more intrepid step needed to be taken. Somebody had to drive a car across.

On 19 May 1903, ten years after Turner had declared the frontier closed, in the University Club in San Francisco, Horatio Nelson Jackson bet $50 that he could drive a car across the United States to New York in less than 90 days. At 4.30 am on 26 July he won the bet when, accompanied by his co-driver and engineer Sewall K. Crocker and his bulldog Bud, he drove across the Harlem River into Manhattan.

There were very few cars in America at the time; there were only 33,000 registrations in 1903. University Club members, like the man who offered Jackson the wager, were sceptical, not just of his chances of making the trip but also of the future of automobilism. To them the car seemed like a rich man's toy; it was inconceivable that it could replace the horse as 'the dependable servant of mankind for travel'. Jackson, however, had 'succumbed completely to a primary enthusiasm for the newfangled horseless buggy'.

Jackson was an almost absurdly heroic American figure. It is unsurprising that none other than Tom Hanks agreed to play Horatio – voice only – in Ken Burns's documentary about the trip. A Canadian-born doctor of modest means, he had married into the richest family in Vermont. His wife's father produced Paine's Celery Compound with the slogan 'It made Mother strong!' This was probably because it was 20 per cent alcohol and, maybe, cocaine. It was the age of patent medicines as well as automobilism. Throughout the journey Horatio would send sweet, devoted and passionate letters back home to his wife Bertha – named 'Swipes' by him for unknown reasons. She had, in effect, made his trip possible by making him rich.

Jackson was a showy, confident, flamboyant type. Such men are common in the history of the car: Barney Oldfield, Henry Ford's crazy, risk-taking driver; Woolf Barnato, the driver who led the Bentley Boys to victory at Le Mans; Tazio Nuvolari, who could not see the point of brakes in cars designed to go fast; and, latterly, Jeremy Clarkson, the supreme alpha male of contemporary car journalism. Horatio Jackson was one of them. Indeed, the drive was rather like one of *Top Gear*'s stunts.

It would have defeated lesser – and less confident – men than Jackson and Crocker. The roads, when there were roads, were appalling and the cars desperately unreliable. Also, there were competitors. In 1899 John Davis, a mechanic, and his wife Louise attempted the crossing from east to west. Their progress was so slow that before they reached Syracuse they were passed by a one-armed cyclist who had left New York ten days after them. The automobile, Louise concluded, 'is a treacherous animal for a long trip'. It took them three months to reach Chicago where they gave up. The same year car maker Alexander Winton set out to drive from west to east. He produced 100 vehicles that year making him the largest car maker in America. But his trip failed; he came to a halt in the sands of Nevada.

On the face of it the Jackson-Crocker attempt was even less likely to succeed. The car he used was also a Winton. It wasn't even new; it had already done 1,000 miles in the hands of a San Francisco Wells Fargo executive who made Horatio pay $500 over the new price of $2,500. Horatio named it 'Vermont' after his home state. It was a two-cylinder, 20 hp car with a chain drive. The top speed was 30 mph and it had no roof or windshield. It was a four-seater but Jackson took out the back seat to make room for his kit. His preparations were minimal. He set out to drive the continent just four days after placing his bet.

Horatio had no corporate backing and zero mechanical competence, though he had Crocker. But he had pride. After setting out he discovered both Packard and Oldsmobile were financing crossing attempts and the cars were chasing him. Winton, realising he was in danger of losing the publicity prize, offered to back him for the remainder of his journey. Horatio, heroically, declined. 'I have informed them,' he wrote to Swipes, 'that we have made the trip so far without their assistance & thought that perhaps two greenhorns could do the rest of it.'

In Peekskill, 44 miles north of Manhattan, there was one last, minor misfortune – they had to patch up a burst tyre. But it was in that town that Horatio, now 20 pounds lighter than when he started, and Swipes were reunited. She, along with reporters and Winton officials, followed Horatio and Sewall in a fleet of cars.

They came to a rest at the Holland House Hotel on Fifth Avenue and 30th Street. He had won his bet in 63 days, 12 hours and 30 minutes. The Winton – battered, spattered and parked in a garage on 58th Street – became an object of devotion to New York's automobilists. The Packard and Oldsmobile teams did both finish after Jackson-Crocker; in fact, the Packard did it a little faster, but on this trip to be first was all that mattered.

In his history of the trip Dayton Duncan notes the unintended significance of its timing. It was exactly 100 years since Lewis and Clark had set out to cross the continent. But Horatio had done it in a car, the machine that was to make the conquered continent accessible to everybody. He never collected the $50 but he spent $8,000 on the trip. 'It was,' he said, 'worth every cent.'

4

After Horatio came Dwight – Dwight D. Eisenhower, war hero and President of the United States from 1953 to 1961. Always a soldier, he was frustrated never to make it to the killing fields of France during the First World War. In 1919 he was considering leaving the army but decided against it when he was assigned to an army convoy that would drive from Washington DC to San Francisco. 'A coast-to-coast convoy,' he said, 'was, under the circumstances, a genuine adventure.' The trip was 'through darkest America with Truck and Tank'.

Having dedicated, near the White House, the Zero Milestone point from which all distances across the continental United States were to be measured, the convoy set off on 7 July. It consisted of a two-mile-long convoy of trucks, staff cars, mobile field kitchens, repair shops and searchlight trucks.

It all went horribly wrong. The convoy's average speed was 5 mph. There were endless breakdowns and the roads, in Eisenhower's words, varied 'from average to ok to non-existent'. They did not arrive in San Francisco until 6 September. It had taken Dwight only a day less than Horatio sixteen years before.

The governor of California greeted them and compared them to the 'Immortal Forty-Niners' – the continent crossers of the Gold Rush. All Eisenhower could think about were 'good, two lane highways . . . the wisdom of broader ribbons across our land'. The idea was lodged in his brain by the trauma of the convoy. And so, as president, he signed a bill authorising the Interstate Highway System in 1956, the greatest encroachment of the wilderness the world has ever seen and a huge subsidy to the American car makers in the midst of their 'golden age'. Or, as John Jerome noted of the interstates, 'We stopped building roads *to* places. We began building roads *for* automobiles.'

The interstates now consist of 48,440 miles of road. Setting out today from San Francisco in a decent car, Horatio Nelson Jackson could make the journey to New York in 41 hours, assuming he didn't stop and he took the I-80. He would scythe through the deserts of Nevada, the Great Plains of Nebraska and pass the cities of Chicago and Detroit as if they weren't there. The interstates formed a rough grid that tamed the continent. In this they can be seen as the climax of a process brilliantly described by David Nye in *America's Assembly Line* as the 'standardization of space'. He added ominously that the 'grid had the effect of erasing the past'.

America had become single, a place you could go to look at or go to look for. Or perhaps there was more work to be done. One Federal Highway Administrator, Francis C. Turner, said in 1996 that the interstate system 'will never be finished because America will never be finished'.

<h1 style="text-align:center">5</h1>

In 1960, as interstate construction was just beginning, John Steinbeck was 58 and a globally established writer, mainly thanks to his two great Depression-era novels, *Of Mice and Men* and *The Grapes of Wrath*. Two years later he would win the Nobel Prize in Literature 'for his realistic and imaginative writings, combining as they do sympathetic humour and keen social perception'. But in 1960 all he wanted was a truck.

General Motors sent him their latest model – a green C25 with a kind of caravan body bolted on the back. Written on the side was 'Rocinante' – the name of Don Quixote's horse. And off he went, quixotically, from Sag Harbor on Long Island to California and then back east to New York where he got lost. There he met a cop: 'Officer, I've driven this thing all over the country—mountains, plains, deserts. And now I'm back in my own town, where I live—and I'm lost.'

In 1962 he published an account of the journey entitled *Travels with Charley: In Search of America* – Charley was his pet poodle. The subtitle is resonant, as is his lostness on the last page of the book. Looking for America sounds absurd; it's there in plain sight, vast and unmissable, on any map or globe. But, of course, Steinbeck means America's soul, essence or identity. This, he feels, cannot be found in New York. There must, he thinks, be some truth about the nation that would magically emerge from these attributes. Many Americans feel this; seeking or yearning for this metaphysical core is a very American habit. But Steinbeck seems to fear that searching for America is futile. He surveys the highways and the traffic that rushed 'with murderous intensity'.

Traffic is alienation and to seek America is to admit that you are lost. Paul Simon's bus journey with his girlfriend Cathy reaches a climax in the Simon & Garfunkel song 'America' when he cries out that he is lost. He concludes that everybody driving on the New Jersey Turnpike is also looking for America. In Lana Del Rey's song 'Looking for America' the whole idea of the country seems to dissolve in the process of searching. Indeed, any quick survey of post-war pop and rock songs with America in the title reveals dozens, perhaps hundreds, of examples. There is a popular conviction, first, that America in particular is a country that needs looking for and, second, that it cannot be found.

Even Steinbeck seems to give up. His journey ends in a fog not just of lostness but of something much worse – amnesia. He forgets most of the journey. All he finally has to hang on to is 'the one shining reality—my own wife, my own house in my own street, my own bed'.

6

Steinbeck's choice of a truck – albeit one converted into a mobile home – had a resonance of its own. The American pickup truck is undoubtedly a useful vehicle but it is also an act of political and geographical defiance. 'Georgians,' proclaimed Brian Kemp in 2018 when he was running for governor of Georgia, 'are sick and tired of these politically correct liberals . . . who are offended and outraged by our faith, our guns and our big trucks.'

Pickups were once simple, utilitarian vehicles but from the fifties they began to change. The Ford F-1 pickup truck, introduced in 1948, had an optional cigar lighter. The F-100, launched in 1953, had deeper door windows so the driver could rest his arm comfortably and elegantly on the sill. The post-war pickup truck was gradually becoming something more than a pickup truck. It was becoming a 'lifestyle' or adolescent choice. When Don McLean wrote of his teenage years in his song 'American Pie' in 1971, his two key possessions were a pink carnation and a pickup truck. By the nineties only 15 per cent of buyers used them for work. The trucks grew ever more elaborate and acquired ever more car comforts. They now account for 18 per cent of all vehicle sales in the USA and the Ford F150 is often the bestselling car.

With astonishing literal-mindedness, car makers have occasionally tried to exploit the lifestyle truck market by making strange car-truck chimeras. There was the Chevrolet Fleetside or, strangest of all, the Chevrolet El Camino, which in the 1969 version looked as though pickup designers had started at one end and car designers

– aiming, I think, at an Impala – at the other and somehow met in the middle. The El Camino, however, now lives on as a cultish oddity on car-fan websites. As such it also became the hero of the film *El Camino*, a follow-up to the *Breaking Bad* TV series. It means simply 'the road', a suitably resonant evocation of the dream of the road that goes on forever.

Such oddities were evidently attempts to tame the appeal of the pickup by blending the sturdy embarrassment of the cargo deck with the baroque golden-age styling of the suburban cruiser. But the discontinuity between the suburban car and the pickup is absolute. The whole point of a pickup is that it's not a suburban car, and vice versa. Never was this better captured than by Martin Ritt in his 1963 film *Hud*.

Somewhere in the Texas Panhandle, bad boy Hud rolls into town in his 1958 Series 62 Cadillac Convertible. He wears the right stuff – big hat, jeans, cowboy shirt and boots – but his car is all wrong, not just because it's a big, flashy car, but also because it is pink (the film is in black and white – the colour is announced in the dialogue). He is in a landscape of pickup trucks and horses with which the Caddy can barely cope – it wallows and slithers when encountering corners. It is, flamboyantly, a terrible car. But Hud is a seducer and this is unquestionably a seducer's ride.

The hopelessness of Hud's pink Caddy demonstrates the geographical defiance embodied in the truck. Pickups are designed to go anywhere, off road or on; Cadillacs are not. Trucks are a sign that the driver is not caged by road planners or suburban manners. People driving them might not be *at* work but the truck signals that they can, if called upon, *do* work, any work. Above all, they are not caged by the wavering grid of the interstates or even the backroads. They are an expression of spatial freedom, the freedom of the wilderness, even when they are cruising down Main Street.

This freedom looks back to the years before the closure of the frontier. John Carroll wrote in his history of pickups that they were 'as American as the cowboy and his horse'. Among pickups the cowboy connection extended to the naming of the models – Silverado, Bronco, Blazer, Rampage, Ranchero, Durango and, of course, the Dodge Ram. And, naturally, mainstream country-music stars drive trucks as outsized and as lavish as their belt buckles.

This urge to link the freedom of the car with the freedom of the horse and in turn evoke the freedom of the West goes way back. It was most vividly represented by the greatest and most ludicrous car ad of all time. Entitled 'Somewhere West of Laramie', it appeared in June 1923. It promoted a car called the Jordan Playboy. The company boss, Edward S. Jordan, had considered calling it the Doughboy – a word used to describe American infantrymen from the First World War – but decided soldiers would want something rather more fun than memories of the trenches.

Jordan cars were seldom highly rated but the marketing was well ahead of its time in its evocation of intangible, quasi-spiritual values. In expressionistic style the Playboy ad shows an open-top car driven by a woman – judging by what appears to be a cloche hat, a flapper – with a wildly trailing scarf. Galloping alongside her is a horse bearing a cowboy whose hat has blown off and whose scarf is also wildly trailing. The text is a masterpiece, a summit of automotive marketing, that I cannot bear not to quote in full:

Somewhere west of Laramie there's a bronco-busting, steer-roping girl who knows what I'm talking about. She can tell what a sassy pony, that's a cross between greased lightning and the place where it hits, can do with eleven hundred pounds of steel and action when he's going high, wide and handsome. The truth is – the Playboy was built for her. Built for the lass whose face is brown with the sun when the day is done of revel and romp and race. She loves the cross of the wild and the tame. There's a savor of links about that car – of laughter and lilt and light – a hint of old loves – and saddle and quirt [whip]. It's a brawny thing – yet a graceful thing for the sweep o' the Avenue. Step into the Playboy when the hour grows dull with things gone dead and stale. Then start for the land of real living with the spirit of the lass who rides, lean and rangy, into the red horizon of a Wyoming twilight.

Having, finally, produced a 'full classic car' – the Speedway Ace – the Jordan Automobile Company folded in 1931. Ned Jordan descended into alcoholism in the Caribbean, recovered, remarried and after spells in military production and advertising – his true talent – he started a column for *Automotive News* entitled 'Ned Jordan Speaks'. He died in New York in 1958.

He is still widely remembered for that one ad because Americans have never quite stopped wanting to wallow in the authenticity of cowboys and cowgirls. The frontier of the imagination never closed; the wilderness was always calling.

7

The cowboy connection gives pickups the authenticity of a distinctively American history. The same cannot be said of the truck's close cousin and another would-be wilderness conqueror, the sport utility vehicle. The SUV does have a history but it lacks the cultural grandeur of the pickup.

All SUVs may be seen as descendants of the 1941 Willys MB – more commonly known as the Jeep – and the 1951 Toyota Land Cruiser. The first was a four-wheel-drive military vehicle; the second was inspired by a Jeep the Japanese Army picked up in the Philippines. This became a light truck – the AK10 – for the army and then the Land Cruiser. There was also the Land Rover, a dignified British ancestor and also a Jeep descendant, that first appeared in 1949.

The legacy of these cars was the idea of a vehicle that, like the truck, could go, within reason, anywhere. When precisely this became a unique category is open to interpretation. The 1962 Jeep Wagoneer is a plausible precursor. It was sold as a station wagon, though it had a pickup truck chassis and four-wheel drive. It had a car- rather than truck-like stance and generally suggested itself as a family car. It was the first four-by-four with the option of automatic transmission, in part because it was targeted at women drivers. It was an SUV *avant la lettre*.

This was already becoming a crowded market. There was the International Harvester Travelall, the Dodge Power Wagon and GMC's Suburban Carryall. But these cars had not yet ceased to be wagons and become SUVs. Google Ngram shows a slight uptick in the use of the phrase 'sport utility vehicle' that lasted from the early to mid seventies to the mid eighties, at which point the chart rises almost vertically until a peak in 2002. SUV does not really get going until 1995, reaching a peak in 2017.

The rise in the early to mid seventies coincides with the launch of the Jeep Cherokee SJ whose advertising brochures defined the car as a sport utility vehicle. In fairness the British Range Rover, launched in 1970, better deserves the title of first SUV. It had a rather literary SUV slogan to make the point – ' A car for all reasons' – but it wasn't called an SUV and, in this category, the initials matter more than in any other.

Looking back on the Cherokee in 2001 Serge Schmemann in the *New York Times* described it as 'an automotive John Wayne . . . a tough, unflustered, ready-to-ride all-American'. He added, 'It was instrumental in creating the sport utility phenomenon and then rode the crest even as other SUVs grew bigger, faster, smoother and better. For eighteen years it went largely unchanged.'

The Cherokee was a direct descendant of the Wagoneer, though smaller. It was said to be 'sporty' perhaps because initially it only had two doors. A TV ad establishes the car's military legitimacy by showing an original Jeep barking questions at the Cherokee in a sergeant-major voice. The Jeep orders him to pick up some boys – 'troops' – with all their camping equipment.

Helped in America by successful industry lobbying to get SUVs classed as light trucks – this made them cheaper to build because they had less stringent fuel efficiency and safety standards than cars – the SUV went on to eat the world car market. In 2020 they accounted for almost 40 per cent of all car sales and were projected to rise still further. In America in 2019 5 million cars were sold and 12 million trucks and SUVs. The three-box sedan was dead; long live the two-box SUV. Not surprisingly, under the circumstances, they were shown to be the second largest cause of the global rise in carbon dioxide emissions in the decade ending in 2020. 'If all SUV drivers banded together to form their own country,' reported Oliver Milman in the *Guardian*, 'it would rank as the seventh largest emitter in the world.'

This SUV mania was baffling, though one can see a glimmer of rationality in the wilderness-seeking mentality prevailing in America. But why should this lead them to prevail in every other country in the world? Perhaps it was just the power of American imagery – gangsters, drug lords, politicians and rock stars were all seen being transported in monstrous SUVs, usually black, though sometimes white, with blacked-out windows.

And they were monstrous. The Chevrolet Suburban started out as a rather cute station wagon in 1935 and ended up as a bloated, lumbering 6,000-pound (kerb – i.e., unladen – weight) SUV in 2020. The

Cadillac Escalade, the supreme rappermobile, started big in 1998 and just got bigger and meaner and hit 5,500 pounds in Premium Luxury spec in 2020.

The one thing that could have stalled the thundering advance of the SUVs – in America at least – was safety. In 2002 Keith Bradsher's book *High and Mighty: SUVs – The World's Most Dangerous Vehicles and How They Got that Way* attempted to do a Ralph Nader on the monsters. One of Bradsher's more subversive revelations was that internal company market research had shown that SUV buyers were insecure, vain, self-centred and self-absorbed, nervous about their marriages and uncertain of their driving skills.

In 2004 the *New Yorker* published 'Big and Bad' by Malcolm Gladwell. He noted the inexplicable and above all unexpected rise of the SUV. One key point about the article was that it showed not that SUVs were necessarily unsafe for drivers and passengers but that they were unsafe for other drivers and passengers. Big, high SUVs make drivers feel immune. This is echoed by Matthew Crawford in his book *Why We Drive*. One way to promote safe driving is to *increase* risk – put a dagger aimed at the driver's heart at the centre of the steering wheel and he/she will drive as if his/her life depended on it. On the same theme Crawford quotes mechanic and author John Muir: 'If we all constantly drive as if we were strapped to the front of the car like Aztec sacrifices so we'd be the first thing hit, there would be a helluva lot less accidents.'

From his own experience Crawford thinks big SUV drivers may be oblivious to risk and in any case they are suspect drivers who had 'no idea how they would behave at the limit of traction'.

Of course, the reality is that these American monsters are neither sport nor utilities – they are just big vehicles. On top of that if they ever did become S and U, handling them would be beyond the competence of their drivers, especially if they were nervous about their marriages.

In Britain SUVs were drawn into class warfare. Greens and just ordinary people trying to navigate urban roads became increasingly angry about the spaces taken up by bloated SUVs, three quarters of which were being used for nothing more strenuous than a shopping trip or the school run. They became known as 'Chelsea Tractors' and, in fact, the figures do show very high prevalence of large SUVs – Range Rovers, Porsche Cayennes, Audi Q8s, etc. – in Chelsea. In

April 2021 a report from the New Weather Institute called for a ban on advertising of SUVs; these cars had become the new cigarettes or, rather, fur coats – wicked but flashy pleasures.

None of which seems to have tamed the flood of SUVs around the world. Very few people will ever need them, and even fewer will have off-road driving skills. Still they fill the streets but at least, in spite of their four-wheel-drive capabilities, they will leave the wilderness untouched.

8

Dennis Hopper's film *Easy Rider* (1969) is about two hippie bikers – Billy and Wyatt – riding round the South on two customised 'choppers' with a pile of cash made from a cocaine deal. They meet a lawyer, Hanson, with a drink problem. Billy notes that everybody seems to be scared of him and his partner. Hanson explains they are not scared of them; they are scared of what they represent – freedom.

The mid to late sixties produced a new breed of automotive wilderness invaders. Anti-bourgeois, anti-big business, anti-government, anti-domesticity, anti-war but pro-drugs and pro the environment and frightened by the end of the world, they were simultaneously nihilists and idealists. The more peaceful of them were back-to-nature, living-on-the-road, camping types whose apotheosis was the Woodstock music festival in 1969. But living on the road with long hair, flared jeans and Native American jewellery could be dangerous; as Billy pointed out, motel owners thought 'we're gonna cut their throat or something'. For these wanderers off-road cars would have been the wrong answer to the wrong question. If you were serious about hitting the trail, conquering the wilderness, the right question was: where do you sleep when you get there?

Woodstock was advertised as a festival of peace and music but, in fact, the mood was defiant. The Summer of Love had become a distant dream in 1967 as Martin Luther King and Robert Kennedy were assassinated, the Vietnam War continued to rage and police were reacting violently to student demos. Clearly the dawning of the 'Aquarian Age' – as celebrated by the hippies – had been postponed.

So, artist and activist Dr Bob Hieronimus painted a Volkswagen Microbus, covering it with arcane symbols intended to show that 'we are all one and connected with the cosmic creator on a vibrational level'.

The Microbus was the descendant of the VW Type 2 Transporter which went into production in 1949. It was the first car Volkswagen built after the Beetle. And it turned out to be just as cool and counter-cultural. The Type 2 retained the Type 1's rear air-cooled engine layout. It was designed not by a German but by a Dutchman, VW's first American dealer Ben Pon. Its styling has something in common with Buckminster Fuller's Dymaxion car, a perverse and dangerous machine which – thank God – never went into production. The front of the Transporter was its most decisive feature – a friendly, art decoish face with a split windscreen. It was this, I am convinced, more than anything else that explains its extraordinary success.

On the side of his Microbus, Dr Bob painted the spread wings of an eagle embracing the world 'Light'. It was known as the 'Light' because it belonged to a little-known Baltimore band called Light. They paid Dr Bob $1,000 for the paint job. The band never actually appeared at Woodstock but they did go there in what they now called their 'Magic Bus'. The police tried to stop them getting in, but Light ingeniously claimed the bus was part of the festival's art exhibition. The 'Magic Bus' was photographed and Dr Bob's imagery was immortalised. It appeared in *Life* magazine and *Rolling Stone*; an AP photograph went round the world. It was an 'art car' that became a logo for Woodstock.

Sadly, Light parted company after Woodstock and the 'Magic Bus' vanished. Dr Bob, however, in 2019 gamely created a replica to mark the 50th anniversary of Woodstock and to challenge the onset of a new dark age under Trump.

In camper form you could cook and sleep in the Microbus. This idea of a sleep-in car was born in the fifties, not in America but in Europe. The British Bedford Dormobile – a name with 'bed' and 'dorm' in it was perhaps ill-judged – was launched in 1957. It had a gas stove, sink and seats which turned into beds. There was also an elevating roof that made it possible to stand while inside the car. The novelist Anthony Burgess had one in which he drove round Europe. He called it 'a miracle of British design' but added that it was much let down by 'slipshod British execution – screws missing, bad wood-planing'. The story of good ideas badly executed was the story of the entire post-war British car industry. It was a pity because the original Dormobile was potentially just as cool as the Microbus, though, crucially, it did not have a friendly face. It might also – see the final chapter – turn out to be a harbinger of the post-car future.

The Dormobile did not spawn a crowd of imitators; the Microbus did. The design feature that was most obviously imitated – notably by the Dodge A100 and the Ford Econoline – was the forward control layout, meaning, basically, that the driver sat over the front wheels rather than behind the engine.

Such sleep-in machines were fine but *in extremis* any car could become your primary residence. The car website Jalopnik.com ran an article in 2008 in the midst of the banking crash entitled 'Ten Cars You Can Live In After Your Home Is Repossessed'. And, indeed, the banking crash threw people out of work and created a population of nomads who drifted from job to job, living in whatever car or van they could keep going.

But the Microbus was different. It had status among the young and it delivered a message. Sleeping in any old car in the wilderness signified failure or at least misfortune. Sleeping in a Microbus signified counter-cultural cool.

The Microbus's stardom endures to this day. Filmore in the Disney *Cars* movies is a hippie Microbus and a yellow one is the star of *Little Miss Sunshine*. And, finally, VW, having cycled through a series of variations without friendly faces, is to resort to something like the original in the all-electric form of the I.D. Buzz concept, maybe becoming a reality in 2022–23.

9

Cars also found new and ingenious ways to despoil the wilderness. Around 1921 in Dallas, Texas, Jesse G. Kirby noticed that 'people with cars are so crazy they don't want to get out of them to eat'. And so with his business partner, a doctor named Ruben W. Jackson, he opened a restaurant on Chalk Hill Road in the city's Oak Cliff area – 'a red-tiled pagoda-like roof set on a rectangular building framed of wood and covered in stucco'. It was called Kirby's Pig Stand. On the menu were burgers and the like, but also a speciality – the Pig Sandwich made from Tennessee barbecued pork.

At the time, just about every car that passed the Pig Stand was a Ford Model T, so the service ritual was straightforward. The car pulled up and a boy – known as a carhop rather than a waiter – wearing a white hat, white shirt and a black bow tie jumped on the running board to take the order. The boy then ran back into the restaurant to pick up the food and ran out to deliver it by hopping back onto the running board.

It was, famously, the first kerbside restaurant in the world. Kirby's had further, less well-substantiated claims to fame – first onion ring, first chicken-fried steak sandwich, first Texas toast, first neon signs in a restaurant and so on. Whether these were true or not, the first Pig Stand was a huge success. Soon there was a chain of Pig Stands and Kirby and Jackson were selling 5,000 Pig Sandwiches a day at a time when the population of Dallas was only 250,000. They expanded beyond Dallas, even as far as Los Angeles. Kirby, ever the innovator, came up with a new way of serving his food. He dispensed with the carhops by inventing drive-through service. It did not take on quite as quickly as the kerbside service but it survived longer – all the way down to contemporary fast-food outlets.

There's another layer to the link between the Pig Stand and the Model T. Both the carhop and the drive-through service have over-tones of industrialised efficiency. Men in the Ford production lines, like the carhops, moved back and forth tending the Ts. The drive-through, meanwhile, evokes the moving assembly line with parts – food – added as the car moved by. Car production had inspired a new way of life, a new way of organising experience.

Most importantly, Kirby's Pig Stand, though located in a city, sig-nalled the start of a new and devastatingly effective way of invading the wilderness. For it is not just the car nor merely the road that conquered the open country. Rather, the combination of the two created an entirely new form of conquest. For the Pig Stand was the forerunner of motorway service stations and of the vast retail accretions that expanded the automotive land grab. It was also the progenitor of fast-food outlets around the world.

But the business itself failed to compete in the new world it had helped to create. Pig Stand went bankrupt in 2006. It is now per-versely memorialised in the Hard Rock Cafe menu. The term 'Pig Sandwich' was trademarked and when Hard Rock tried to use it on its own menu in 1992 they were taken to court. They lost and now they sell not a Pig Sandwich but a 'BBQ Pulled Pork Sandwich'.

10

Having been fed, there was one other thing the driver needed – petrol. This was, initially, a haphazard business. At first, like Bertha Benz, drivers bought fuel wherever they could find it – pharmacies, hardware shops, livery stables. Fuel was hand-pumped into a bucket and then poured into the car. Or, occasionally, it was dispensed from wagons that travelled from house to house. This was the most risky method, as these wagons tended to explode.

In 1905 in Fort Wayne, Indiana, Sylvanus Freelove Bowser simplified matters with his Self-Measuring Gasoline Storage Pump. This allowed drivers to fill up much as they do now. Cars would simply stop at kerbside pumps. As the car population grew, thanks to the Model T, this became a problem as long queues formed at pumps and blocked the roads. But the whole modern system fell into place when the drive-in filling station was invented. There are multiple claims for the date of the first drive-in – 1905 in St Louis, 1907 in Seattle and 1913 in Pittsburgh. The last is the most satisfying, as it was a surprisingly pretty, pagoda-like structure which anticipated the later decorative extravagances of the genre. Wherever its birthplace, the creation of the filling station was a momentous event.

Around the world hundreds of thousands of filling stations were built to the now familiar formula of pumps, canopies and shop fronts. By 1920 there were 100,000 places selling fuel in the USA, half of them the old store operations; by 1929 there were 300,000, almost all of them filling stations, and 143,000 drive-ins. Oddly, the Great Divide was reflected in the names given to these places: east of the Rockies they were called filling stations; west of the Rockies they were service stations.

They began to grow ever more ambitious – bigger with grander signs. These signs – combined later with the signs of fast-food restaurants and motels – provide, especially at night, evidence of the grid the car has cast over the wilderness.

(I remember driving north to Chicago at night in torrential rain.

I could see nothing but the small pool of light from my headlights. Then, in the distance, glowing and beautiful as never before, a McDonald's sign. It was the poetry of the American road at night. I stopped more out of gratitude than hunger and watched a trucker in dungarees surreptitiously slipping the plastic cutlery into his pocket.)

The filling stations soon offered more than fuel, notably TBAs – tyres, batteries and accessories. Air and water were free services. They also offered free road maps of their areas, a huge leap forward for cartography. Bruce Barton, an advertising executive, urged on the attendants in life-changing terms redolent of Ned Jordan's 'West of Laramie'. He advised selling petrol as 'the juice of the fountain of eternal youth'.

They needed no encouragement. The car land grab was all but limitless. Drive-in filling stations, in the USA at least, created a drive-in cult. There were drive-in churches and, of course, drive-in cinemas, known as 'passion pits' by the teenage regulars. Kirby's inspiration for the Pig Stand – 'People with cars are so crazy they don't want to get out of them to eat' – turned out to be a general truth. Then there was the drive-in hotel, the motel. The word is said to have emerged from the name Milestone Mo-Tel, which opened in 1926 in San Luis Obispo, California. A single architectural innovation defined the genre – there was a parking space or a garage directly outside every room and bungalow. The word 'motel' couldn't be trademarked and as a result it freely spread across America and the world.

Unfortunately, their anonymity and the high occupancy turnover aroused suspicion. J. Edgar Hoover, director of the FBI between 1924 and 1972, alerted the nation to their dangers, calling them 'camps of crime' and 'dens of vice and corruption'. Not only did criminals hide out in motels, people also had sex in them. A 'hot pillow trade' had developed and, warned Hoover, some motel rooms were rented out as many as 16 times a night.

In spite of such lurid enticements the motel trade did not really get going until after the war. By 1964 there were 61,000 motels in America. The subsequent decline was explained in part by the Alfred Hitchcock movie *Psycho* in 1960. The Bates Motel was where the murderous psycho lived. It had no customers because it was on a road that had been made redundant by the advent of the freeways and interstates.

In the fifties and sixties in California these new building types created their own architectural style known as googie doo wop or populuxe. This was a development of the streamline moderne of the thirties. But this time the influencers were not ocean liners or railway engineers – they were the space age and jet aircraft. Roofs swept upwards and starburst motifs were everywhere.

The point about limited or controlled-access highways – inter-states, autobahns, motorways, etc. – that spread across the world in the fifties and sixties is that they were also limited-egress highways. You couldn't just stop if you saw a nice-looking restaurant or a convenient filling station; you had to wait until you were granted a slip road by the road planners. The motorway service area and the truck stop – a fuel, food and parking complex – emerged to combine all these into a one-stop shop. Combined with a new motel, it offered the possibility of never having to leave a road that went on forever.

Britain's first motorway opened in 1958. But it had been first conceived 20 years earlier when an engineering delegation from Lancashire visited Germany to examine the autobahns. It was not far from my carless childhood home. Then known as the Preston Bypass, now subsumed into the national motorway network, it was 8.5 miles long and an adult with a car took us to see it. I remember nothing more of that trip. I do remember, years later, passing the Forton Services near Lancaster with its enclosed bridge and a massive concrete hexagonal tower.

Such landmarks celebrated a climactic moment. They were full expression of what Kirby had but dimly seen in his pagoda-shaped Pig Stand – the car's rebuilding of the world. But there was one even more massive land grab, one more justification of the life of what Daniel Yergin calls 'Hydrocarbon Man'.

11

In its issue of 6 June 1999 *Time* magazine named William Jaird Levitt as one of the 100 most influential people of the twentieth century. He was in the category 'Builders and Titans' alongside Bill Gates, Henry Ford, Walt Disney, Akio Morita and Louis B. Mayer. Born in 1907 in Brooklyn to a Jewish family, his grandparents were immigrants from Russia and Austria. His father had started an upmarket building company, Levitt & Sons, of which William became president. Returning from the war – he had been in the navy – he saw a need for cheaper housing both for returning veterans and the families created in the baby-boom years. He had tried a low-cost housing development before the war and failed. But, starting in 1947, he succeeded. On 4,000 acres of what had been potato fields near Hempstead on Long Island he constructed Levittown using mass-production techniques. By 1951 he had built 17,447 houses occupied by 82,000 people and made a celebrity of the town as well as himself. 'It is a poor week when Levitt houses aren't featured in at least one full-column story in the New York newspapers,' remarked *Fortune* magazine in 1947.

Levitt compared his operation to that of General Motors – his assembly line just happened to be outdoors. He was a showman, not just a developer; he was offering a complete way of life. 'William Levitt,' commented Richard Lacayo in *Time* magazine, 'a man who just about never read a novel, turned out to be the author of an entire world.'

In Levittown depression and war were in the past. Ahead lay the sunlit uplands of peace, prosperity and cars. Buying his houses would even defeat the new enemy. 'No man,' he said, 'who owns his own house and lot can be a Communist. He has too much to do.' He had created a post-war vision of paradise – a house, a yard and a Chevy in the drive. People living there liked it a lot; their neighbours didn't. They felt the tone of the whole area was being lowered by these incomers. Non-whites cannot have liked it much either. In clause 25 of the town's standard lease agreement there was a restrictive covenant stating that the house could 'not be used or occupied by any person other than members of the Caucasian race'.

Modern suburbs were born of the Industrial Revolution. The rural working classes moved off the land and into the factories. Urban populations grew uncontrollably – there were 860,000 people in London in 1801 and 3.8 million in 1881 – and this happened without any expansion in the size of the cities. The ensuing chaos was the world of Little Jo, the crossing sweeper.

The railways had made commuting possible but they also added to the populations of central urban areas by transporting manufactured goods out and food in. With the advent of the car and the twentieth century, progressive thought began to turn to the possibility of an extra-urban paradise beyond the reach of the urban poor. This wasn't, however, progressive in the contemporary sense of the word. 'To the Anglo-Saxon race,' wrote one enthusiastic observer of the new American suburbs in 1898, 'life in the great cities cannot be made to seem a healthy and natural mode of existence.'

There were two distinct suburban solutions, one largely British, the other largely American. The British – as at Letchworth – favoured the construction of self-sufficient towns serviced by trains; the Americans favoured domestic developments dependent on the city centres and serviced by cars. This was clearly because there were far more cars in America, though the new-town movement in Britain did claim that their developments were more socially idealistic and medically beneficial. Either way, after the Second World War as economic growth soared so did car ownership. Urban and suburban development responded by making the car even more necessary. Now there are 838 cars per 1,000 people in the USA, though a mere 471 in the UK.

The suburbs were sold as little paradises of middle-class gentility or pioneering realisations of the American dream. Since these places also encouraged giving the car to the kids, both aspirations were self-subverting. For in their cars the kids had sex, plotted against their parents or fomented revolution. This kind of tension – seething urges and anger beneath the immaculate lawns and driveways – was to provide rich suburban material for critics, dramatists and satirists over the ensuing decades. But, as a pure land grab, the suburbs could not be stopped. Between 1945 and 1959 9 million people moved to the suburbs. Between 1950 and 1976, the number of Americans living in the centres of cities grew by 10 million while the population increase in the suburbs was 85 million.

Suburbs appeared across the world, annexing ever greater tracts of land. But it was not just the houses. To replace the walking distance to local stores new forms of driveable retail appeared. Huge shopping centres sprang up to cater for the new suburbanists. There were eight shopping centres in America in 1946; by 1980 there were 20,000. Everywhere, everything seemed to be responding to and defined by the car.

12

Paradise, maybe, but not if you didn't have a car. The very idea of a modern metalled road and its attendant luxuries is discriminatory, of a controlled-access highway doubly so. You need a car to join the club. But some are too poor or too young to have cars. To rub salt in the wound, cars are often extravagantly and visibly unoccupied – they almost always have empty seats. The injustice of the road could be remedied by filling those seats with the carless.

Hitchhiking is probably as old as the wheel or the tamed horse but it became a distinct culture in the early twentieth century with the advent of the car and the roads on which it could run. An English novelist, nature writer and vicar was among the first to document this development. Sussex born and bred, Tickner Edwardes was vicar of Burpham from 1927 to 1935. Before that he had been a prolific writer, mostly about bees. His novel *Tansy*, the tale of a young shepherdess, was filmed by Cecil Hepworth in 1921.

Before all that, however, he was a pioneer of motorised hitching. He determined to travel the southern counties of England relying entirely on the kindness of strangers. He wrote about the experience in *Lift-Luck on Southern Roads*, published in 1910: 'I got me, to tell the truth, through the whole two-hundred-mile stretch of the way, with camera and pack on shoulder and at surprisingly little expense, by means of Lifts, taken in any chance vehicle that might be faring in my direction.'

Only once does he travel by car and he hates it, but the tone of his description of the experience is significant. Reluctantly deciding not to hitch a lift on a 'comfortable basket-chaise', he succumbs to the novelty of a 'Juggernaut of excruciating modernity', the owner of which is determined to demonstrate its performance. Edwardes, a man besotted by nature, is appalled. The natural world was whipped into a frenzy by the car: 'The trees and the hedgerows got themselves legs and race by in an indistinguishable streak of green.'

Finally, having determined to revisit on foot all the places that he had passed in a motorised blur, he retired to a pub in Exeter. Speed, for Edwardes, negated the experience of the traveller. But this was little England and his trip was only 200 miles; in America you needed speed to get to know the country.

In spite of the example of Edwardes, historian John T. Schlebecker could confidently declare in 1958 that 'Hitchhiking originated in the United States' and the hitchhiker was 'first of all a product of the American automotive industry'. Schlebecker says true hitching – actively soliciting rides rather than accepting offers from passing drivers – began in 1917 among soldiers. That military connection lasted through the Second World War and beyond.

Hitching for civilians did not really take off until the twenties when improved roads and the exponential growth in car ownership made serious hitching possible. J.K. Christian, for example, hitched 3,023 miles in 27 days in 1921 and was rewarded with membership of the Adventurers Club of Chicago. In 1927 two hitchers crossed the continent from west to east in 14 days. At about the same time the extended thumb, pointing upwards or in the direction of travel, became the recognised gesture of the hitcher.

With the advent of the Great Depression in 1929 hitching became commonplace as the dispossessed sought better ways of life, usually somewhere in the West. Suspicions emerged at once. Newspapers warned drivers of the dangers of hitchhikers and some police forces took to arresting hitchers for obstructing traffic. In part this was because the distinction between bums, tramps or beggars and hitchers was not yet clear. Once it was understood that hitchers wanted nothing more than a ride, the driver-hitcher deal became a little less fraught and a little more romantic.

By 1934 the hitching deal had become comfortable enough for Frank Capra to use it in a movie. In *It Happened One Night* Clark Gable's thumb fails to win a single ride. Claudette Colbert steps forward, raises her skirt to reveal a daring amount of stocking and the first passing car skids to a halt.

This erotic dynamic, incidentally, was neatly reversed in Ron Howard's *Rush* (2013 but set primarily in 1976). Again, the male, Daniel Brühl, steps forward and again fails to thumb down a lift. Again, the female – Alexandra Maria Lara – steps forward. A Lancia 2000 screeches to a halt. But now there's a twist. The two men in the Lancia had not stopped because they were inflamed by the sight of Alexandra. They walk straight past her and greet Brühl. For he is playing their hero, Niki Lauda, then one of the most celebrated racing drivers in the world.

But hitching could never be entirely comfortable. The displacement of the social encounter from the certainties of the home or the workplace to the contingencies of the highway is necessarily risky. The assumption of hitchhiking is that human sympathy, mutual aid and general good manners will prevail. This, in turn, makes an assumption about the cohesion of society – not necessarily a safe one in the context of the anonymity and long-range mobility of cars on the open road. Also, films need drama. Ida Lupino's tedious film noir *The Hitch-Hiker* (1953) features a murderous hitcher who kidnaps two pals on a fishing trip. The action mostly takes place inside a 1951 Plymouth Cranbrook, not the most thrilling of cars.

The chances of a hitcher being a psychopathic killer are slim but not completely deniable. Rutger Hauer played a hitching murderer in Robert Harman's *The Hitcher* (1986), a very violent film that is said to have contributed to the decline of hitchhiking. Again, this was tedious but at least it introduced the strangely enticing phenomenon of the drive-away car. Hauer's primary target is a young man in a 1977 Cadillac Seville, a car obviously beyond his means. He is taking it from Chicago to San Diego for some rich guy who can't be bothered with the effort of the 2,000-mile journey. This was – and remains (see Cardriveaway.com) – a fringe business in America. It is, in its way, the ultimate hitch with the added bonus that the hitcher actually drives the car.

Paranoia-inducing movies, however, were not enough to defeat the newly discovered romanticism of hitching in the post-war period. As the interstate, motorway and autobahn networks were extended, and as the young aspired to newer, freer lives, an ideal of unending mobility was born. The new truth wasn't to be found on the road; the truth was the road.

For one generation this romance was expressed in 1957 by Jack Kerouac's novel *On the Road*. The drifter, having once been a bum, a tramp, a mere beggar, became a philosopher hero in search of meaning, identity and, most of all, the company and consolations of strangers. At one point Sal Paradise, the novel's narrator, is confronted by a cop who insists on the importance of law and order. Paradise cannot refute the argument but he has a higher mission – to move on to the now accessible beyond, to discover the teeming millions of others. Hitchhiking, with its elements of chance and risk, was the solution to the regimented certainties and strictures of the growing suburban sprawl.

13

Remains have been found of constructed human dwellings that are almost 20,000 years old. Agriculture, which requires lasting settlement, seems to have begun about 12,000 years ago. Prior to that humans were, like other animals, inhabitants of the wilderness. After that, they were colonisers.

In the next phase, now known as the Anthropocene, humans became engineers on a planetary scale. This began slowly in the early eighteenth century and accelerated furiously in the late nineteenth and twentieth centuries. Many technologies were involved in this but the one that most successfully colonised and engineered the earth was the internal-combustion engine. The car subdued the wilderness to human demands.

Anxiety about human intrusion into the wilderness was widespread from the early nineteenth century. Dismayed by the inroads of industry – notably the railways – the romantic movement celebrated nature and ancient ways of life. In America this urge to protect was dramatised by the discoveries revealed by the westward advance of the frontier. When the explorers encountered the sublime beauties of Wyoming, Montana, Idaho and California they paused. This pause was a combination of aesthetic wonder and the shock of deep time. The combination was captured in a speech made by President Theodore Roosevelt in 1903: 'Leave it as it is. You cannot improve on it. The ages have been at work on it, and man can only mar it. What you can do is to keep it for your children, your children's children, and for all who come after you, as one of the great sights which every American, if he can travel at all, should see.'

The assertion 'man can only mar it' implied the establishment of an internal frontier that surrounded an area of land that could not be bought or sold or even cultivated. In fact, the principle had already been established with the creation of Yellowstone National Park, the first in the world, in 1872 under the presidency of Ulysses S. Grant. Almost 3,500 square miles of land across three states was 'withdrawn from settlement, occupancy, or sale'. The idea was inspired by art – the photographs of William Henry Jackson and the paintings of Thomas Moran, imagery later reinforced by the greatest of all landscape photographers, Ansel Adams.

But it was the writing of John Muir – the 'Father of the National Parks' – that had the most lasting impact. In his essay on the High Sierra of California he wrote:

> No excursion can be made into the Sierra that may not prove an enduring blessing. Notwithstanding the great height of the summits, and the ice and the snow, and the gorges and canyons and sheer giddy precipices, no mountain chain on the globe is more kindly and approachable. Visions of ineffable beauty and harmony, health and exhilaration of body and soul, and grand foundation lessons in Nature's eternal love are the sure reward of every earnest looker in this glorious wilderness.

Nature's untouched sublime could save the human soul. The message was heard. There are now 63 national parks in America and the idea has spread around the world, though usually not with quite the same purist zeal. Britain's national parks include human habitations and even in America the Muir/Roosevelt ideal has had to be modified. You can drive around – as I often have – Joshua Tree and the land is littered with the debris of abandoned gold mines. But at least this debris is left untouched; it is left to bleach away in the dry desert.

The 1964 Wilderness Act defined wilderness as 'the earth and its community of life untrammeled by man' which 'retains its primeval character and influence, without permanent improvement or human habitation'. But the truth is a national park is made by humans, a designation that marks out a space that can no longer be a wilderness. Parks have rangers, climbers, hikers, information boards, toilets and they need constant care to ensure visitors find what they want to find – even if it's themselves.

The further problem for the wilderness purists was the fact that the spiritual and health-giving virtues of the wilderness were, by their own definition, for everybody and they would therefore be invaded by millions. They could have taken the ethical high road by fully adopting the intrinsic value argument – that the wonders of nature were valuable *in themselves* and irrespective of the recreational demands of humans. They were not there to 're-enchant' human life by introducing us to the sublime and to deep time; they were there because they had their own enchantments, impenetrable to the short-lived turmoil of the human imagination. Humans become, in this context, an invasive alien species, a form of pest. We should be satisfied by the knowledge that wilderness is there whether we see it or not. Or they could have played the green card: the planetary benefits of truly untouched wilderness are human benefits.

In the end the riddle was solved not by humans nor by nature but by the car. It was the car that provided human access to and from and in and out of these protected beauties. Keeping people at bay was no longer an option. The parks had become attractions – like ancient buildings, museums or galleries. What they contained had become a series of display cabinets or framed canvases, works of art.

This is not a terrible fate but it is a loss. All these automotive-enabled demands – freedom to drive, SUVs, pickup trucks, filling stations, motorways, parking areas, malls and mini-malls, Pig Stands, fast-food outlets, sleep-in cars, urges to find ourselves and our countries, vacations, attractions – have destroyed and are destroying much of the untouched wilderness. The idea of nature as intrinsically valuable has, meanwhile, gone forever. The car, the Anthropocene's battering ram, has dewilded the world.

Hot Rod

Chapter Seven

MORE THAN JUST CARS

1

By 2003 Rolls-Royce was owned by BMW and Bentley by Volkswagen. This left Mercedes out in the cold as the one big German car maker without a super-premium marque. The company had seen it coming so in 2000 it responded with the Maybach, named after Wilhelm Maybach, the co-creator of the Mercedes 35hp in 1901.

The Maybach was introduced to America with a good deal of non-trivial corporate bling. Enclosed in a glass case, it sailed to New York on the *Queen Elizabeth II*. Fireboats welcomed its arrival and a helicopter lifted the exhibit onto the dock. 'Brand ambassadors' were the golfer Nick Faldo and Ulrich Schmid-Maybach, a descendant of the great engineer.

In 2011 Kanye West and Jay-Z 'chopped' – or, more politely, customised – a Maybach 57, said to have cost West $517,000, for use in the music video for their song 'Otis'. The chopped car, basically stripped of its body panels and roof and provided with battered, unpainted wheel arches, was later sold at auction for $88,000. The video was really the Maybach's finest hour. It had been a fatally flawed project that was discontinued in 2012. The car just looked too much like a stretched and funereally pimped Mercedes S-Class whereas Rolls and Bentleys both looked like exactly what they were – uniquely expensive and aggressively sculpted cars. The only time I travelled in a Maybach the underlying boredom and tastefulness of the thing was deafening. It was, says motoring journalist Gavin Green, 'a spectacular failure'. The Maybach was, unchopped, boring; chopped, it became a masterpiece.

Kanye West has had quite a few cars in his time: a Mercedes/ McLaren SLR Stirling Moss – one of a limited edition of only 75 – a

Dartz Prombron Red Diamond Edition – a bizarre and enormous jewel-encrusted Latvian SUV – and, most conventionally, a Bugatti Veyron and a Lamborghini Urus. Bling, automotive or otherwise, is a complex gesture, showy and at the same time dismissive. In the case of great urban/hip-hop stars like West and Jay-Z it signals success and wealth while simultaneously undermining both. You can have it all if you are me; but if you are me, you don't need it all. Breaking expensive stuff is a way of showing your freedom from empty consumer aspiration. Flaunt it but simultaneously diminish it.

In any case, a broken Maybach 57 is infinitely more interesting than an unbroken one. In the 'Otis' video, with West and Jay-Z in the front seats and four laughing girls in the back, it gives the car something Mercedes didn't even know it needed – insolent fun.

Cars cannot be left alone – they exist to be chopped, hot-rodded or just blinged up. Or they are there to be so valuable, so refined, so fast and so uninsurable that they can barely ever be driven. Or they are there to signal you are not one of the crowd. Or they are there to signal virtue with bumper stickers or 'baby on board' signs. Above all, they are not there to be the showroom shiny products that become, on the road, just more anonymous, messed-up mediocrities. They are there to be more than just cars.

2

The cunning ambivalence of bling reflects the wider ambivalence of popular culture towards post-war wealth and consumption. To the young, cars initially offered freedom and a new, showy form of courtship and seduction; later, they offered only capitalist greed and environmental catastrophe.

In the first phase it was OK – it was in fact admirable – for pop-music stars to spend their money on automotive glitz. At the top of this pile was Elvis Presley with his countless Cadillacs he bought during his lifetime – he died aged 42 in 1977 – many of which were simply given away. While in the army between 1958 and 1960 he bought a Lincoln Continental Mark V and had it shipped out to Germany so he could be chauffeured around in comfort behind privacy glass. He had a Rolls-Royce Phantom V, naturally, but his Series 75 Cadillac Fleetwood Limousine was where he felt most at home. He also, bizarrely, had four Stutz Blackhawks, which were really just pimped-up Pontiac Grand Prixs designed to revive the name of an old American car. This kind of crazed – though apparently generous – excess worked because the young wanted to be famous like Elvis and they wanted to buy stuff like Elvis. Cars were cool. When a Fleetwood passed a school, the kids, as Harley Earl intended, whistled.

This post-war moment of young, automotive splendour was celebrated in George Lucas's partially autobiographical film – made in 1973 but set in 1962 – *American Graffiti*. It's a day in the life of the teens with cars.

Fabulously adorned, they parade down the street like carnival floats. When not parading they cluster round Mel's Drive-In. There's a '54 Buick Special, a '58 Chevrolet Bel Air, a '56 Chevrolet Biscayne, a '60 Chevrolet Impala, a '56 Ford Fairlane Victoria, a '32 Ford Model B (the Deuce Coupe, hot-rodded) and many more. From Europe there's a couple of eccentricities – a Volkswagen Beetle and a Citroën 2CV.

This is not really, as it is often described, a teen or coming-of-age movie; it is, in reality, a car movie. The cars – most of them – are drawn from the golden age of American automotive baroque. That design tide was already turning. The following year President Kennedy was to be shot in a very long but much more chastely styled Lincoln Continental. Drifting down the main street in Modesto, California, while the occupants chat and flirt with each other, the teens' cars are sculpted expressions of the extravagance and awkwardness of teenage eroticism. They are absurd, unreal creations, steel dreams, born of a single night in which the stories happen.

As are the characters. One of the lead figures, Curt Henderson (Richard Dreyfuss), repeatedly catches glimpses of a beautiful blonde in a white '56 Ford Thunderbird – in the real world a black version of this car once belonged to Marilyn Monroe. The T'Birds always had a dreamlike quality; in his film *Thelma & Louise* (1991) Ridley Scott chose a turquoise '66 model in which the two heroines flee the cops. But Curt's dream car is not fatal. Each time his dream blonde appears she mouths 'I love you' at him. He never finds her; she really is a dream.

On top of that there is the casual, drifting, directionless quality of the dialogue: 'Well, I gotta go. Where you going? Nowhere. Well, you mind if I come along?' The cars and the people are creatures of a floating world.

The film was a reminiscence for Lucas. Three of the characters – the student, the nerd and the hot-rodder – are all versions of his own late fifties, early sixties self. Their world floats because all such young moments seem in retrospect fragile, ill-judged and unreal. But in those years the floating was intensified, almost literalised, by the cars.

The fifties, as Joni Mitchell once pointed out to me, were all about the kids getting the car. She wrote a song – 'Ray's Dad's Cadillac' – about it. Meat Loaf looked back from 1977 with a similar erotic longing in his song 'Paradise by the Dashboard Light'. The car was a new space outside the home where the kids could have sex or just talk. But it also provided access to an infinite space into which the kids could travel. Such freedom was unprecedented; it upended family dynamics.

Various theorists have attempted to explain what can now be seen as the emergence of post-war youth culture. The historian Theodore Roszak classified it as an individualist moment comparable to the Renaissance or romanticism. Another historian, William L. O'Neill, suggested it was a case of neglect; parents, caught between the carnage of the Second World War and the threat of nuclear annihilation, just didn't pay attention to the kids. More specifically in *A Cycle of Outrage* James Gilbert argued that the war had sent fathers away from home and mothers into the workforce – children were left to look after themselves. Post-war teens were thus a trapped generation. Their parents had known nothing but economic depression and war for fifteen years and they wanted security above all. They were scared.

The mellifluous legal term 'juvenile delinquency' emerged to inspire a moral panic that sought to suppress, among other things, rock 'n' roll. But the truth was that if you wanted to suppress youth culture, music was the wrong target. The inventors of youth culture were not Elvis Presley or Jerry Lee Lewis; they were Henry Ford, with his car for the masses, and Alfred Sloan, with his fancy styling and financing deals. It was they who had laid the foundations for the explosion of car ownership and freedom for the kids. In the post-war period, when Britain, France, Germany and Japan were struggling to reconstruct their economies, Americans were just buying cars. L.J.K. Setright pointed out that there were then so many cars in America that the entire nation could have been 'simultaneously carborne'. They were also, crucially, moving to the suburbs where everybody needed a car to do anything – not least, for the teens, have sex.

Sex in cars comes in two forms: while moving and one of the participants is driving or while parked. Both are frowned upon by the authorities but the former especially so. Nevertheless, both forms seem to happen a lot. Cindy Struckman-Johnson, a University of South Dakota psychologist, found that 33 per cent of men and 9 per cent of women had engaged in some kind of sex while driving. While not driving, the figure rises to 60 per cent of all people and over 8 per cent had lost their virginity in a car.

The figures are not that surprising. If home is impossible and a hotel too expensive, where better to indulge than in these rooms on wheels? Indeed, in 2019 *Cosmopolitan* ran an article entitled '20 Ways to Have the Best Car Sex of Your Life'. Joylessly, the first way is not to do it while the car is moving. There are also a number of lists of the best cars to have sex in – disappointingly the UK winner on the Askmen website was the Mitsubishi L200 Long Bed (Animal), a truck.

The words 'date' or 'dating' used romantically seem to be exactly the same age as the car. A 'liaison at a particular time, by prearrangement' had evolved into 'date' by the 1890s according to one source, or, according to another, by the 'roaring twenties'. The car had shifted the ritual of courtship away from the home and family and out into the world and beyond the reach of parental disapproval. The car had given the kids not just a private space, it had given them the road, the never-ending road.

Jack Kerouac was 35 when *On the Road* was published. It was – and still is – the bible of the post-war teens. Superficially it might have seemed to be another looking-for-America book like John Steinbeck's *Travels with Charley*. But it was Steinbeck unhinged; he might have concluded with a sense of loss but he had one reality to cling to – 'my own wife, my own house in my own street, my own bed'. It was precisely what the kids weren't looking for. Sal Paradise, the narrator of *On the Road*, found no such reality, only the road. You won't find any truth there because, once again, the road *is* truth.

3

The teen machines in *American Graffiti* are suburban cars: flashy, capacious and built for cruising rather than cornering. They are for families but in the hands of these kids they become celebrations of a new opportunity for sex and street display. This is novelty, certainly, but it is not full-blooded rebellion. The real drive-free-or-die rebels were the engineers or hackers, as they would now be called.

The odd one out at Mel's Drive-in is the 1932 Ford. It was a big year for new Fords. The Models B, 18 and 46 were wholly new. The 18 was powered by the first V8 engine – the celebrated 'flathead' – in a mass-produced car. One list of the 100 greatest cars of all time put it at number one. It was in one of these V8s that the outlaws Bonnie and Clyde were gunned down by Texas Rangers and Louisiana cops in 1934. After the war, the Bs and the 18s, especially the roadsters and the coupes, became popular among a new breed of automotive engineers – the hot-rodders.

Hot-rodding is not, like Elvis, pop; it is heavy-metal rock. It is a radical branch of just plain customising, started up before the war. Modifying cars had begun during Prohibition when bootleggers needed something quicker than the cars of the revenue agents and cops. True hot rods first appeared in the thirties. They raced on dry lake beds around Los Angeles. After the war abandoned airfields were used and drag racing first appeared. Then the races moved, dangerously, to the streets. In an attempt to keep things legal Wally Parks, the first editor of *Hot Rod* magazine, founded the National Hot Rod Association in 1951.

Straight-line performance – delivered by the Ford V8s – defined the cars but also a new form of decoration. Hot rods appeared covered in flames with exposed engines polished to a brilliant, mirror-like sheen. Hot-rodding had become a new automotive subculture that rejected the treadmill of bourgeois conformity imposed by Detroit. In this first phase hot-rodding lasted until the 1980s when, as Matthew Crawford observes, electronic engine management made everything under the bonnet 'a little opaque'. It is hard to rod a computer.

Both Crawford and earlier Tom Wolfe saw hot-rodding as a new art form. In his essay *The Kandy-Kolored Tangerine-Flake Stream-line Baby* Wolfe compared them to European architecture of the eighteenth and nineteenth centuries. But Crawford locates the art not in the paintwork but in the engineering.

The supreme hot rod was the Deuce Coupe, a 1932 Ford – the 'deuce' refers to the two in the model year. It was the perfect machine for hot-rodding, being cheap, available and almost infinitely customisable. Its popularity made a pre-war look acceptable to the rodders in the floating world – perhaps because such a vintage vehicle represented a rebuke to the obsession with the annual model change that had hypnotised their parents. The Deuce need never be planned into obsolescence. It became a Beach Boys song – 'Little Deuce Coupe' – and album. It also appears in the Bruce Springsteen song 'Blinded by the Light' in the line 'cut loose like a Deuce'.

Rodders spread to Sweden as *raggare* – roughly 'greasers' – though there it was more middle-aged and definitely more right wing. The Nordic greasers tended to get into fights with punks and hippies. Meanwhile, some Swedes seem to have fallen in love with American automotive excess. Annually, in the first week of July, the Power Big Meet is held in Lidköping. It's a show purely for American cars, mainly of the fifties and sixties.

The sheer showy vulgarity of American car design – as opposed to the practical rationalism of Swedish cars – inspired the *raggarists*. Christmas trees, Davy Crockett raccoon tails and pink leopard-skin seat covers became the design signature of the *raggare* and when in the seventies the Swedish middle classes were appalled by the Vietnam War, they displayed American flags and heckled anti-war demonstrators. In the hands of the *raggare* American cars have become the great symbols of dissent from Swedish good taste.

Hot-rodding came to other parts of Europe but with nothing like the style and the panache of the American version. Perhaps the young hunger for speed was sated here by a clever invention from the mainstream manufacturers. The hatchback – a car with an upward-swinging rear door – was first seen in the Citroën 11CV Commerciale in 1938. This was a version of the justly celebrated Traction Avant. In the sixties the format entered the mainstream and then in the seventies the hot hatch appeared. These were the souped-up variations of the basic hatchback. The first was the Simca 1100 Ti in 1973. Then there was the Renault Gordini in 1964, the VW Golf GTi in 1976, the Renault 5 Turbo in 1980, the Honda Civic Type R in 1997 and many others. The power rose to a peak in 2017 of 395 hp in the Audi RS3 Sportback. But all of these were corporate-controlled excesses available only to the teens of richer, more indulgent families. On the other hand, as the cars aged they found their way into the hands of the poor who resurrected the rodder way of life by pimping them up with paint jobs, aerodynamic wings and side skirts.

One final example of crazed customising: the lowrider cult was born in the 1940s in Los Angeles and later in Japan. Production cars are fitted with smaller wheels and the suspension is lowered. They are covered in intricate designs, often with a Mexican theme, and they are driven 'low and slow'. Variable suspension allows them to lean over, to bounce up and down or raise the front or rear several feet in the air. Unlike hot rods or pimped-up teen machines, these are cars adapted to do precisely what cars are not supposed to do. Kanye West's chopped Maybach looks, in this context, relatively restrained.

4

Hot rods, lowriders, pimped hot hatches and Kanye West's Maybach are more than just cars – they are demonic improvisations that make the car express something quite different from anything the manufacturer intended. But there's another way of making something that is more than just a car, a way of fleeing mere practicality by making something very expensive, entirely new and better, and which doesn't even need to be driven.

In 1992 McLaren, primarily a racing-car company, released the fastest road car ever, the F1. It was also the first million-dollar car and judging by the reviews it may well have been worth it. 'One of the great events in the history of the car,' said Andrew Frankel in *Autocar*, 'and it may possibly be the fastest production road car the world will ever see.'

The F1 created a new car genre. The supercar category had been created by the Lamborghini Miura in 1966. But this was something different; it was a hypercar. Only 106 F1s were produced and they now sell for many millions at auction. But Gordon Murray, the designer of the F1, has a deal for you. He is offering you the entire F1 driving and owning experience for just $2.36 million – a huge discount on the F1's auction value. This is the price of his GMA (Gordon Murray Automotive) T50 and it is, he says, much better than the F1. There will only be 100 of these and they all sold out before the car was released.

Murray is an automotive Platonist. He believes in the existence of the ideal form of the car, though he must know he will never attain it. Others thought the F1 was the *ne plus ultra* of car making; he just lists its shortcomings – hard to get in and out of, air-conditioning 'rubbish' and the lights were 'pathetic': 'At anything over 100 mph you couldn't really see where you were going.'

One of his heroes was Colin Chapman, founder of Lotus Cars, who, like Henry Ford, believed in lightness above all things. It was said that Chapman's ideal racing car would fall apart the moment it crossed the finishing line. If it lasted longer than that, it must be carrying unnecessary weight.

'A heavy car,' Murray tells me, 'will never give you the transient handling that a lightweight car will give you. It's impossible because the laws of physics unfortunately don't change.'

'Adding power makes you faster on the straights,' Chapman said. 'Subtracting weight makes you faster everywhere.'

Murray is, in engineering terms, a direct descendant of Chapman. He used to drive a tiny Smart Roadster with a kerb weight of 790 kilograms. It was not, on paper, particularly fast – 0–60 in over ten seconds – but he took delight in beating very fast Porsches on roundabouts. It's all done by lightness.

Simple straight-line speed, though necessary, was not the point. I met Murray when he was in the midst of designing the F1 and, like every simple-minded car nut, I asked about its 0–60 time. 'It doesn't matter,' he said. (It was, in fact, 3.2 seconds.) What mattered to Murray was the unrelenting lightness of the car.

About the F1 itself there were obvious oddities – the driver's seat, for example, was in the centre with a passenger seat either side of him – but the true originality was the austerity demanded by the pursuit of the ideal. This meant, among other things, removing driver aids like traction control, the system that prevents wheelspin.

It needs, as a result, good drivers. It did not always get them. Most famously Rowan Atkinson twice crashed his F1. In 1999 he ran it into the back of a Rover Metro, a sad but entertaining case of the best car in the world ramming one of the worst. In 2011 he hit a tree and a road sign – the repair bill was £1.4 million. Ownership was, nevertheless, profitable for Atkinson – the car was sold for $12 million in 2015.

The engineering wisdom of the dematerialising philosophy of lightness is subservient to the aesthetic perfection, the ideal form, which Murray seeks. Each hypercar feels like a step closer to automotive paradise. There is, however, a tragic side to this. These supremely refined aspirations to the ideal form of the car will rarely be driven.

'When people first bought the F1,' he says, 'I would say 90 per cent of the owners drove them. Because it was meant to be a driver's car. And although it was relatively expensive then, it was still possible to insure it and service it and run it relatively inexpensively. But as the cars grew in value, so driving them became more and more iffy – let's say because of the insurance premiums. When I had my prototype car the insurance premium went up every three months. And then as spare parts became difficult to find, and the car's value is so high, people drove them less and less. Today probably only half a dozen cars are used on the road.'

Many super/hypercars are kept in hermetically sealed garages and never driven. The rest are only ever driven a few miles because every mile reduces the second-hand value. These barely mobile machines have become sculptures in galleries of other worldly ideals, Platonic forms, static images of an unattainable automotive paradise.

Unfortunately, their sheer performance is now being threatened by electricity. Some Teslas have a setting called 'Insane' which reduces the 0–60 speed to 3 seconds; some have a setting called 'Ludicrous' which reduces the figure even further to 2.6 seconds. The new Tesla Roadster reaches 60 mph in 1.9 seconds. A possible version of the Roadster with cold gas rockets would do it in 1 second, more than half a second faster than a Formula 1 car.

But, then again, are such things really cars?

5

This 1968 Lamborghini Miura P400 is orange. It is seen speeding along Italian mountain roads driven by a man who clearly knows what he is doing. This Miura has a 3.9-litre V12 engine that produces 345 hp. Its maximum speed is 163 mph, it can accelerate from 0 to 60 in 6.3 seconds and it cost around $20,000. The stereo is playing 'On Days Like These' sung by Matt Monro. This is a dreamy, aspirational scene – everybody wants to drive a Miura through the Italian Alps listening to crooner Matt. But then the song fades and the Miura enters a dark tunnel.

Tyres screech as the driver brakes furiously. He dies as the car crashes into a bulldozer which then slowly reverses out of the tunnel, the mangled car attached. At a signal from a man in a sharp suit, car and driver are pushed over a steep cliff. The Miura rolls over, parts flying off in all directions, before finally tumbling into a fast-flowing river. It was a Mafia hit job.

Suffused with romance, violence, death and beauty – the Miura, unlike later Lamborghinis, was very beautiful – this opening scene from Peter Collinson's film *The Italian Job* (1969) announced the arrival of a new type of car. *Car* magazine in the UK claimed naming rights for these exotic, rarefied, fast but impractical machines – they were supercars. The Miura – the name comes from Eduardo Miura, who had a ranch full of fighting bulls in Seville – was officially the first. All the more amazing, then, that its first starring appearance should involve its destruction. In reality, the car that rolled down the cliff was already pretty much a write-off as a result of a real-world crash. The driven car was fine and in fact sold as new after the film.

There had, of course, been plenty of fast, expensive cars before the Miura. One clear precursor for these machines was the Mercedes SSK in 1928, a glamorous roadster. It was Ferdinand Porsche's last car for Mercedes before he set out on his own. The SSK was the fastest car of its time. It won many races and was involved in almost as many crashes. The crashes worked wonders for its after-sales value. Just 40 were made and only a handful survived of which one briefly became the most expensive car of its time, selling for $7.4 million in 2004.

In the twenties and thirties there were the mighty 'Blower' – i.e., supercharged – Bentleys. Their drivers were known as the 'Bentley Boys', a small platoon 'united by their love of insouciance, elegant tailoring, and a need for speed'. There was the 30/98 built by Vauxhall between 1913 and 1927 before GM took over the company. It became known as the first and best British sports car. From 1931 to 1939 there was the fabulous Alfa Romeo 8C that looked rather like the Bugatti Aérolithe of 1935.

The theme of these cars was that they were intended to be more than mere sports cars but they could not be all-out racers as they had to be driven on public roads. After the war the idea flourished in the form of long-nosed – i.e., front-engined – cars like the Ferrari GTO, the AC Cobra and James Bond's original car, the Aston Martin DB5.

But a new car type was emerging. Designers of Formula 1 cars were now putting the engine behind the driver and in the sixties the designers of Le Mans cars like the Ford GT40, the Ferrari P4 and the Chaparral 2F followed suit. A mid-engined – i.e., behind the driver but in front of the rear axle – car is better balanced than one with an engine at the front. For a very fast car it is the logical format and it made the long-nosed bruisers look old-fashioned.

And so the Miura emerged to announce the arrival of the road-legal, mid-engined racer known as the true supercar. These were obviously rich people's toys but, unlike the toys of the early days when almost nobody but the rich had cars, the supercars appeared as adjuncts to a consumer culture in which almost everybody has a car or access to one. The speed, impracticality, even the danger of the Miura and its successors are super-refinements of the ordinary, affordable cars that fill our streets. In fact, this was literally true in the case of the Miura. The gear box and the engine were made in one casting and mounted transversely, a technique borrowed from the British Mini. L.J.K. Setright began his majestic review of the Miura in *Car* magazine by describing it as 'a Mini Cooper turned back to front'.

Supercars now exist in popular car-owning and aspiring culture as objects of envy and wonder. They are uncanny in that they appear to be a car but also something else, something from another, higher realm. No motoring magazine can be expected to survive if it does not have supercars on some or indeed all of its covers. And TV shows, pre-eminently *Top Gear*, use supercars as unattainable idealisations of the cars their viewers own. Indeed, *Top Gear* drove the point home almost cruelly with its 'Star in a Reasonably Priced Car' segment in which celebrities drive as fast as they can round a track in a very humble, very everyday car – a Suzuki Liana, Kia Cee'd or Vauxhall Astra. It's a joke – a good one – at the expense of the ordinary.

The Miura emerged from the mind of Ferruccio Lamborghini, who started out in tractor manufacturing before launching Automobili Lamborghini in 1963. He disliked the Ferraris then available – or he was suffering from the pandemic of Ferrari-envy – and he decided to build something better. His inspiration came from Le Mans. This was not easy. The trick of turning a long-distance racing car into a road car could fail. The Ford GT40 also became a road car after its triumphs at Le Mans but it was a bad one – 'to drive it was to feel a spell breaking', remarked a reviewer. 'Better to let a GT40 stay in the land of your dreams.' That was the point about supercars; for almost everybody they could only exist in a land of dreams. But

Lamborghini started with the idea of a road car that could also be a racer and succeeded.

Increasingly elaborate forms of these 'mid-engined exotics', as car journalists used to call them, dominated the supercar seventies. Lamborghini produced the Countach in 1974, the styling of which – wedge-shaped with the driver and passenger seemingly buried in a complex of steel and glass angularities – looked like an act of defiance, a rejection of any demand for road-car practicality or for the feminine, flowing lines of the Ferraris. Then there was the Maserati Bora and the Ferrari Berlinetta Boxer, the company having finally accepted the mid-engined architecture required by the supercar. There was also the Porsche 911 Turbo, but was this really a supercar?

Possibly there was the 959, a 911 variation. Released in 1986 it reached around 200 mph and 0–60 in 3.6 seconds. Many still think it was the greatest Porsche ever. Bill Gates seems to have thought so. He bought one in Germany and shipped it to San Francisco, where it was impounded by US Customs. It had not been cleared as a roadworthy car – crash-tested and so on. It was, in fact, a slightly altered street version of a rally car so the customs people might have had a point. For 13 years Gates fought to drive the car out of Customs. Eventually, in 2001, he succeeded by having the law changed. Unapproved cars could now be imported for show or display, though they could only be driven for 2,500 miles a year.

But, on the whole, Porsches are not supercars. The great motoring journalist Gavin Green agrees. 'Probably Porsche's only real supercar was the 918 Spyder. They did something called the Carrera GT, and that would be categorised as a supercar as well. But they tend to operate at a slightly lower price point – usually much cheaper than Ferraris. I think they're probably seen as more honest, utilitarian, useable high-performance sports cars than supercars.'

This is a crucial insight. The list of attributes of a supercar do not include real-world roadworthiness or useability. Storage space is a joke; reviewers often declare there's room only for a 'packet of fags' or in the case of the GT40, as Nick Brittan suggested, 'if you're thinking about a dirty weekend, send all luggage on ahead'. Instead, these cars offer a paradisal level of competence which is neither of the race nor the road. For Green this idealistic tendency attained perfection with the McLaren F1. This, along with the Ferrari F40 – the first road car ever to be capable of 200 mph – launched in 1987, marked a new supercar phase. From this point onwards a supercar was for the moderately rich; for the stupendously rich there were these hypercars.

The F1 cost $1 million when new in 1992; five years earlier the F40 was $400,000 and many more were produced. The latter is often celebrated as one of the greatest ever Ferraris but nobody ever seems to have pointed out that it looks nothing like a Ferrari. It has a huge, distinctly vulgar wing at the back and the rest of the car is angular rather than flowing. The F1, meanwhile, has the air of a spacecraft built out of granite; it looks as though it was polished rather than built into existence. In short neither of these hypercars looked quite like their supercar predecessors. These were cars of delirious engineering perfection from which appearance simply emerged. Their appearances no longer felt like empty gestures, as did the Ferrari Testarossa launched in 1984 or all Lamborghinis, and neither did they look stolidly practical like Porsches. Rather they eschewed both cosmetics and practicality in favour of something more purposeful. The cars had to look this way because they sprang out of the imaginations of artist-engineers like Murray and Nicola Materazzi, designer of the F40. Their forms do not follow function – they follow feeling.

The F1, because it came from a famous Formula 1 racing company and because of its extraordinary originality, was the car that really created the hypercar category. It was, unlike the F40, a limited-edition car. This at once set the car apart from the conventions of the car market. Rather than celebrated cars accreting value over time, becoming infinitely more valuable than when new, an F1 was priceless from day one. If you missed out on the edition, you had no choice but to pay over the odds in the after-market.

On the simplest metric of hypercarness, the Bugatti Veyron, launched in 2005, surpassed the F1 when it reached 254 mph and hit 60 mph in under 3 seconds. Nevertheless, the Veyron does not represent any real progress over the F1 primarily because it is as ugly as sin – its rear end looks as though it is eating its front end.

6

Henry Royce, born in 1863, did not have a good start in life. His father's flour mill failed and the family – Henry was the youngest of five children – moved from Peterborough to London. His father died when he was nine and with only one year of formal education Henry was sent out on the street to sell newspapers and deliver telegrams. He moved back to Peterborough to take up an apprenticeship with Great Northern Railway, then to Leeds and London with the Electric Light and Power Company. In 1884, in partnership with Ernest Claremont, he formed an electrical business in Manchester called F.H. Royce and Company.

The business suffered from imports and the aftermath of the Second Boer War. Royce worked furiously to stay afloat. Claremont, strangely but clairvoyantly, suggested he buy a car to help him relax. France was the automotive world leader at the time so he imported a De Dion in 1901 and later a Decauville. But Royce was an engineering perfectionist. 'Strive for perfection in everything we do,' he was later to say. 'Take the best that exists and make it better. When it does not exist, design it. Accept nothing nearly right or good enough.'

He wasn't happy with either of the French cars so he produced his own 10 hp two-cylinder car. He drove the first one out of his factory in Manchester on 1 April 1904. A month later he met Charles Rolls. Unlike Royce, he had an excellent start in life. The youngest child of four, he was born in Berkeley Square to Baron and Lady Llangattock, whose ancestral home was in Wales. He was educated at Eton, where he was known as 'Dirty Rolls' because of his fascination with engines. After studying mechanical and applied science at Cambridge, he went to Paris in 1896 to buy a car – a Peugeot Phaeton. It became, simultaneously, the first car based in Cambridge and one of only three cars owned in Wales. With the backing of his father, in 1903 he opened one of the first car dealerships in Britain, C.S. Rolls & Co, which imported Peugeots from France and Minervas from Belgium. Meanwhile, he had helped create the Royal Aero Club. Also in 1903 he won the Gordon Bennett Gold Medal for the longest single flight. He filled what was left of his time by ballooning.

Rolls had a friend at the Royal Automobile Club called Henry Edmunds who happened to be a director of Royce's company. On 4 May 1904 they met at the Midland Hotel in Manchester, an alarming Edwardian baroque heap opened the year before. On 23 December Rolls agreed to take all the cars Royce could make; two years later he obliged with the best car in the world.

This was, at first, simply a chassis – coachbuilders in those days added the bodywork. It was known as the Rolls-Royce 40/50hp. An

actual car appeared the following year, now with a proper name –
Silver Ghost. The reviewer at *Autocar* magazine was ecstatic. 'The
running of this car at slow speeds is the smoothest thing we have
ever experienced,' he raved, 'while for silence the motor beneath the
bonnet might be a silent sewing machine.'

The review concluded that this was 'the best car in the world', a
term that was subsequently applied not just to this model but to every
Rolls-Royce. That might have later become marketing exaggeration
but from 1907 until production ended in 1926 the Silver Ghost really
was the best car in the world. Just under 8,000 were made at a time
when Ford was churning out Model Ts by the million. It was the best
but at a price that reserved it for aristocrats, royalty and potentates.
It was, wrote L.J.K. Setright, 'entirely ordinary in its administration
and equally extraordinary in its execution'.

The engineering was astounding. The Ghost just ran and ran –
nothing much ever seemed to break at a time when all cars routinely
broke down. T.E. Lawrence – Lawrence of Arabia – was very fond of
his Ghost. He had an armoured version in which he rushed romantically around the desert during his war with the Ottoman Empire.
'We knew it was nearly impossible to break a Rolls-Royce,' he wrote.

The Ghost was also probably Jay Gatsby's car in F. Scott Fitzgerald's novel *The Great Gatsby*. The uncertainty arises from the
fact that Fitzgerald only says a Rolls-Royce. But, since the book was
set in 1922, a Ghost would have been the only choice for a man of
Gatsby's wealth and ambition. It certainly *sounds* like a Ghost: 'a
rich cream color, bright with nickel, swollen here and there in its
monstrous length with triumphant hat-boxes and supper-boxes
and tool-boxes, and terraced with a labyrinth of wind-shields that
mirrored a dozen suns'.

This lush, quasi-architectural description is accurate. To be in the
presence of a Ghost is to be stunned by its size, its obvious weight
and its confident air of being perfect, as if everything from the wheels
to the smallest nut or bolt was certain to be the best of its kind.
To the contemporary eye, accustomed to smoothly integrated car
design, all cars of that period seem festooned with a rococo chaos
of bolted-on extras – lights, mirrors, trunks, horns and colossal
mudguards flowing into running boards. They look more like do-it-
yourself houses or, in the case of the Ghost, palaces. And, indeed,
the deeply buttoned seats do look like a rich man's sofa.

Ghosts did not all look the same. Customers bought the chassis and then made their own decision about the bodywork. Usually they ended up at Barker & Co in London, founded by a guards officer in 1710. Barker's masterpiece was the Silver Ghost Roi des Belges. The first of these was commissioned by Claude Johnson – a company man known as the hyphen in Rolls-Royce – in 1907.

'It was specified,' reported the *Rolls-Royce Magazine* in 1990, 'that the coachwork would be painted silver and that upholstery would be in green leather. Lamps and other external fittings were to be silver plated. Price of the body was £110–140 and the chassis retailed at £950 plus £7 10s for the aluminium dashboard fitted as an alternative to the usual polished teak.'

But, in spite of such lush variations, the point of the Ghost was not that it looked different from the cars of its time – it was that it just looked better. It was a summation of the developments in car design that had begun with the Mercedes 35hp; indeed, in its four-seater version, the Mercedes looked pretty much the same as the Ghost. Between them the two cars were the finest flowering of Europe's automotive ascendancy before the rise of Detroit.

Both the Ghost and the Mercedes were of a time when cars were for the rich. They were just the best of a single genre. That was all to change with the launch of the Model T in 1908. At that point the Ghost, which was in continuous production until 1926, became not just the best but also a separate car category. This category was christened 'luxo-barge' in the eighties, though the use of the term seems to have peaked in 2000. Rolls-Royce and Bentley were at the top of this expensive pile – neither America nor Europe really competed at this level, though the Europeans do now compete because BMW have bought Rolls and Volkswagen have bought Bentley.

America has had luxo-barges like the Duesenbergs but the most famous premium brand, Cadillac, always languished at the top of the mass market rather than in the paradise of luxo. Elvis Presley would have disagreed. 'A Cadillac,' he said, 'puts the world on notice that I have arrived.' Ford's Lincolns were a little more impressive but having a few times rolled around in the back of a Lincoln Town Car, I concluded it was not a player in any best of list. Japan's most impressive luxo-effort was the Toyota Century – produced almost unchanged from 1967 to 2017, a new version appeared in 2018. It was built to mark the 100th anniversary of Sakichi Toyoda's birth.

Nissan with the President and Mitsubishi with the Debonair also went luxo.

But, in essence, Rolls-Royce remains at the top of the luxo pile. And on the website it celebrates this ascendancy in a lather of ecstatic transcendence. 'Beauty and comfort combine,' the website explains in prose hereafter known as plutocrat sublime, 'beneath the celestial canopy of Phantom's iconic Starlight Headliner. Whether you take the wheel or recline in the Phantom Suite, the harmonious collaboration of technology and engineering delivers exquisite poise. In every moment of every journey, Phantom exists beyond previous conceptions of automotive perfection. Phantom is beyond time.'

7

A couple of levels below, starting in Japan in 1986 with Honda's Acura brand, was the creation of premium, near-luxo brands by mass-market producers. This was followed by Toyota's Lexus in 1989, Nissan's Infiniti in the same year and Hyundai's Genesis in 2015. This was tried by Chrysler in 1955 when it split off the Imperial model name as a separate brand with limited success.

Clearly the assumption was that merely rich people would want something more than a car with a mass-market name. German car makers – Audi, BMW and Mercedes – by somehow not exuding a mass-market vibe managed to bridge this gap without any 'badge engineering'. But for Gavin Green the problem with this kind of rebadging is that it produces ugly chimeras: 'A Lexus is basically almost always riding on the platform of the Toyota, and that's why I find the styling, personally, fairly hideous. And that's partly because they're sitting on platforms that they weren't designed to sit on so the general stance is pretty terrible. And to compensate for that they make them very busy and over-styled.'

Premium brands are a variation of GM's marketing. That was a way of creating the ideal customer – one who was willing to upgrade once a year – and the ideal car was one that didn't last too long. This was, according to a chapter title in Heon Stevenson's book on car advertising, 'Selling the Dream: A Neurosis Unleashed'. The neurosis was *being seen*. The advertising drive was relentless: 'Eyes instantly pick out a 1934 Nash', 'Wherever you go, People know . . .

Packard', 'It's a "who's who" of the Highway' (Cadillac). The wrong or old car was shameful; the right one signalled success, good taste, engineering savvy. So, it is better to be seen in a Lexus than a Toyota.

The more socially secure can easily overcome this neurosis. I once knew a very successful American businesswoman who drove a Toyota Camry. When I asked her why, she said, 'It's a Lexus.' Beneath the skin the two cars were identical. And some cars sell by being entirely classless. Princess Margaret – the 'rebel royal' – drove a Mini. Even James Bond in *For Your Eyes Only* makes an escape in a Citroën 2CV. 'I'm afraid we are being out-horsepowered,' he says but the car, for the moment, was the star. The Queen, a countrywoman, has often been seen driving a muddy Land Rover but she can only go so far – she spends her time in public in a Bentley Mulsanne.

Meanwhile, the luxo-barge has mated with the SUV in the forms of the Rolls-Royce Cullinan and the Bentley Bentayga. These are unhappy marriages – both are hideous – and they are absurd. Going off road and encountering a mishap in these things risks appalling repair costs, but very few people do. I heard of one Bentley salesman being struck dumb when a customer asked for a tow bar on the back of a Bentayga. The truth is these cars are closer to the blacked-out, faux SUVs – the Suburbans and Escalades – of the rock stars and rappers than an early Range Rover that was actually intended to go off road.

Increasingly hyper- and supercars have also mated with luxo-barges. Ferraris, Lamborghinis, Bugattis, Aston Martins and even the hypercars all have a mass of technology – elaborate infotainment systems – and comfort features. They are no longer the stripped-down near-racers of the early days.

One early attempt at this was the unremittingly eccentric 1976 Aston Martin Lagonda. The company was in trouble and it decided to take a step back from its usual supercar/GT format by building a luxo-barge, a four-door saloon. The designer, William Towns, took the need for a new direction very seriously. He adopted the folded paper style of the 1967 De Tomaso Mangusta by Giorgetto Giugiaro. This was all about straight lines and sharp edges. There was barely a single curve in the Lagonda's bodywork and it was said Towns had to be talked into making the wheels round.

Its eccentricities did not stop there. It had two fuel-filler caps, one on each side of the car, two different horns and a handbrake between the driver and the door. But most astoundingly it had the first digital dashboard in the world. This last was wildly premature. After months of trying to make this work, the car was sent to Javalina in Texas, an aircraft instrument specialist. They found an electronic package weighing 180 pounds and computer boxes under the rear seats. They chucked it all out and 90 days later working Lagondas were delivered to customers. At £50,000 the price was at the summit of the luxo market. But it did sell, not least because Towns's folded paper actually looked rather impressive. Sadly, however, the Lagonda came 28th in *Time* magazine's list of the 50 worst cars of all time: 'Mechanically it was a catastrophe.'

But the ultimate hyper-barge fusion is surely the Koenigsegg Gemera. Koenigsegg is a Swedish company that only make hypercars. The Gemera, unveiled in March 2020, is a hyper-family car – it has four seats but it also has 1,700 hp. It has a top speed of 249 mph and a 0–60 time of 1.9 seconds. It has four heated and four cooled cup holders. It costs $1.7 million.

8

Everybody wanted to give Marilyn Monroe a car. Her first was a 1948 Ford Super Deluxe Convertible, a chunky pre-war styled number with a big boot/trunk and a split windscreen. In fact, she bought this herself. She had been making money doing photo shoots and a few small films.

She later acquired a 1952 Pontiac, another convertible. It still looked a bit pre-war but now there was a touch of Harley Earl. She came into her own, as did her car, with another convertible, a 1954 Cadillac Series 62 Eldorado, a lengthy beast with two little bumps at the rear prefiguring the finmania that was to follow. It was a gift from her second husband, baseball star Joe DiMaggio. Her third husband, the playwright Arthur Miller, gave her a more sophisticated machine, a Jaguar XK140. After shooting *The Misfits* (1961), the studio gave her a Chrysler 200 convertible. She also had – a startling touch of earthy authenticity here – a Land Rover for driving in the desert.

The most potent picture of her with one of her cars was a black-and-white shot with the Cadillac. She was standing and leaning back against the car's multiple horizontals, her legs crossed and her body angled to the right. The woman's body and the car's were an invitation – come ride with me. This was reprised many times, notably in the final dream sequence at the end of Edgar Wright's film *Baby Driver* (2017). The hero walks out of prison to see his girlfriend standing, legs crossed and arms spread along the long horizontal of a convertible 1959 Chevrolet Impala – white with a red flash and the door opened to reveal blood-red upholstery.

Monroe liked her cars black. The Cadillac was black as was her 1956 Ford Thunderbird, though she was also photographed in a pink T'Bird. The black one was sold for $490,000 at auction in 2018.

Famous owners and drivers are the last and most nebulous way in which cars become more than mere cars. Nebulous because you can label the hypercar as fast, the luxo-barge as comfortable and the hot rod as crazy, but the stars' cars are just ordinary machines made special by celebrity contact. In a way undetectable by science, that black T'Bird was different from any other – it was replete with Monroe's allure.

Of course, their specialness may be very detectable. In 1964 Beatle John Lennon bought himself a Rolls-Royce Phantom V, one of only 517 made. It was entirely black but for the radiator – Lennon wanted that black as well but the company refused. The following year he came up with a seven-page list of changes – the back seats became a double bed, and a record player, cassette deck and radio telephone were installed. Weirdly, speakers were mounted in the front wheel wells so that people inside could talk to people outside.

After filming *How I Won the War* in Spain in 1967, Lennon realised the car needed a new paint job. Abandoning black, he went for yellow with sixties psychedelic/rococo patterns. The car was shipped out to New York when Lennon moved there and in 1977 he gave it to the Cooper Hewitt Smithsonian Design Museum to cover a tax problem. In 1985 it was sold for $2.3 million and it now resides, capriciously, in the Royal British Columbia Museum in Canada.

This was celebrity customising with a touch of urban bling – I can do this because I am who I am – almost 50 years before Kanye West's Maybach was chopped. But, in general, celebrity cars are, like Monroe's, simply production models touched by the undetectable residue of fame.

On the other hand, the choice of the car does show how the

famous want to be seen. A Toyota Prius – George Clooney, Ryan Gosling, Julia Roberts, Leonardo DiCaprio, etc. – clearly signals green sensitivity; any SUV – Scarlett Johansson, Charlize Theron, Jessica Simpson, Matthew McConaughey, David Beckham, Wyclef Jean – is just kind of showy mainstream practicality veering, in some cases, into entry-level bling; a classic Chevrolet Corvette – George Clooney – signals American authenticity. And so on.

But the award for most comically exact alignment of car and star must go to Arnold Schwarzenegger and the Hummer. AM General, a somewhat specialist automotive firm in South Bend, Indiana, had been making the High Mobility Multipurpose Wheeled Vehicle – HMMWV or 'Humvee' – for the army from 1984. People began to notice its implausibly wide stance on TV reportage of assorted US overseas adventures in the nineties and early 2000s. Schwarzenegger noticed one when he was shooting *Kindergarten Cop* in Oregon in 1990. 'He just went ape for that machine,' said his agent. He contacted the company, suggested they sell it to civilians and from 1992 that's what they did.

Now called the Hummer, it was either – take your pick – a steel vision of toxic masculinity, a brutal assault on the environment or a rather cool street cruiser. It had a 6.2-litre diesel engine and a kerb weight of 2,800 kilograms. It took 21.8 seconds to get to 60 and its top speed was just 68 mph. In the H1 versions it looked pretty much like its military predecessor, H2 looked slightly more like a conventional SUV and the much smaller H3 just looked awful, possibly a prisoner transport vehicle. As a domestic car sale it made no sense whatsoever. As a political gesture it was downright offensive. 'Hummer's H3 is mightily effective off the road,' said *Autocar* magazine when it was introduced into the UK, 'but not good enough on it to risk taking a smack in the mouth for.'

None of which troubled General Motors, which bought the Hummer name in 1999 and introduced the H2 and H3. This was the company that three years earlier had made the eco-virtuous EV1, a full electric car. The H3 emitted 336.5 grams of carbon dioxide per kilometre. Schwarzenegger, meanwhile, is reported to still have an H1 'slant back' in his garage, as well as an M47 Patton tank. But, if it's any consolation, he also has a Tesla Roadster.

Perhaps the most noble expression of a celebrity-touched car is a brilliant-red 1990 Mercedes 500 SE. On 11 February 1990 Nelson

Mandela was released from prison. Workers at the East London Mercedes plant in South Africa decided to celebrate by making him a car. Management agreed to donate the parts and in return the staff worked one hour a day extra overtime free of charge. It was a hand-built car and was said to be the best Mercedes ever to leave the factory. The workers danced and sang around the car as it was driven out onto the streets. Mandela was moved and called the car 'a tremendous gesture that was convincing evidence that in South Africa, there are many who are willing to work together and make sacrifices to build our nation'. In 1998 the car was retired and went on display at the Apartheid Museum in Johannesburg.

One of the workers said, 'We made more than a car for Nelson Mandela.'

9

'As long as we are driving,' said Gordon Murray, 'and we're allowed to drive our own cars and steer our own cars, there'll always be room for an extreme version of whatever we're driving.'

These cars that are more than cars are all about extremity – of comfort, luxury, speed, sex, pimping, hot-rodding and, in a few cases, real beauty. The celebrity-blessed ones are about the contemporary metaphysic of fame. They are all intended to lift the journey from A to B into a different realm, a realm where there is no A and no B, just the drive. Or in the case of a hypercar in a hermetically sealed garage there isn't even that; there is only the artistry of the bodywork and the engine that never starts.

Ultimately the Rolls, the Ferrari, the Deuce Coupe, the pimped hot hatch, the Hummer and the Koenigsegg are all expressions of the need to free the car from the surly bonds of practicality, convention, reason and, sometimes, the law. Like the writer of the plutocrat sublime prose on the Rolls-Royce website – 'Phantom exists beyond previous conceptions of automotive perfection. Phantom is beyond time' – the rich, the famous, the poor and the rebellious all want the car to be more than just a car. They want it to be *me*.

There is, however, one other way to make a car more than a car. You can die in it.

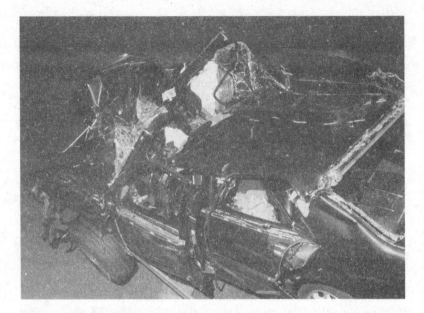

Princess Diana's Mercedes S280

Chapter Eight

THE DISPLACED HEART

1

The 1961 Lincoln Continental came as a relief – first, for anybody tired of chrome and fins and, second, for the Ford Motor Company whose Lincoln division had just lost $60 million. In response, Robert McNamara, president of Ford, cut the number of Lincoln models from three to one. The future of one of Detroit's most revered brands hung on this one car.

It was originally meant to be the latest Ford Thunderbird but the Lincoln division was desperate for something special. And this was a genuinely beautiful car. After years in the rococo wilderness, Detroit had at last made a car that inspired not a gasp but a sigh. It did not look like a carnival float; it looked like a car. Among many other improvements, it was 15 inches shorter than the previous Continental, an ungainly confection of chrome and meaninglessly creased steel. The shortness of the new car became a selling point – one ad showed it could be parked *by a woman*.

This was a car of the sixties, not of what Hannah Arendt called 'the disgusting posturing fifties'. In fact, you could say that the awkward old Conti was Richard Nixon, Republican presidential candidate in 1960, and the new one was the man who beat him – John F. Kennedy.

A convertible version was chosen as Kennedy's presidential 'parade' car. It was a predictable choice; his three predecessors – Eisenhower, Truman and Roosevelt – all had Lincolns. Kennedy's car was given a Secret Service code name – SS-X-100 – and lengthened by 41 inches. It also had a larger engine, two steps on the rear bumper and grab handles on the boot lid.

FBI Special Agent Clint Hill stood on one of those steps and grabbed one of those handles just after 12.30 pm on 22 November 1963. Lee Harvey Oswald had fired three shots, one of which had hit Kennedy's head. Hill found himself on the boot lid facing the First Lady Jackie Kennedy, who was scrabbling to reach something which Hill thought was a fragment of her husband's skull.

A Gräf & Stift 28/32 PS Double Phaeton now languishes in the Museum of Military History in Vienna. Next to it is the blood-stained uniform of Archduke Franz Ferdinand, heir to the throne of the Austro-Hungarian Empire. It was a car of its time – a design descendant of the Mercedes 35hp and the Rolls-Royce Silver Ghost – with deep-buttoned seats, prominent running boards and a vertical windscreen. It was also open-topped, like Kennedy's Lincoln. The Gräf brothers and their investor Willy Stift produced cars for Austrian aristocrats and royals. This one was bought by Count Franz von Harrach, who was standing on the car's running board when the Archduke and his wife Archduchess Sophie were driven through Sarajevo on 28 June 1914.

This was, as historian Michael Burleigh writes, 'the most fateful assassination of all' – it precipitated the mud- and blood-bound insanity of the First World War – but it was also the most comically incompetent. The first assassin failed because the car was moving too quickly and there was a policeman nearby. The second tossed a grenade into the car but it bounced off and exploded under the following car. Finally, after the Archduke had given a speech complaining about the attacks, he foolishly set off again. This time the car stalled in front of, astoundingly, yet another assassin, Gavrilo Princip, a Serbian nationalist with a 9 mm Browning. He shot both Sophie and Franz but, oddly, neither seemed to notice it. Franz kept repeating, 'It's nothing.' They both died. Princip tried to kill himself on the spot but failed. He died of tuberculosis in prison in April 1918, seven months before the end of the war he had started.

American presidential parade cars are now, in essence, military vehicles. The current one – known as 'The Beast' or 'Cadillac One' – seems to be the bloated bastard child of a CTS saloon and an Escalade SUV. Full specifications are not officially available. But it is said that the way to open its doors is known only to the Secret Service. It has 5-inch-thick bulletproof glass and only the driver's window opens – apparently to pay tolls but I find this unlikely. In the boot there is an oxygen supply and firefighting equipment. There are pump-action shotguns and tear-gas canisters on board. At 18 feet it is slightly shorter than Kennedy's Lincoln but it is said to weigh 8 tons, which would make it more than twice as heavy. It is a lugubrious beast, attaining a top speed of only 60 mph and reaching that in 15 seconds. It also is said to carry bottles of the president's blood type.

The Austro-Hungarian Empire collapsed as a result of the events precipitated by Gavrilo Princip. Kennedy's death helped turn America into a security state, enervatingly obsessed with conspiracy theories.

2

Apart perhaps from garage suicides involving carbon-monoxide asphyxiation, every car death is a public event. After crashes, police cars, ambulances, hazard tape and gawping pedestrians mark the scene as significant, worthy of our concern. In the cases of the president and the Archduke, they are events of global significance. Beneath them are the celebrity deaths and beneath them are the anonymous millions killed on the roads. All happen in public.

Celebrity car deaths are romantic. Except perhaps in the course of a cavalry charge, death on a horse could not compete with the crushed-metal spectacle of death in a crash, especially when high speed and glamorous cars are involved. I do not know whether cars kill celebrities more often than ordinary people but it is obvious that these violent, famous deaths take on high mythical and moral significance. They also spread confusion and yet more conspiracy theories.

James Dean died at 5.45 pm on 30 September 1955 when his Porsche 550 Spyder – he called it his 'Little Bastard' – ran into Donald Turnupseed's Ford Tudor. The Porsche was a 1,200-pound, fast, tricky car with a lack of torsional rigidity that could lead to dangerous oversteer. Ken Miles, the British driver who led the charge of the Ford GT40s at Le Mans, said, 'You were never quite sure where in the turn the car would finish up.' This might not have troubled

Dean, a 24-year-old actor for whom taking risks was all part of his shtick. 'Life is short, break the rules,' he said. 'Dream as if you'll live forever; live as if you'll die today.'

In contrast to the Little Bastard, the Tudor was a lugubrious 3,000-pound sedan and Turnupseed was a 23-year-old student who was driving home from California Polytechnic in San Luis Obispo to his hometown of Tulare. He suffered mild bruising.

Turnupseed's age was poignant. He was of the generation of which Dean was said to be the spokesman, the symbol. Dean's death became, and remains, the primal gesture of the post-war live-fast-die-young-leave-a-beautiful-corpse subculture. Before Jim Morrison, Janis Joplin, Jimi Hendrix, River Phoenix, Kurt Cobain and many others, he showed that death could just be the beginning of real, lasting fame.

He is usually said to have been travelling at 85 mph. An officer at the scene, however, estimated 55 mph, which was the speed limit. Later research suggested the officer might have been right. Dean had been given a speeding ticket when earlier on the drive he passed through Bakersfield at 65 mph so perhaps he was being cautious. But all of this is unclear.

Like the Archduke's Gräf & Stift, which was involved in all sorts of violence after the assassination, the Little Bastard has acquired a reputation as a 'cursed car'. In the Porsche with Dean was Ralph Wütherich, a mechanic. In fact, he might have been driving. Either way, the crash ruined his life. Deluged with hate mail calling him a killer and hearing stories of suicides of Dean fans, he became a depressed alcoholic. He went through four wives – the fourth he stabbed in her sleep. In 1981, having just signed a TV contract to make a show about Dean's death, he died when he crashed his Honda Civic into a wall.

On the fatal day Dean was in convoy with a Ford station wagon containing a photographer, Sanford H. Roth. Arriving at the crash site, Roth took pictures of the scene, thereby planting the image of the eviscerated Porsche in the popular imagination. The wreckage then had an afterlife as a sacred relic but it somehow vanished around 1960. Parts from the car, it is said, have been used in other cars which subsequently crashed.

There are competing narratives about all of the above, as there were about Kennedy's death, but that hardly matters now that people have become accustomed to the spectacle of the fatal celebrity drive.

The list is long. Here are some of the highlights: Isadora Duncan died on 14 September 1927 in an Amilcar CGSS; her trailing scarf was caught in one of the wheels and she was yanked out of the car, her neck broken. A year after Dean's crash, on 11 August 1956, Jackson Pollock died when he overturned his Oldsmobile 88 convertible while driving drunk. On 29 June 1967 Jayne Mansfield died when her Buick Electra 225 smashed into the back of a tractor-trailer. Mary Jo Kopechne died on 18 July 1969 when Senator Edward Kennedy drove his Oldsmobile into Poucha Pond on Chappaquiddick Island. Marc Bolan died on 16 September 1977 when the Mini 1275 GT in which he was a passenger hit a tree in Barnes, south-west London; the tree became known as the 'Bolan Tree'. And Diana, Princess of Wales, died on 31 August 1997 when the Mercedes S280 in which she was being driven crashed at 65 mph into a pillar in the Pont d'Alma tunnel in Paris.

Diana's death is the one that overshadows them all, even Dean's. Its effect was to mobilise not just the culture of youth but the whole of popular culture. The manner of her death seemed an affront to all that she had become – the blessed victim of royal cruelty, a fashion goddess, somebody who, like Jackie Kennedy, seemed to be just what everybody wanted her to be. All this was brought to a climax in that tunnel.

Her S280 was driven by Henri Paul, deputy head of security at the Ritz Hotel, whose blood alcohol level was found to be 3.5 times over the legal limit. Diana had no visible injuries but internally she was bleeding profusely from a tear in her pulmonary vein caused by the displacement of her heart to the right side of her chest on impact. The invisible wound and the displaced heart seem, in retrospect, to summarise her life.

Diana would have been saved if she had worn her seat belt. Indeed, many people on that celebrity list would also have been saved if the three-point seat belt had been in general use. This points to the absurdity of death in a car crash. A seat belt would have prevented it but many things could have prevented it – the mechanical condition of the car, a different route, 5 mph less speed, not drinking . . . Cars are intrinsically dangerous but not as dangerous as human folly and miscalculation. Which is why, as many people have noted, the death of Albert Camus on 4 January 1960 was peculiarly sad but appropriate.

He was only 46 and at the peak of his powers. He had won the Nobel Prize in Literature in 1957. The Facel Vega HK500 in which, as a passenger, he died was asking for trouble. The owner's manual contained some remarkably demanding advice: 'Not to look at anything else but the road, not to change the radio programme, not to smoke.' And it was a remarkably demanding car. At 4,000 pounds it was heavy. Weight in a car is often seen as a safety feature; it isn't – at speed weight is an added risk factor. Nevertheless, it was beautiful, a combination of American bulk and European styling. The fact that both Picasso and Dean Martin had one makes the point. So did Jackie Collins, who compared driving a Facel Vega to great sex: 'you want the moment to go on forever'. It was also, thanks to its Chevrolet V8 engine, fast, the quickest four-seater in the world.

Michel Gallimard, the publisher who was driving, might have said 'Merde!' according to his wife Janine. She felt a violent wobble as the car left the road at about 90 mph, hit one tree and then wrapped itself round another, having torn up 150 feet of the road surface. Camus in the front seat flew through the windscreen and died immediately. Gallimard died days later. Janine and their daughter Anne were unhurt.

It might have been a worn rear tyre on a wet road but, whatever it was, the death was absurd and Camus was the philosopher of the absurd, of the discontinuity between humanity's obsessive need for meaning and the meaninglessness of the universe. Or between humanity's obsessive need for movement and the pitilessness of the open road.

3

In *Rebel Without a Cause* (1955) James Dean played Jim Stark, the troubled teenage son of troubled parents. It was an early 'moral panic' film, this panic being caused by disaffected youth or 'juvenile delinquents' as bad boys and girls had come to be known.

Charles Starkweather, born and brought up in Lincoln, Nebraska, was 17 when the film came out and he loved it. He wanted to be Jim

Stark; he also wanted a car and a girl. He got the girl when he was 18 – 13-year-old Caril Ann Fugate. He had also befriended Bob von Busch. Friends were a scarcity in the life of ill-favoured, ill-mannered Charles. Together they bought a car, a 1941 Ford. Later he found a better car, a '49 Ford.

His first kill was on 30 November 1957. He had decided to rob his local filling station. Late at night he pointed his 12-gauge shotgun at Robert Colvert, the 21-year-old attendant, and took the money in the cash register. He also wanted the money in the safe but Colvert didn't have the combination. He took Colvert outside and told him to drive the Ford. In Superior Street Colvert was to get out and as he walked away Charles shot him in the back. He followed up with a shot to the back of his head. One thing led to another and in January 1958 he went to Caril's house and killed her father, mother and baby sister. The couple hung out at the house for six days before heading out when the cops were closing in.

In the end Charles, accompanied by Caril, killed 11 people. They went through three more cars – another Ford, a Packard and a Buick – before they were caught after a 100 mph chase in Natrona County, Wyoming. They chose to be extradited to Nebraska, a mistake because the governor of Wyoming opposed the death penalty, the governor of Nebraska did not. Charles died in the electric chair in his hometown of Lincoln on 25 June 1959. Caril received a life sentence. They achieved one beautiful thing – Terrence Malick's great film *Badlands* (1973) was loosely based on their story.

They also endorsed two prevailing sentiments: that all these new roads brought new dangers and there was something amiss with the kids. In fact, as the historian Ginger Strand makes clear, the fear of the road was made by the movies. It is certainly true that highway killers did seem to make good films.

Caril and Charles's story echoed that of Bonnie Parker and Clyde Barrow, who passed their time in the Great Depression robbing banks, filling stations and stores, killing at least 13 people in the process. And they really loved their car – a Ford V8. It was known as the Ford Flathead because of the flat top of the cylinder block. Clyde loved it so much he wrote to Henry Ford to thank him:

> While I still have got breath in my lungs I will tell you what a dandy car you make. I have drove Fords exclusively when I could get away

with one. For sustained speed and freedom from trouble the Ford has got every other car skinned and even if my business hasen't been strickly [*sic*] legal it don't hurt anything to tell you what a fine car you got in the V8.

Some say this is a fake but it sounds authentic to me.

The couple died riddled with 130 bullets fired by a posse of Texas Rangers and Louisiana cops on 23 May 1934. They too inspired a good movie – Arthur Penn's *Bonnie and Clyde* in 1967.

Perhaps the predecessor of these automotive killers was the Bonnot Gang. Unlike the Americans, these guys, being French, had a philosophy of bank robbing – they were anarchists. Formed around the Paris magazine *L'Anarchie*, they chose banks as their targets as a matter of principle. Bonnot, a criminal since his teenage years, joined the gang then led by Octave Garnier in 1911. Bonnot was a good shot and the gang used repeating rifles not then available to the police. He also invented the getaway car – the first being a stolen Delaunay-Belleville. This was, by the standards of getaway cars, a distinctly showy set of wheels with an extravagantly cylindrical engine bay and the usual big running boards and deep-buttoned seats. This would have suited Bonnot, who was known to his friends as 'Le Bourgeois' because of his fancy suits. Later they stole a De Dion-Bouton, another *haut bourgeois* machine.

It was all very classy but it didn't last long. The first robbery was in December 1911. The gang split up the following April and Bonnot found himself besieged by 500 *flics* and a lynch mob of angry citizens in a house in Choisy-le-Roi. The police decided to blow up the house, an unusual manoeuvre. In the ensuing wreckage Bonnot was found, still alive, underneath a mattress. He died later at the Hôtel-Dieu. The inevitable film, *Bonnot's Gang*, was made in 1968 followed by another, *The Tiger Brigades*, in 2006.

The Bonnot Gang did have one – in automotive terms – remarkable successor. This was the Gang des Tractions Avant. The Citroën Traction Avant is widely regarded by engineers as one of the most interesting cars ever made and by aesthetes as one of the most beautiful. It had front-wheel drive – as the name suggests – independent suspension, monocoque construction and rack-and-pinion steering. For 1934, the year it was launched, this was a revolutionary package. It took, writes L.J.K. Setright, 'rationalist France by storm'.

Superficially it had roughly the same shape of other cars of the time but its curved lines and the way the passenger compartment flows into the car removes the boxiness and bulk of the average thirties car.

Two of these beauties screeched to a halt by a Crédit Lyonnais van in the Avenue Parmentier on 7 February 1946. This would have been scary in itself; the Gestapo had used these Citroëns in Paris during the war. The whole thing became even scarier when the cars disgorged a gang of men with submachine guns demanding cash. That and their ensuing raids on vans, tax collectors and post offices earned them around £6 million.

The mastermind was Pierre Loutrel, an all-purpose thug, Nazi collaborator and useful assassin for the Gestapo. He switched sides once the Germans were clearly losing and shot a German officer in a café to prove his conversion. He acquired a nickname – 'Pierrot le Fou' – that became the title of a Jean-Luc Godard film in 1965 which, disappointingly, was not about Loutrel. He was also named as France's first 'Public Enemy Number One'.

His death was not as spectacular as Bonnot's. He accidentally shot himself in the stomach during a jewellery-shop raid and died five days later on 11 November 1946. The gang buried his body, which was found after three years by police.

All these stories were determined by cars and celebrated in films. In the popular imagination this fixed the car as a common criminal accessory. In fact, it became so fixed that it's amazing any gangster could be stupid enough to give the game away by using a Traction Avant or the Jaguar Mark X driven by the London hoodlums Ronnie and Reggie Kray or a Cadillac Town Sedan like Al Capone's or the Ford Model A driven by John Dillinger when he escaped from a gunfight in St Paul, Minnesota, to lie low in Chicago.

In fiction the car-crime connection was most gruesomely celebrated by Quentin Tarantino's *Death Proof* (2007). This is about a stuntman who drives around in a 1970 Chevrolet Nova customised so that a crash won't kill him but will kill the girls he picks up and places in the steel box he has built where the front passenger seat should be. The Chevy was also death proof for the driver in the event of a head-on crash. This leads to the most technically brilliant and utterly sickening car-crash scene in movie history. Whatever it means, it is a superb display of the deadly dynamics of flesh and steel in a high-speed crash.

The truth is, as Tarantino knew well, people like the idea of cars and death. Even Ford's driver Barney Oldfield thought that people only went to races to see someone killed.

4

In the unromantic and less filmic world of warfare cars could also take on a more positive role as murder weapons.

Nestor Ivanovych Makhno was commander of the Revolutionary Insurrectionary Army of Ukraine. He was an anarchist. During the civil war in Russia that followed the Bolshevik revolution of 1917, he took on the Ukrainian government, Germany, Austro-Hungary, the White Army and the Red Army. After the Reds defeated the Whites they turned on Makhno. He fled, ultimately, to Paris where he wrote and developed the anarchist idea of 'platformism', whereby platformist groups should exclude anybody not in agreement with the group's core ideas. Today's no-platforming students inherited this idea from Makhno.

His other most lasting achievement was his invention of the drive-by shooting. In his case this did not involve a car but a horse-drawn carriage on which was mounted a heavy machine gun, an arrangement known as a *tachanka*. These proved very effective and were widely used in the civil war. The trick was rapid movement towards and then away from the target, so the *tachanka* was first an assault weapon and then a getaway car.

During the Prohibition era gang boss George 'Bugs' Moran perfected the drive-by shooting, using the devastatingly effective Tommy gun. Like Makhno he found reasons to kill almost everybody and gave everybody reasons to kill him. Al Capone knocked off seven members of Moran's North Side Mob in the St Valentine's Day Massacre of 1929. Annoyingly, however, Moran lived to the fairly advanced age of 63, finally expiring in prison of lung cancer.

Motorcycle drive-bys were favoured by Colombian drug boss Griselda Blanco, a truly horrific individual even by the standards of the Medellin Cartel. Her own weapon came back to haunt her

– a motorcyclist gunman relieved the world of her presence in 2012. The Ku Klux Klan were also drive-by killers and a lot of rappers died from drive-by bullets – Tupac Shakur, Notorious B.I.G., Big L and Mac Dre. In 2000 50 Cent was shot nine times by a car-bound gunman but survived.

Nevertheless, as the Arizona State University's Center for Problem-Oriented Policing noted in 2007, you are much less likely to be shot from a car than by somebody who just walks up to you. Also, you are less likely to die – of 2,000 drive-by shootings in Los Angeles in 1991 only 5 per cent were fatal. Half sustained leg wounds. It is, therefore, a method that is picturesque – it looks great in films – rather than effective.

5

The finest stunt of the Clarkson-May-Hammond era of *Top Gear* came in 2010 with its multiple attempts to destroy a 1988 Toyota Hilux pickup truck with 190,000 miles on the clock. This involved driving it into a tree, drowning it in seawater, dropping a caravan on it, hitting it with a wrecking ball and, finally, placing it on top of a 23-storey tower block which was then explosively demolished. Each time, with minimal repairs, it survived as a driveable machine.

The Americans might have monopolised the pickup but with the Hilux the Japanese produced its most celebrated and enduring model. The name evokes not the showy might of a Dodge Ram or the street credibility of a Ford F150 but simple, reliable sturdiness. Clarkson and friends did those stunts because everybody already knew the Hilux was unkillable.

But it was also an appalling war machine, the direct, horseless descendant of Makhno's *tachanka*. 'The Toyota Hilux is everywhere,' one former US Army Ranger commented. 'It's the vehicular equivalent of the AK-47. It's ubiquitous to insurgent warfare. And actually, recently, also counterinsurgent warfare. It kicks the hell out of the Humvee.' Even American special forces used them in Afghanistan until improvised explosive devices forced them to switch to armoured military vehicles.

During the war in Somalia in the early 1990s NGOs bought

protection from local fighters who mounted their weapons – machine guns, anti-aircraft guns, rocket launchers – on the back of pickup trucks. They were known as 'technicals' because the NGOs used government money defined as technical-assistance grants to buy them. Their formal classification is NSTV – non-standard tactical vehicle. A warlord's power, it was said, is measured by how many technicals he has.

Technicals – before they earned the name – were used by British special forces in the North African desert in the Second World War. They used light vehicles mounted with machine guns. The Hiluxes appeared in Morocco in 1975 and in 1987 in Chad's war with Libya, which as a result became known as the Toyota War. On 22 March of that year 2,000 Chadian soldiers on technicals overran the Libyan air base at Ouadi Doum. Libya was hit one more time by technicals when rebels attacked using mostly Chinese Zhongxing trucks in 2011. At the Beijing Motor Show in 2012 Zhongxing advertised its truck as 'Stronger Than War'. The display was built around international film footage of their truck at war. 'Yup, that's another Zhongxing there, with a machine gun on the roof to kill. Brilliant marketing indeed,' reported *CarNewsChina*.

But it was the name 'technical' and their use in Somalia that made trucks globally famous and feared. In the case of the Hilux it was the queasy oddity of such a domesticated brand becoming the automotive equivalent of the AK-47 assault rifle.

The true significance of technicals was the evidence they displayed of the rise of asymmetrical warfare in which local armies, militias and terrorists deployed highly effective improvised tactics and weapons. The reason the Hilux 'kicked the hell' out of the heavily armoured Humvee was that it was lighter, faster and more manoeuvrable. The Humvee showed more concern for the safety of its occupants; the technical had no such qualms.

6

On 17 August 1896 Bridget Driscoll, aged 44, her teenage daughter May and her friend Elizabeth Murphy were in the grounds of the Crystal Palace, which by then had been moved from Hyde Park to Penge Common in south-east London. Driscoll was visiting a

Catholic League of the Cross fete. Whether she knew there was a motoring exhibition going on at the same time is unknown.

Three German-made, French-assembled cars were being demonstrated on the Dolphin Terrace where Bridget was walking. One of the cars was being driven by Arthur Edsall, who worked for the Anglo-French Motor Company but, like most people at the time, had little experience of actually driving a car. There is some dispute about what happened next – primarily about Edsall's speed – but what is beyond dispute is that Bridget died and became the first automotive fatality in Britain.

The car was capable of 8 mph but it was said to have been limited to 4 mph for the show. Nevertheless, at the inquest a servant, Florence Ashmore, said it was going at a 'tremendous pace . . . as fast as a good horse could gallop'. A passenger in Edsall's car, Ellen Standing, said afterwards that she heard him shout 'Stand back!' and then the car swerved giving her 'a peculiar sensation'. Driscoll looked bewildered – she might not have seen a car before – just before she was struck.

The first claimed death of a British driver was in Harrow on the Hill on 25 February 1899. This was 31-year-old Edwin Sewell. A rear wheel of his 6 hp Daimler collapsed and the car careered into a brick wall. Sewell died on the spot and his passenger, Major Richer, died three days later. A plaque marking the spot on the 70th anniversary of the event is headed 'TAKE HEED'.

The claim was false. As the *Brighton Evening Argus* reported, on 12 February 1898 Henry Lindfield, a retired builder, lost control of his car on a downward slope. The car swerved, ran through a fence and struck a tree. Henry's son Bernard was thrown out of the car but Henry died in Croydon Hospital the following morning. Henry's seems to have been the real first driver death in Britain.

The coroner at the inquest into Bridget Driscoll's death had said he hoped this would be the last death of its kind. He hoped in vain. Between 1926 – the first year that national figures were recorded – and 2019, 128,000 died in road accidents in Britain. As the years before 1926 were the most dangerous on the roads, the true figure is much higher. The Royal Society for the Prevention of Accidents once estimated the actual total is 550,000.

On 13 September 1899 America had its own first automotive death. Henry Hale Bliss, a 69-year-old realtor, stepped out of a trolley car at West 74th Street and Central Park West in New York City and was hit by an electric-powered taxi. He died in hospital the next morning. A plaque placed at the site in 1999 calls Henry's death 'the first recorded motor vehicle fatality in the Western Hemisphere'. This was not true either. Penge Common lies fractionally to the west of the Prime Meridian. Bridget's was the first motor-vehicle death in the western hemisphere. The plaque has since been changed.

When the streets were filled with horses, they were also filled with pedestrians and children playing. They were truly public spaces and traffic controls were non-existent to minimal. Bicycles joined in, causing consternation and some accidents, though people usually got back on their feet and walked away. But cars changed everything.

The automotive conquest of the streets is vividly demonstrated by old pictures of street scenes in London. In 1900 there was a casual confusion of cars, carriages and people occupying the road space almost at random. By 1920 regimented lines of cars and motor buses have taken over. This was primarily to do with speed. If cars were to serve any purpose at all, they must be allowed to travel faster than pedestrians or horses. This meant creating and annexing space.

Also, there was a general unfamiliarity with the behaviour of cars and their drivers at first. This is probably what ended the life of two-year-old Louis Camille, the first child to be killed by a car in New York City. It was on the Lower East Side and the car was carrying financiers on their way to Wall Street. Crowds attacked the driver but he was saved by police and subsequently found not guilty, because, it was claimed, Louis ran out in front of the car. A thousand children were to be killed by cars in New York in the first decade of the twentieth century.

Of course, it was not just children. Peter D. Norton writes in his book *Fighting Traffic* of a revolution in street use between 1915 and 1930 accompanied by a 'wave of blood, grief, and anger in American city streets'. This was partly a class problem – few people could afford cars at the time and those that could suddenly seemed to be annexing the common land of the poor. In American cities anti-car sentiments were expressed by stone-throwing, shots fired and riots. In Britain they were expressed as parliamentary outrage. 'Harmless men, women and children, dogs and cattle,' cried Cathcart Wason

MP, 'have all got to fly for their lives at the bidding of these slaughtering, stinking engines of iniquity.' In the same debate Brampton Gurden MP said, 'I would almost consent in some cases to the punishment of flogging.'

The car lobbies, convinced correctly that they owned the future, struck back. The Automobile Club of America reacted to any restriction on motorists rather as the National Rifle Association does today to any suggestion of gun control. They fought off any minimum age for drivers until 1919 and a New York City speed limit of 12 mph was thrown out to be replaced by one of 25 mph. In Britain the Automobile Association resorted to vigilantism to prevent the police enforcing speed limits – cyclists were sent to patrol roads to ensure drivers were safe from prosecution.

The advance of the car seemed to be unstoppable; the vision of the automotive future was just too seductive. People, in Jane Jacobs's words, were 'captivated by the vision of the freeway Radiant City'. In the interwar years there was a burst of techno-futurist optimism driven, not least, by the need to sell cars. In 1919 General Motors had produced its one millionth car – an Oldsmobile coupe – and in that one year Ford produced half a million Model Ts. Growth in the previous decade had been explosive in spite of the global disruption of the Great War.

Visionary cities started to appear in fiction. Fritz Lang's film *Metropolis* was typical in the assumptions it made about the urban future. Metropolis was a vast million-acre city full of walls of densely packed skyscrapers between which scurried cars, trains and planes, all controlled by monstrous underground machinery.

The car had introduced a new urgency into city life. It must have space for roads, parking and fuelling. It was the future; it could not be impeded in any way, not even by death. As Robert Moses, New York's ruthless master builder in the mid twentieth century, put it, 'When you operate in an overbuilt metropolis, you have to hack your way through it with a meat axe.'

7

Total car deaths in the USA are now approaching 4 million; it is one of the most dangerous developed countries in which to drive, with an annual rate of 12.4 fatalities per 100,000 inhabitants. Britain's rate is 2.9, Germany's 3.7, France's 5.0, Spain's 3.7 and Japan's 4.1. The US death rate is primarily explained by the fact that they drive so much – 5,500 miles a year per capita against 1,100 miles in Japan. According to the World Health Organisation, traffic accidents kill about 1.35 million worldwide every year, more than 90 per cent of them in low- and middle-income countries. It is the leading cause of death in the 5–29 age group. Clearly humanity has made an un-spoken deal – the annual benefits of the car are seen as worth the price of 1.35 million deaths.

One could reasonably say that just as many people would have died from accidents and disease if we had stuck with horses. Urban horses were indeed involved in many fatal accidents. Ulrich Raulff in his book *Farewell to the Horse* quotes the French author and dramatist Louis Sébastien Mercier. On 28 May 1770 he witnessed a horse-powered pile-up in Paris: 'Its cause was a mass of vehicles blocking the road, across which poured the most enormous stream of people, a huge crowd in the dim light of the boulevards. By a hair's breadth I avoided losing my life. Twelve to fifteen people were killed, either on the spot or later as a consequence of their injuries, having been crushed so terribly.'

A hundred years later four people a week were dying in New York because of horse transport. *Harper's Weekly* reported in 1899 that 'a good many folks to whom every horse is a wild beast feel much safer on a machine than behind a quadruped, who has a mind of his own, and emotions which may not always be forestalled or controlled'.

Or, from another perspective, almost 60 million people die every year so car deaths are just 2.25 per cent of the total. Stuff happens. People die. They behave badly; if you give them guns, they will shoot each other; if you give them Twitter, they will abuse each other; if you give them cars, they will crash into each other. So why we made this deal is obvious – it's just the sort of thing modern humans do, the sort of sacrifice they make.

There are other kinds of car deaths, as we have seen. A subset of the traffic deaths is the celebrity crashes around which coalesce rumours, conspiracy theories and a sickly necrophilia. Car-bound assassinations produce similar responses. There are drive-by killings, and murderers thrive on the road, their work made safer and more productive by getaway cars and fast roads. And the car is recruited by asymmetrical warriors who load Toyota Hiluxes with machine guns and rocket launchers.

Cars amplify human capacities for good or ill. But with traffic accidents they don't just amplify, they also create new ways of dying. People were not catapulted through a windscreen like Albert Camus, nor did they have their necks broken by a scarf like Isadora Duncan, nor have their hearts fatally displaced like Princess Diana before the advent of the car.

Modern car dealers must just hope for the best when they hand over the keys to thousands of pounds of metal that can be accelerated to 100 mph or more to barely trained drivers. If they die, they die – life goes on.

In 1949 Reuben Jacob Smeed, a British statistician, tried to disentangle the death–car deal. He came up with a simple calculus showing that increased traffic volume led to an increase in fatalities per capita but a decrease in fatalities per vehicle. By the time of his death in 1976 he had applied his theory in 46 countries; all confirmed Smeed's Law. Many have since refuted this law. Notably the physicist Freeman Dyson, who had worked with Smeed during the war, suggested it was an expression of his fatalistic nature. Smeed also forecast that the average speed in London would always be 9 mph. If it fell below that figure people would abandon driving and it would not rise above that figure because so many people did drive.

Over time, Smeed's work has not survived scrutiny; too many other factors – notably improved safety features – are involved. But the way he thought takes us to the heart of the matter: what are the calculations people make when they get into a car, either about their own risk of death or about the number of acceptable deaths? The answer, if there is one, lies in what people think about cars and how those thoughts change over time.

8

Dealing with car deaths in a less abstract way than the equations of Smeed is not easy. Matthew Crawford writes of a 'larger risk ecology – speed limits, traffic density, the quality of drivers and so on'.

On top of all that there is now the distraction of technology. Having to touch one of the many buttons – on screen or dashboard – produces seconds of inattention to the road. Using a mobile phone, especially for texting, is suicidal. Eating the fast food picked up at the filling station even more so. Writing in the *New York Times* in 2010, automotive journalist Jamie Kitman summed it all up as a capitalist death trap: 'As a courtesy to our telecommunications industry, Americans have de facto permission to be distracted by texts, calls and other focus-compromising data.' Faced with this malign alliance of marketing and human folly, the only way ahead was to forget the folly and fix the physics.

Sir George Cayley, born in 1773, seems to have invented everything – fixed-wing aircraft, self-righting lifeboats, tension spoke wheels, caterpillar tractors, automatic railway signals, an engine powered by gunpowder and, above all, seat belts, which he fixed on a glider he had built. Nobody took much notice.

In 1885 Edward J. Claghorn of New York was granted a patent for a belt 'designed to be applied to the person, and provided with hooks and other attachments for securing the person to a fixed object'. In 1946 Dr C. Hunter Sheldon, a neurologist, had the idea of a retractable belt in cars to prevent head injuries. In 1949 Nash offered the option of seat belts in their cars. Buyers hated them. The same thing happened at Ford in 1956. And so it went on. People, it seemed, would rather die than strap themselves in.

Finally in 1959 the modern three-point seat belt, invented by Nils Bohlin for Volvo, was introduced as a standard item. Its effectiveness is spectacular. Seat belts reduce deaths and injuries in crashes by 50 per cent. Air bags, collapsible steering columns, crumple zones, safer fuel tanks and so on followed. On top of that there were devices to stop crashes happening in the first place – better tyres, better brakes, traction control, antilock brakes etc.

Road traffic deaths in the UK declined from 8,000 in 1966 to 1,800 in 2019. In the same period in America they fell less impressively from 51,000 to 36,000. The lower fall in the USA may be due to a reversal of the decline from 2005 caused by distracting technology. Deaths from distracted driving in the USA rose by 28 per cent between 2005 and 2008. Even physics cannot prevent the intrusion of the all too human.

9

The automotive mortality equation is incalculable. There must be a death rate at which people stop driving out of fear. It has not yet been found but it is evidently pretty high. The car offers so much and death always seems, to the individual, so remote, so unimaginable, so inconvenient.

NEW POWER FOR EASIER UPS AND DOWNS! Corvair's strong-and-silent new engines never quit showing off. They do it in three sizes for '64: the standard Turbo-Air 164 now with 95 hp, the high-performance Turbo-Air 164 now with 110 hp (extra-cost option), and that absolute braggart, the 150-hp Turbocharged Spyder engine. Best way to humor all three is to find yourself some hills and dales, then just relax as Corvair takes 'em at a canter. Unchanged saving habits in all three, too. All of Corvair's famous features —rear-engine traction and handling ease, 4-wheel fully independent suspension, and flat floor for extra roominess—are back again. Extra added attractions include classic styling refinements and new interior design with pleasing details like map pockets in both front doors of Monzas. If you thought Corvairs were fun to drive before, try one of these new ones! . . . Chevrolet Division of General Motors, Detroit, Michigan.

Chevrolet Corvair advertisement

Chapter Nine

BACKLASH

1

Launched in 1960, the Chevrolet Corvair looked like the right car at the right time. It ticked, as they say, all the boxes. It was by Detroit standards small and mechanically original. Even better, after the carnival-float extravagances of the fifties, it looked clean-lined and neat. In fact, it looked European. The NSU Prinz 4 that appeared at the Frankfurt Motor Show in 1961 could have been its chubbier younger brother.

It was a true 'compact', an American term for cars that look to European eyes quite large. At the same time as GM launched the Corvair, Ford and Chrysler had also been trying to produce compacts but they were just shrunken versions of their big sedans; they signalled to the buyer that he was, frankly, a loser. The Corvair made the buyer look smart, cool. It was a US original, if not a European one. Its configuration – a rear-mounted, air-cooled engine – was taken from VW and Porsche as was the swing-axle suspension.

GM knew this car was special; marketing soared to new levels of hysterical overkill. In 1960 a short film – *The Corvair in Action* – claimed the car could 'go just about anywhere'. After it had careered down a stream for 20 miles the voice-over demanded, 'What more could a Corvair do?' The answer seemed to be that it could survive brutal crashes with much larger Chevrolets. Then, ominously, 'They tried to make the Corvair roll over – it wouldn't.'

A 1964 ad showed the car being flung about among 'the oldest living things on earth' – bristle cone pines. 'The incredible Corvair of 1964 – if there's a sceptic left let him watch now.' A 1965 ad of the old blonde-in-the-desert genre implied the usual link between the car and a woman's body, adding a claim that driving the car was superior to sex: 'There is no feeling in all the world like the one behind this wheel.' When the new '65 model appeared with the absence of the 'B' pillar – always a sporty signifier – *Car and Driver* magazine went over the top, calling it 'the most beautiful car to appear in this country since before World War II'.

Also in 1965, a 31-year-old, Connecticut-born-and-raised, Princeton-and-Harvard-educated lawyer called Ralph Nader published his book *Unsafe at Any Speed*. Chapter one was entitled 'The Sporty Corvair – The One-Car Accident'. This made the Corvair one of the most famous cars in automotive history but not in a good way. At a stroke all the boxes were unticked.

First there was the swing axle. This was invented in 1903 and first appeared in the unfortunately named Rumpler Tropfenwagen. Basically, the two rear wheels at either end of the axle could move independently up and down. If one wheel went up, it didn't make the opposing wheel go down. It seemed like a very good idea at the time and for Porsche in particular it indeed was. The handling of their rear-engined, swing-axled 911s is spectacular, if tricky for the inexperienced.

Most of the suburban drivers of the Corvair would have been inexperienced. The problem was that when combined with a rear-mounted engine, the swing axle can cause strange things to happen. Sixty per cent of the Corvair's weight was over the rear – swing – axle. The advertising sold this as a huge advantage for the owner. It made the steering lighter and the handling more agile. This was true but it also made rather specialised demands of the driver. For a start the front and rear tyres had to be maintained at very precise and widely differing pressures – 15 (cold) to 18 (hot) pounds per square inch at the front and 26 to 30 psi at the rear. Since the average American car mechanic would unthinkingly inflate all four tyres of any car he saw to 24 psi, this meant there must have been quite a few Corvairs speeding along the freeways on dangerous wheels.

There were further demands to be made of the Corvair driver. The weight over the rear wheels caused the back end of the car to move outwards – 'oversteer' – on corners. The natural response of most drivers when feeling this happening would be to take his or her foot off the throttle. This could make matters worse. Sudden deceleration shifts the weight forward and can precipitate a spin.

The further problem is that the swing axle could cause one wheel to 'tuck-in' and that could fling the car into a roll. The design of the Corvair, Nader concluded, was 'one of the greatest acts of industrial irresponsibility'.

Considered as a car review, it was the most effective in automotive history. Nader's assault produced two reactions from GM – one disastrously stupid and the other too little too late. The stupid move was made by James Roche, who had become GM president in the same year as *Unsafe at Any Speed* appeared. Roche had already made his name with what turned out to be a fabulously complacent remark: 'America's romance with the automobile is not over. Instead, it has blossomed into a marriage.' Perhaps one should cut the man a little slack. He was new to the job and he might have assumed Nader's book was just another fleabite on the thick hide of GM. He also knew that the world had changed – the consumer movement, he said, was 'a form of harassment unknown to businessmen in other times' – but he didn't adapt.

Either way, his stupid course of action was the employment of private detectives to discredit Nader. This involved, first, tapping his phone and, second, hiring prostitutes to get him into a compromising situation. Unfortunately for Roche, for the Corvair, for General Motors and for the entire US car industry, Nader realised something was going on and he reported it to Senator Abe Ribicoff for whom he was then acting as a consultant. Ribicoff set up an inquiry at which Roche was forced to confess. Nader sued for invasion of privacy and settled for $425,000, which he used to found the Center for the Study of Responsive Law to continue holding Roche and people like him to account. In 1966, meanwhile, Congress enacted the National Traffic and Motor Vehicle Safety Act, the first time federal safety standards would be set for American cars.

Roche's too-little-too-late manoeuvre was to fix the problems of the Corvair. In fact, the problems had been partially fixed by the time Nader's book came out. But the name was tarnished and in any case the car's sporty credentials had been overshadowed by those of the Ford Mustang, a 'muscle' car that made the euro-style of the Corvair look downright unAmerican. Production fell from 220,000 in 1965 to 110,000 in 1966 and slumped to 15,000 in 1968. The car was discontinued in 1969.

All of which was radical enough but just as radical was Nader's impact on car culture and the car's place in society. In terms of car culture nobody would ever – could ever – again try to produce over-styled, under-engineered and unsafe cars like those floats of the fifties. For Nader's book was not simply an attack on automotive engineering, it was also a brutal onslaught on the dangers inherent in certain styling decisions. Brightly finished dashboards could cause driver-dazzling reflections; poor designs of gear shifts could cause drivers to reverse unexpectedly; 'second collisions' of passengers with car interiors in a crash were made worse by sharp edges, poor steering columns and door design.

And then there were the fin-and-dagger shapes common in the exterior design of the baroque era. A nine-year-old girl on a bike bumped into a '62 Cadillac whose fin ripped through her body and killed her. A 13-year-old boy running to catch a ball was stabbed in the heart by a '61 Cadillac fin. Killing children in the name of a stylistic superfluity was not a good look for Detroit. The underlying brutality behind the glamour of the fifties aesthetic was being exposed.

There can be little doubt that Nader was right. Too little attention had been paid to car safety and too much to Sloan's most prized innovations – styling and marketing. But was he right about the Corvair? Possibly not. Several subsequent studies showed that it was no more dangerous than many other cars of the time. Furthermore, there was – and still is – a strong pro-Corvair lobby among petrol heads of all kinds. But they are missing the bigger point, made by Timothy Noah in the *New Republic* in 2011. It may be true that it was not especially dangerous *at the time* but that was because no car at the time was 'remotely safe by contemporary standards'.

Nader went on to join the assault on the Ford Pinto, a 'subcompact' launched in 1970 – its rear-ended fuel tank was liable to catch fire in collisions. He also ran several times for president, and campaigned for clean water, freedom of information, product safety, control of foreign corrupt practices and whistleblower protection. He established several institutions, including the American Museum of Tort Law, in which the main attraction is a cherry red '63 Corvair, and won many awards. He had become the secular saint of the consumer movement. He never married and has famously lived the life of an ascetic devoted to his cause of making corporate America answerable for its actions.

In this he succeeded, especially in the car industry. In 1965 his book launched a backlash against the car that is with us to this day and which will soon remove the fully driver-controlled internal-combustion-powered machine from all our lives. 'I think,' he said in 2015, 'the internal combustion gasoline engine is on the way out.'

In 2016 he was, improbably, inducted into Detroit's Automotive Hall of Fame. 'That Nader's name,' says the ambivalent citation on the website, 'still draws some ire among certain car enthusiasts highlights how significant his influence was on the automotive industry.'

2

After Nader came a deluge of anti-car feeling. In 1972 John Jerome published *The Death of the Car: The Fatal Effects of the Golden Era, 1955–1970*. In 1973 Emma Rothschild published *Paradise Lost: The Decline of the Auto-Industrial Age*. In 1972 the cover of *Motor Trend* magazine carried the headline '20 Auto Defects That Can Kill You!' There had been earlier anti-car tracts, notably John Keats's *Insolent Chariots* in 1958 in which the car was compared to a nagging, demanding wife – 'She grew sow-fat while demanding bigger, wider, smoother roads.' But the new automotive critics went deeper and wider and they were very serious.

The car was on the run. Pro-car feelings of speed, comfort, leisure and freedom were now counterbalanced by anti-car feelings of fear, distrust, scepticism and environmental alarm. Consumerism had arrived and the car was its most visibly guilty party. The world of Ford and Sloan was gone to be replaced by something much more complex, more technically demanding and less easily controllable. Nader was the hero of the car's third act and an army of car doubters and haters had suddenly filled the stage.

Emma Rothschild notes that anti-car feeling had an effect on marketing that was both subliminal and comical. An inspired TV ad for the tiny Honda N600 in 1970 gave advice on 'how to prepare your town for the new Honda sedan'. It recommended planting more parking meters – the Honda was so small; placing vases of flowers on fuel pumps – the Honda made a gallon last 40 miles; lanes could be narrowed – again the car was so small: 'A couple of more basic adjustments and you'll have a perfect town for Honda.'

As Rothschild comments, the ads turned automotive culture into a counter-automotive culture. The Honda, as opposed to Detroit's big boats, was a *good* car.

More spectacular and a good deal less cosy were the astounding yet subliminal TV ads for his Seattle Chevrolet and Fiat dealership made by Dick Balch from 1970 onwards. In one he appears in a multi-coloured suit carrying a sledgehammer. 'Hi, I'm Dick Balch, and if you can't trust your car dealer, who can you trust?' he cries before smashing his hammer into the front wing and then the wing mirror of a new Chevy truck. He emits a maniacal laugh and, jazz hands spread, yells, 'That's show business! Ta da!' It worked. Balch became not only famous but also, surprisingly, rich. He spent $30,000 a year on fixing the cars he had smashed and the customers wanted to buy them even more than untouched, pristine models. Then there was Cal Worthington, who flooded the airwaves around Los Angeles with ads for his dealership in the seventies. He was announced as 'Cal Worthington with his dog Spot', but it was never a dog – it was a chimpanzee, gorilla, tiger or elephant.

Balch indicated, says Rothschild, 'some mysterious perception of automotive discontent'. This makes sense. There was no dignity, no grandeur, no exciting newness about Balch's or Worthington's cars; their actions mocked the cars. They were just stuff like any other stuff. Detroit had been disenchanted.

There was also growing awareness of the absurd extravagance of most of what Detroit offered. A survey had found that 85 per cent of all trips were of 13 miles or less and they were for essential purposes. Who needed Detroit's carnival floats or muscle cars for that? Or, as Christy Borth of the American Manufacturers Association said, it was folly to build 'two tons of automobile to transport a 105-pound blonde'.

Furthermore, the strategy of planned obsolescence inaugurated by Alfred Sloan in the twenties reached some kind of mad climax in the fifties. Cars became flimsier. On 1 July 1955 80.5 per cent of cars made by the Big Three were still on the road after nine years. Twelve years later the figure had dropped to 55.23 per cent. Planned obsolescence meant planned waste.

Deluged by these and many other developments and revelations, including Nader's, consumers began to strike back. In the first four months of 1973 small-car sales shot up to 39 per cent of the market.

This was a nightmare for Detroit – they just couldn't find a way to make a profit out of 'sub-compacts'. But later that year came even worse news.

In October the 'oil shock', caused by the Yom Kippur War, was traumatic, an existential threat to a way of life. Henry Kissinger said the shock 'altered irrevocably the world as it had grown up in the post-war period'. From 1945 up to 1973 big oil and big car makers had dominated Western economies. They had seemed unchallengeable; now they looked like bewildered extras in a drama much bigger than even their inflated profit margins.

Of course, things went back to a kind of normal, a condition somewhat altered by a new awareness of the fragility of our comforts and by a deeper scepticism about big company intentions and inventions. Perhaps the oil shock had just been a little local difficulty, a teaching moment, nothing more. But for cars, worse, much worse, was to come.

3

On 22 August 1981 there was a front-page story by Walter Sullivan in the *New York Times* with the headline 'Study finds warming trend that could raise sea levels'. Scientists had 'detected an overall warming trend in the Earth's atmosphere . . . They regard this as evidence of the validity of the "greenhouse" effect, in which increasing amounts of carbon dioxide cause steady temperature increases.' In the second paragraph Sullivan used the phrase 'global warming'.

It was not the first use of the phrase – it had been current in specialised circles since the early seventies – but this was the *New York Times* and this was the front page. Also, 'global warming' is a much more effective phrase than 'greenhouse effect'. The latter is about causes and does not explain anything in itself; the former is about an event and explains precisely what it is. From that point onwards the image of humanity's death by heat was burned into the popular imagination.

Environmental anxieties had been around for much longer – they were an aspect of the romantic movement's defence of nature in the early nineteenth century. In the sixties and seventies they became a more science-based popular obsession. Acid rain caused by industrial emissions was found to be killing plant life. The ozone layer that protects the planet from excessive ultraviolet radiation was being depleted by the chlorofluorocarbons used in fridges. Now greenhouse gases were threatening catastrophic global warming. One gas in particular stuck in the mind – carbon dioxide.

Car exhaust fumes are an impressive chemical cocktail. They consist of particulates – soot, etc. – benzene, hydrocarbons, sulphur dioxide, nitrogen oxides, carbon monoxide and carbon dioxide. None of these is good for you and some – nitrogen oxides, carbon monoxide – are terrible. But because its effect is planetary, the worst is carbon dioxide.

CO_2 in the upper atmosphere stops heat being radiated away from the earth's surface – hence global warming. Transport accounts for about a fifth of global CO_2 emissions – cars and trucks account for about three quarters of that.

Gradually, through the eighties, this began to attract ever more attention, though not on a scale large enough to move governments. Then, in 1988, NASA scientist James Hansen appeared before the US senate. Although Hansen had spoken out before, the timing of this event was critical. In the summer of that year a terrible fire had burned in Yellowstone National Park, tinting the skies red for hundreds of miles. In addition, both Washington and New York had suffered temperatures of 38 degrees Celsius. Water levels in the Mississippi had sunk to a new low.

America was primed to hear the global-warming message and Hansen was the man to deliver. Even outside the room where he spoke the temperature was at a record high. He told the senators that he could state with '99 per cent confidence' that long-term warming was happening and the greenhouse effect was the cause. He said to reporters afterwards that it was time to 'stop waffling so much, and say that the evidence is pretty strong that the greenhouse effect is here'. Global warming was now on the political agenda and cars were to be accused, not quite accurately, as being the prime warmers.

Warming, though the biggest, was not the only issue. Pollution from fossil fuels in general, including oil, was found by one study to have killed 8.7 million people in 2018, accounting for one in ten deaths in the USA and Europe. This is more deaths than from smoking and malaria combined. Pollution was even said to lower

IQ. Pollution effects took over, briefly, from global warming as the big environmental scandal when one of the two biggest car makers in the world was caught cheating. This one brought the backlash against the car to Europe and raised it to a new level.

4

In petrol engines the fuel–air mixture is ignited with a spark. In diesel engines it is ignited by compression. This is mechanically efficient and consumes less fuel. As a result, European car makers, supported by the green lobby and green-minded politicians, spoke out for diesel. The manufacturers responded to the point where in the last decade petrol-powered cars became a minority of those on offer. In the UK incentives to buy diesels were so effective that by 2017 there were 12 million diesel cars on the road compared to 3 million in 2000.

Overlooked, ignored or simply unknown to car buyers was the inconvenient truth about the poisons that came out of diesel exhaust. True, carbon-dioxide emission is lower than petrol exhaust but diesel exhaust as a whole is classified as a Group 1 carcinogen associated with lung and bladder cancer. Then there are the particulates – soot, ash, abrasion particles, sulphates, etc. – which are inhaled deep into human lungs causing respiratory diseases. Carbon dioxide might, through global warming, kill millions in the future but diesel was killing people now.

America, however, did not make the same mistake. US makers and customers resisted diesel engines, partly because of a bad performance reputation dating back to the seventies and partly because of alarm about their high exhaust emission of particulates and nitrogen oxides (NOX). From 2005 European makers, especially Volkswagen, the leader in diesel technology, were eager to break into the American market. They announced the creation of new, cleaner diesel engines.

This was going well until researchers at West Virginia University rented two VWs to test emissions in 2013. They found the cars were emitting NOX at much higher levels than they had done in laboratory tests. The VWs were found to be equipped with a software 'defeat' mechanism which reduced emissions of NOX under regulatory test conditions; in the real world driving emissions were up to 40 times higher.

The truth was that it had proved impossible to combine fuel economy, performance and low emissions. The West Virginians, who had previously been 'diesel guys', were shocked. In 2014 they presented their findings at a conference in San Diego and in September 2015 the US Environmental Protection Agency accused Volkswagen of a violation of the Clean Air Act. This was not just happening in American imports. VW admitted that 11 million cars had defeat devices and 8 million of those were in Europe.

This was the company that had once made the Beetle and the Microbus, the preferred transport of the generation that believed in hitting the road and fighting capitalist oppression. But now VW had become a giant company – alongside Toyota it was the biggest car maker in the world – and it had cheated on a monumental scale.

The company was convulsed by the scandal but so was the entire car industry. Angela Merkel, the German chancellor, complained about the demonisation of diesel cars but the damage had been done. NOX is a more immediate, more urgent threat than carbon dioxide. People understood cancer and respiratory disease better than they did global warming. Diesel began to die. But so did cars as a whole – diesel made people sick and petrol made the entire planet sick. In 2018 Volkswagen announced that its next generation of internal-combustion cars starting in 2026 would be its last.

If diesel wasn't the road to lower emissions, then what was? Electricity obviously. 'What Volkswagen is really showing,' said Elon Musk, 'is that we've reached the limit of what's possible with diesel and petrol. The time has come to move to a new generation of technology.'

The assault on the car accelerated and expanded. Even electric cars were targeted. In the *Guardian* the outspoken and radical environmentalist George Monbiot said they were also part of the problem. Microscopic particles are thrown up by the friction between tyres and the road surface. These particles also end up in rivers and oceans. Electric cars are in this respect as bad as ICE-powered cars. Production of cars, any cars, generates emissions. Also, cars, any cars, create traffic.

In the *New York Times*, Farhad Majoo argued that it's not merely petrol that is the problem, it's the car. Cars are ridiculous objects that spend most of their time parked, they are no less ridiculous if they are being charged while parked. Such thoughts go back to the defenders of the wilderness and to the dismay of Lewis Mumford and others at the way cities have become places for cars rather than people. It is time, say the eco-radicals, to stop tinkering with the car and get rid of it entirely.

For whatever reason, this idea seems to have been adopted by the young. In the UK in 2018 a meta-analysis of transport trends by the Department of Transport found that the number of 17- to 20-year-olds with driving licences had fallen by 40 per cent since 1990. There was also a significant but smaller fall among 20 to 29 years old. Car usage had also fallen – there were 36 per cent fewer trips in cars.

There were various reasons suggested for this but the most significant was the rise of ride-hailing companies like Uber and Lyft – Transport Network Companies as they are known in the USA. They are much cheaper than taxis or car ownership and they are superior to public transport in that pick-ups and drop-offs are exactly where you need them to be. Who would need a car in the future? And, by then, who would need a driver?

5

The material bases of anti-car sentiment were clear. But deeper and older was an imaginative and spiritual disgust.

Patrick Hamilton was an English playwright and novelist. His play *Rope* (1929) became, though radically altered, an Alfred Hitchcock film. Another play, *Gas Light* (1938), was filmed twice, first by Thorold Dickinson and then, again, by Hitchcock. The term 'gaslighting', meaning a malign form of psychological manipulation, has now entered popular discourse.

Hamilton was a troubled man, the child of an alcoholic father, a trait he inherited and which, via cirrhosis of the liver, killed him at the age of 58 in 1962. Aged 27, he was badly disfigured when he was hit by a car when walking with his wife in Earls Court Road in London. It left him with an enduring dislike of cars.

The final part of his novel *Mr Stimpson and Mr Gorse* (1953) is a startling after-effect of that incident. Gorse is a psychopathic fraudster who has been given a car, a 'ravishingly new Sunbeam'. With no particular place to go he drives off, mulling complacently over his crimes. He 'thought himself as very much the master of himself and of his car. But he was the deluded victim of both – particularly of his car.'

Hamilton's focus then pulls back from Gorse to take in the whole of the country, a place invaded by 'beetles', the word he uses for cars. Gorse is diseased but so is the landscape made by cars. They have taken 'complete control of the country'. A war waged between beetles and humans. Humans surrendered and became the slaves of cars – 'their crawling yet pitilessly exacting new rulers'. Ever more people are killed by the beetles.

This monstrous image of cars as conscious, sadistic conquerors of humans and colonisers of the world reappeared in 1992 in a book-length illustrated poem entitled *Autogeddon* by Heathcote Williams. Born as John Henley Heathcote-Williams and educated at Eton, he became a ruthless anti-establishment writer, a hero of the arts world of the London left. He was not, therefore, a mover of mass sentiment. Nevertheless, in retrospect *Autogeddon* is a superb distillation of all the post-Nader sentiments that became, in our time, the funeral dirge of the car.

Williams starts out with the number of people killed by cars since 1885 – 17 million – and then imagines an alien visitor to earth who sees what Hamilton saw in his beetle invaders. The car is the dominant life form and people are just fuel cells, taken up by the car when it wishes to move and ejected when their power has gone.

The visitor goes on to anatomise the sexual, social, economic and religious desires that the car satisfies. He takes apart advertising images and slogans. An MG ad proclaims 'Beautiful body. A joy to handle. And rumoured to be rather fast.' 'Car as marital aid,' comments the visitor.

The visitor is mystified by 'the frequency/With which these containers are gouged open/And spattered with the blood of their contents'. He is intrigued by the psycho-sexual powers of the car: 'And the automobile becomes an orgone-accumulator/Stimulating shallow sexuality'.

Then he considers the full list of environmental crimes of the car. The work ends with dozens of quotes from newspapers, magazines and books lambasting the car and the world it has made. The last one, however, precedes the car. It comes from Lao Tzu, the author of the *Tao Te Ching*, a foundational text of Taoism: 'Give up haste and activity. Close your mouth. Only then will you comprehend the spirit of Tâo.'

So, for Williams the car's most heinous crime, a crime demanding the death penalty, is that it induces spiritual failure. In Lao Tzu's terms, in the frenzy of movement we are blind to the Tâo – the 'way', the supreme form of existence – or in the secular terms of environmentalism, we are fatally blind to the destruction of the planet. He was prescient; over the next 30 years this was to be transformed into anti-car sentiment strong enough to end the automotive era.

6

Robert Zemeckis's film *Who Framed Roger Rabbit?* (1988) was a brilliant slapdash combination of live action and animation. But it had a surprisingly serious theme – the destruction of the public transport system of Los Angeles and its replacement by a car monoculture. The animated characters are known as 'Toons' and their home is a district of LA called Toon Town. The villain of the piece is Judge Doom. His dream of the future is a city entirely taken over by the car and its needs – petrol stations, motels, fast food, billboards: 'My God, it'll be beautiful.'

The Toons represent a vibrant, chaotic urban culture which is being driven out of existence by the crazed car plans of Judge Doom. Zemeckis was probably familiar with the works of Jane Jacobs, who celebrated the organic grain of old city streets, and Lewis Mumford, who confronted the theme of spiritual failure and loss in the face of technology. The car was at the heart of Mumford's two-volume work *The Myth of the Machine*, which was published in 1967 and 1970. In the second volume, *The Pentagon of Power*, he almost goes as far as Hamilton and Williams in treating cars as sentient conquerors, desecrating the primeval landscape.

In this Mumford is following a long tradition of writers and adventurers who celebrated the natural world and feared for its future under industrialisation – the poet William Wordsworth, the transcendentalist philosopher Ralph Waldo Emerson, the 'Father of the National Parks' John Muir, Henry David Thoreau, author of *Walden*, the naturalist John Burroughs who accompanied Henry

Ford on his picnics and many more. This was a theme in Europe as well as the USA but it was particularly poignant for the Americans who saw their wilderness treasures as a match for the art and architecture of old Europe.

In the short film *Cars or People?* Mumford describes cars as 'the most influential of all our city planners'. They mutilate and deform not only cities but entire city regions – scattering fragments of the city over the whole countryside. Inside the city he noted the weird synergy between the car and elevator technology. High buildings were needed to suck up the drivers and passengers of the cars that daily invaded city centres.

The city, in the process, had become accessible but uninhabitable as cars demanded ever more space. The planners' solution – to build more roads – played into the hands of the tyrannical car. More roads just mean more traffic. And more cars mean more parking. According to Anthony Townsend, surface parking in Los Angeles now provides spaces for 19 million cars, consumes 200 square miles of land and has an estimated market value of $350 billion.

This tyranny became more effective because of the rise of the second-car family. Between 1950 and 1970 car ownership in America grew three times faster than the human population and the number of families owning more than one car jumped from 7 per cent to 29 per cent. By 2017 the figure had risen to 57 per cent. This has had a traffic multiplier effect. New roads became jammed as soon as they were built. Cities, once centres of human contact, have been redesigned in favour of a machine that reduces human contact to a bare minimum.

But spiritual forebodings and urban hells would not on their own be enough to turn the tide against the tyranny of the car. As Nader showed, to really threaten the automotive ascendancy you need bad engineers and good lawyers.

7

Half-time at the annual Super Bowl provides the most valuable TV advertising slot of the year. In 2012, with the world still recovering from the financial crash, the slot was taken by Chrysler and its three very American brands – RAM, Dodge and Jeep.

Clint Eastwood is walking the street at night – 'It's half-time
. . .' He speaks in a barrel-aged growl. 'It's half-time in America
too. People are out of work and they're hurting.' There's a low-key
montage of people out of work and hurting. But, he goes on, Motor
City is fighting back.

This is not quite what happened. In April and June 2009 Chrysler
and General Motors both crashed. They were saved by an $85 billion
government bailout to allow the companies to reorganise themselves
and break free of debt. GM emerged with the government holding
a majority of stock – it had been nationalised – and Chrysler was
owned by the United Auto Workers union and by Fiat. Ford survived
intact, though it still tried to be included in the bailout so that it
would not suffer from unfair competition.

The absolutist free-market ideology of neo-liberalism seldom
survives first contact with reality. This was an unusually graphic
example. These two great emblems of American capitalism were
just not very good at capitalism. The Japanese invasion had landed
more than 40 years before but Detroit still wasn't competitive with
the Asians.

Eastwood's startling script is rhetorically simple but politically
complex. The left were irritated because the government source of
the bailout wasn't mentioned; the right were even more irritated
because it celebrated the bailout as a great effort of the people. There
is another theme in the script – automotive nationalism. Industrial
power is at the heart of American identity and the car is its most
potent expression. So, bailing out GM is not just saving jobs – it is
also saving America in a sense that goes beyond politics. Charles
Wilson, when president of GM, once said, 'For years I thought what
was good for our country was good for General Motors, and vice
versa.' In other words, GM was more than a company; it was an
integral part of the state and of American success. No wonder it
was nationalised.

The negotiation of the bailout exposed, often comically, the
tone deafness of the Big Three. At one point all three CEOs flew
to Washington in their private jets – a gesture both extravagant and
environmentally unsound. The ensuing derision made the Ford boss
drive on his next visit and, finally, all three had to sell their planes
and work for $1 a year.

More importantly, the bailout exposed the failings of Detroit.

Toyota passed GM as the world's biggest car maker in 2007. A few years later GM would be languishing somewhere beneath Toyota, Volkswagen and Hyundai/Kia. The Big Three were still struggling with the idea of a small car and foreign competitors had better dispersed production facilities. Furthermore, 20 years after James Hansen's senate testimony, they had not embraced energy efficiency.

'If these companies,' said David Brooks in the *New York Times*, 'aren't permitted to go bankrupt now, they never will be.'

The economist Thomas Sowell drily observed that the owners and workers in the horse industry were not bailed out when after thousands of years, almost overnight, horses were made redundant by the car.

The bailout did work to the extent that the companies recovered. GM emerged from bankruptcy in 2009 and Chrysler now survives as a division of the Stellantis group that also includes Fiat, Peugeot, Citroën, Alfa Romeo, Opel and Maserati. But whether it was a good idea remains an open question. If GM and Chrysler had been allowed to fail, would that have led to the birth of smarter, better companies freed of the shackles of Detroit's complacent assumptions?

Whatever the answer to that question, the bailout was a pivotal moment for the car in the world. The great American makers had been humbled precisely because of their inability to take seriously or even recognise how different the twenty-first century was from the twentieth. And as Silicon Valley rose to become the newest, richest summit of American capitalism, Detroit, the previous summit, shrank in significance. Never again would GM bestride the world; never again would the Big Three lay claim to the future.

8

The backlash against the car will prove fatal, not just because of global warming and not just because of the end of the internal-combustion engine. Rather, it will be because technology will change the world of movement beyond recognition – first through increases in autonomous driving systems and second through a public transport environment based on developments in ride-hailing. Beyond that, maybe a world of virtual experience will remove the need to move at all. What cars remain will become like those scarcely driven hypercars in their garages or like horses, eloquent and beautiful reminders of a vanished way of life.

Audi design for interior of driverless car

Chapter Ten

ELECTRIFIED AUTONOMY

1

In 2019 Ross Hunt, a Dublin man, left Loki, a poodle, in his car, a Tesla Model S, while he went to a lunch meeting. It was a hot day and a passer-by was outraged by what he saw – a dog in a car without so much as a half-open window. He called the police to report this flagrant act of animal cruelty. Hunt was charged with violating Ireland's Animal Health and Welfare Act. He was cleared because, he explained, he was able to control the temperature inside his car from his phone. He had ensured Loki was comfortable at 20 degrees Celsius. It was quite clear, concluded the judge, that Hunt was a 'very loving, responsible and caring dog owner'.

This should have been obvious to the passer-by. The Tesla's huge touch screen would have been displaying in very large letters, 'My owner will be back soon. Don't worry! The A/C is on and it's 20 degrees C'. This was the Model S's 'Dog Mode'. It combines care for the dog and for the car – car windows were sometimes smashed by pedestrians desperate to save the life of a dog. Dog Mode was part of the V10 software update released by Tesla in 2019. This also included Caraoke – a singalong app – Automatic Lane Change, Tesla Theater and Joe Mode. The last – named after the man who brought up the problem – muted the alert and navigation sounds so that children in the back seat would not be disturbed.

No oil-spattered mechanic had to touch the car to install these features; the eager owner didn't even have to say he wanted them. V10 was an automatic download. Like the overnight updates on your phone, it arrives as an invisible gift delivered by no one from nowhere.

2

In November 1989 Sunraycer, a General Motors solar-powered machine with the appearance of an elongated cockroach, won the Solar Challenge in Australia. This was a 1,900-mile race from Darwin to Adelaide. Sunraycer completed the course in just over five days with a running time of 44.9 hours at an unprecedented average speed of 41.6 mph.

The Sunraycer had a highly efficient electric motor and a battery pack to smooth out performance and provide extra speed for over-taking slow-moving trucks. Solar was obviously not likely to power future cars on its own; people need to be able to drive at night, in fog and on cloudy days. But the battery and motor technologies were very promising. They inspired Roger Smith, then CEO of GM, to exhibit an electric car named the Impact at the 1990 Los Angeles Motor Show.

At this point Smith needed, as did all GM bosses since Nader trashed the company, some positive PR. Now more than ever, in fact, because also in the year of the Sunraycer success Michael Moore's career as a subversive filmmaker had suddenly taken off with his documentary *Roger & Me*. This was about GM's decision to close its factories in Flint, Michigan – Moore's hometown – and relocate to Mexico. The film is full of harrowing stories. It portrays a city eviscerated by mass unemployment. Moore goes in search of an interview with Smith to demand an explanation. Finally, he confronts him in Detroit. Moore insists his victim should travel to Flint to see the damage he has done. Smith, embarrassed, declines.

Once again GM was being portrayed as a cold-blooded corporate monster. So, a year after the Flint debacle, Smith's Impact was just the right sort of response to bad publicity; it was a car that felt young and free. It was well-received and GM launched itself into electric-car production. In 1996 the Impact became the EV1, a friendly-looking machine with a 55-mile range on lead-acid batteries and 105 miles on Nickel Metal Hydride (NiMH). It could hit 80 mph and accelerate from 0–60 in 9 seconds. This so impressed the California Air Resources Board (CARB) that they decided to require the production and marketing of zero-emission cars by seven car makers who wished to sell in California.

But then it all went horribly wrong and in 2006 GM was again pilloried by an alarmingly good documentary film – *Who Killed the Electric Car?* by Chris Paine. This was not the guerrilla filmmaking of Moore; this time big stars were involved – Martin Sheen, Ed Begley Jr, Mel Gibson, Ralph Nader of course and Tom Hanks, who at the time had never seen an electric car he didn't like. Hollywood had gone very green indeed.

GM's killing of the EV1 was more comical than sinister – though it was still sinister. In fairness, GM wasn't the only culprit. The EV1 was destroyed by politics, corporate greed and governmental cowardice. Many powerful people just didn't want it to work. That was bad enough but its end was so bizarre and so horribly handled that once again GM looked like the only bad guy.

Customers had only been able to acquire EV1s on leases and only in the cities of Los Angeles, Phoenix and Arizona – later San Francisco and Sacramento were included, as well as, to a limited extent, the State of Georgia. The idea was that this was an engineering and marketing evaluation. The leases freed GM of any responsibility for the parts-supply and service infrastructure for 15 years mandated by the State of California.

Chris Paine's film shows that the marketing aspect of the evaluation produced very positive results. People seemed to love the car. Simple to drive, it did all that an average lifestyle required of it. 'The electric vehicle is not for everybody,' said the Hollywood endorser Ed Begley Jr. 'It can only meet the needs of 90 per cent of the population.'

As a result, there were howls of protest when GM announced in 2002 it was to remove all 1,117 EV1s from the road. Customers tried to pay for extensions of their leases but GM returned their cheques. In contrast, Honda had also run a lease programme for its own electric EV Plus and when production ended the company promised to extend leases and continue to service the cars. But GM ploughed on with the removal and destruction of the EV1s, though 40 were donated to museums and educational institutes. It was a spectacular display of dumb wastefulness.

The whole project was finally cancelled in 2003 when the CEO was Rick Wagoner, a man whose name surely predestined him to become a car boss. He later said his worst decision was 'axing the EV1 electric-car program and not putting the right resources

into hybrids. It didn't affect profitability, but it did affect image.'
In 2009 Wagoner resigned at the request of the White House. It
was required as part of the Obama rescue package that saved GM
from bankruptcy. GM, it was felt, just wasn't making the right
cars.

3

The tide, as Wagoner must have realised, had turned but not yet
to the fully electric vehicle. The point often made about the EV1
was that clever though it was it needed people to pay good money
for a car that offered less than the car they already had. Primarily
it offered range anxiety and long recharging times. In return for
making you feel good about yourself, the electric car demanded
significant sacrifices.

The solution – a feelgood car requiring minimal sacrifice – had
already appeared a year before the launch of the EV1. In what
came to seem like a replay of the Corona that broke the American
market in 1964, Toyota launched a very odd-looking car at the 1995
Tokyo Motor Show; it was a curious, vaguely bean-shaped object.
It was known as the NHW10 or, more amiably, as the Prius, a Latin
word that means precursor. The Prius was indeed to be the great
precursor, John the Baptist preparing the way for the coming of the
saviour – the fully electric car. It is the second most important car to
be mentioned in this chapter.

Sadly, its importance was scarcely noted at the show. It was the
year of the Great Hanshin Earthquake and the nerve gas attack on
the Tokyo subway. The latter caused the show – entitled 'Dream the
Dream, a Car with That Feel' – to be shortened by two days. But
Toyota knew this was a revolutionary car and the launch in Tokyo
was extravagant. Huge video screens displayed scenes of birds and
skies – untouched nature – and a giant globe rotated on the stage
which then opened like an egg to hatch the planet's automotive
friend, the Prius. The unusually tall Toyota president Hiroshi Okuda
eased himself into the front passenger seat and Takeshi Uchiyamada, Toyota's chief engineer, drove the first Prius down the ramp onto
the ballroom floor of the ANA Hotel.

The Prius went on sale in 1997. The car was technologically

unique – a hybrid with a 1.5-litre petrol engine and an electric motor, a combination managed by a power-split device. And it was, by the standards of the day, very fuel efficient, attaining 40 miles per gallon in the city and 51 mpg on the highway. In spite of which, as a car, it was a package of pristine ordinariness – a four-door saloon. But it did look different; Uchiyamada had ordered designs from all of the company's studios. A focus group had chosen the winner, a design by a Japanese subsidiary.

The design choice was crucial. Later iterations changed the curvy saloon shape into more of a wedge shape and latterly a wedge with some spikey rear-light arrangements. But always the Prius stood out from the mass of small saloons and hatchbacks. Ordinary as it was, it was never anonymous, not least because some vociferous people hated it.

Jeremy Clarkson said the Prius is the car he would give to his worst enemy: 'Because that is a cynical marketing exercise for the gullible and the stupid.' After the launch of the Prius in America in 2000 and its prodigious success in California, it became a pawn in the bitter culture wars that still afflict that country. Owning a Prius was not just the opposite of owning a truck and a gun – it was an affront to truck and gun owners.

'The Prius is known as a hybrid,' said TV host Craig Ferguson, 'because it can run on either electricity or the smugness of the owner.' Then there was comedian Mo Mandel, who came up with this brilliant distillation of divided America: 'Yeah, that's my Prius, the one with the gun rack and the McCain sticker on the back and the dead deer carcass roped to the hood. Wouldn't that be sweet? Driving around in a Prius, throwing garbage out your window? "It's a Prius; I already helped the Earth, hippie!"'

None of which would have worried Toyota executives. Indeed, the sneers probably thrilled them. Not only did they keep the Prius front and centre, they also signalled that this was something different, a car for people who cared for the environment, not a virtue that was high on the list of an industrial culture still in thrall to the imaginations of Ford and Sloan.

Twenty-two years after the launch Toyota has been fully vindicated, having sold 15 million hybrid cars worldwide.

4

But to bring on the full electric era another automotive novelty was needed. The hybrid was a revolutionary car but it was also a green compromise with driving reality. GM was right to the extent that the EV1 could only ever be a niche product because not many people were ready to accept limited range and long charging times. The Prius solved those problems but it still consumed fossil fuel and emitted greenhouse gases.

Toyota was accidentally involved in the next big step. Scion was a Toyota marque launched in 2003. These were cars aimed at millennials born between the early eighties and the late nineties. The Scion xB, a conventionally powered five-door hatchback, had the square, toy-like appearance to which the Japanese are mysteriously drawn. There had previously been the Nissan Cube, launched in 1998, which also looked like a toy or, as some suggested, a clown car; it could have been driven by Hello Kitty. The xB, like the Cube, looked friendly, non-aggressive, different. Fatefully, it caught the attention of AC Propulsion, a California company specialising in electric drive trains.

In 2006 AC unveiled the eBox, an xB converted into an EV. A few months later the first production model was delivered to Tom Hanks. It was his second electric, the first being a converted Toyota Rav4. AC couldn't have found a better celebrity endorser. Everybody loves Hanks and he seemed to love EVs, making a sweet video about the joys of the xB. Environmental virtue-signalling had taken hold of Hollywood at the time but giving money to green causes and working with green NGOs did not catch the imagination quite as much as good ol' Tom scooting about LA in his eBox.

Long before the eBox, however, AC had made another, rather different EV. This was the tzero – the name is derived from a mathematical symbol denoting a starting point in time. It was a two-seater which could reach 60 mph in 4.07 seconds and, with care, could be driven without ever using the brake pedal – easing off on the throttle caused the car to lose speed rapidly as 'regenerative' braking kicked in to recharge the batteries. But only three were ever built and the tzero never made it into production. The tzero used lead-acid batteries – the same as the ones that start the internal-combustion car – which meant its range was poor.

In 2001 Martin Eberhard, an engineer and businessman, turned up at the AC works. He said it looked 'like a ghost town' but he gave the company $500,000 to build a car for him with lithium-ion instead of lead-acid batteries. Lithium-ion batteries had been quietly developing since the seventies. They are lighter and have much higher energy density than any previous batteries. Eberhard was a big fan. As a reward for his $500,000 investment AC built him a one-off lithium-ion-powered tzero. This had a 300-mile range and did 0–60 mph in 3.6 seconds.

Eberhard, along with Marc Tappening, another engineer/entrepreneur, had founded an electric-car company in 2003. It was called Tesla Motors in honour of Nikola Tesla, the strange genius behind alternating current, the Tesla coil, radio remote control and countless other devices. He is still surrounded by the quasi-magical aura of a seer and keeper of strange secrets rather than a mere scientist or engineer.

Eberhard and Tappening needed a new, big investor to keep their company going. Tom Gage at AC said he had heard of somebody who wanted to invest in electric cars, an 'angel' – i.e., enthusiast – rather than a straight moneymaker. They flew down to Los Angeles to meet a rather odd, blankly bland-featured man. After peppering the two men with questions, Elon Musk said, 'Okay, I'm in.' He gave them $6.5 million.

Musk saw the tzero on a visit to AC. He loved it in spite of the best efforts of the management to interest him in the eBox. He was never going to choose the eBox over the tzero. South African born, he was in his early 30s and rich thanks to his time at Zip2, an online city guide, and X.com and Paypal, online financial service systems. He had also started a space company, SpaceX, with the aim of turning humans into an interplanetary species, starting with Mars. His imagination, like the tzero, did not need brakes. He was only ever going to fail miserably or spectacularly succeed.

He became the lead investor in Tesla and rapidly rose to dominate the company. He has just become, at the time of writing, the richest man in the world. Forbes estimated his real-time net worth in January 2021 at $183.8 billion. The market value of Tesla, currently $800 billion, is consistently far higher than any of the Detroit,

Japanese or German car makers. This may be froth, an aspect of a post-pandemic 'innovation narrative' that marketing professor Scott Galloway believes has driven up all tech companies. But even without froth Tesla would still be way ahead of Detroit. Meanwhile, SpaceX has sent a crew to the International Space Station, saving America from the embarrassing problem, since the cancelling of the Space Shuttle programme, of relying on Russian rockets. Musk has not, so far, failed.

But it is still too early to tell if he will one day be seen as an automotive figure of the stature of Henry Ford, Alfred Sloan or Taiichi Ohno. If he is any of those, he is Ford. Sloan was about management structure first and cars second; Ohno was about production methods; Ford, in his supremacy, was only about a car, the Model T. It cannot be a coincidence that, like Ford, Musk calls his cars 'Model' with a following letter.

What his customers needed, in Musk's interpretation, was speed. In July 2006 he put his first car on display, the Tesla Roadster in bright red. It was, apart from its other virtues, hair-raisingly fast – 0–60mph in 3.7 seconds. The 2006 Ferrari F430 Berlinetta took a sluggish 3.8 seconds. Musk's first car was not aimed at the mass market – it was an electric supercar.

'Until today,' Musk said when he announced the Roadster, 'all electric cars have sucked.'

This chutzpah was part of the revolutionary novelty. He wasn't offering electric cars because they gave you less and were virtuous. He was offering them because they gave you more – primarily more speed. Going electric was not the opposite of owning a truck and a gun – it was much better, even much more macho. To ram the point home, in 2020 Musk unveiled the Tesla Cybertruck, a confection of points and angles more savage-looking than the most savage Lamborghini. Next to this the 6.4-litre Dodge Ram 2500 truck looks, frankly, childish. And even the Cybertruck will be absurdly fast – 0–60 in 4.5 seconds in the dual motor version. Finally, enough never being enough for Musk, his promised full-sized semi (tractor–trailer) is said to do 0–60 in 5 seconds.

Even geographically Musk is an outlier. The American car industry is based in the Mid-West; Detroit is its capital. But Musk's Tesla is in California where the capital is Silicon Valley. His cars are made of electronics more than they are of steel or carbon fibre. He built the iPad long before Apple – his version was the touchscreen controller of almost every function in his next car, the Model S, the most important car in this chapter. Conceptually, it was a big iPad with a car attached.

Furthermore, Musk didn't sell his cars through dealers but through stores modelled on the Apple store – clean modernist design combined with a clean modernist sales staff. No Dick Balches or Cal Worthingtons here.

In popular culture the sheer bland-featured exoticism of the man turned him into a superhero. Jon Favreau's film *Iron Man* (2008) starred Robert Downey Jr as a prodigiously gifted inventor and businessman who designed a suit for himself that turned him into a new iteration of Superman. At once the assumption was made that Downey's performance as Tony Stark was based on Musk – they certainly met when Musk gave the actor a tour of the SpaceX plant. Riding this wave, in 2010 Musk appeared in *Iron Man 2* as himself. Stark meets him at a reception. Musk says he has an idea for an electric jet. 'You do?' replies Stark. 'Then we'll make it work.' He even appeared, again as himself, in the comedy show *The Big Bang Theory* as a volunteer kitchen hand in a charity shelter. As an actor, he was terrible, but who cared? He just had to turn up.

5

In spite of all that there was an alarming gap between the Roadster and the Model S, which did not go on sale until 2012. It looked as though Musk was losing the initiative and allowing the established manufacturers to own the electric future. The all-electric Nissan Leaf, released in 2010, was ominous.

The Leaf was everything the Roadster and the S were not. It was, in appearance, extravagantly ordinary – a small, five-door hatchback like numerous other small, five-door hatchbacks. Aerodynamically it was somewhat unusual – the strange, bulging headlight enclosures, for example, were designed to deflect airflow away from the wing mirrors. But, other than that, there was nothing to alarm the average car buyer. The performance, meanwhile, was even less alarming – 0–60 in 9.9 seconds and a top speed of 93 mph. Carlos Ghosn, chairman and CEO of the Renault–Nissan Alliance, was not, like

Musk, going for the speed-freak market. He believed that if the EV had a future, it lay with the mass market. 'He was,' says car writer Gavin Green, 'the first established car company CEO to spot the upcoming revolution, though even he underestimated how profound it would become.'

The Leaf endures, but sadly Ghosn is now a fugitive from Japanese justice. He was accused of claiming 'questionable expenses' amounting to €11 million. In December 2019 he was 'exfiltrated' from Tokyo by former US special forces soldiers and is now in Lebanon.

Elon Musk, meanwhile, is free and one of the richest people in the world. He somehow managed to navigate the intervening profitless years between the Roadster and the S amidst the mounting incredulity of his critics. This was, basically, a story of extreme brinkmanship, of doing two of the most expensive things in the world – building cars and rockets – while tap-dancing his way round all obstacles and even having the nerve to float Tesla on the stock market in 2010. Jalopnik.com, the car website, was incredulous, dismissing the move as a Hail Mary pass.

The scepticism was reasonable but, in the event, misplaced. An astounding ten-year turnaround had begun when Tesla rounded a financial corner in 2010. First, the company won a $465 million loan from the Department of Energy and, second, Musk managed to buy a factory in Fremont, next to Silicon Valley, at a knock-down price. This had, since 1984, been the home of New United Motor Manufacturing Inc., a joint venture between General Motors and Toyota intended to bring together Japanese and American car-making skills. It did produce millions of cars like the Chevrolet Nova and the Toyota Corolla but GM pulled out as the financial crash drove it into bankruptcy. Tesla paid $42 million for most of the site and in return Toyota bought a 2.5 per cent stake in Tesla for $50 million. Musk had, in essence, acquired the factory and its very useable tools for nothing.

6

Finally, in 2012, the Model S came on the market and everything changed. The S upended the motor industry, not least by showing that the Nissan Leaf was not the only possible or inevitable type of EV.

'It proved,' says Gavin Green, 'that EVs don't have to be little city runabouts, which is what the "old school" car industry thought, although many thought battery electric cars had no future at all. Musk showed EVs could be cars for the highway as well as the high street. He also proved they could be premium in pricing, spec and performance. These were major shocks for the old guard carmakers.'

This was, as Bradley Berman noted in the *New York Times*, a Model T moment: 'Put simply, the automobile has not undergone a fundamental change in design or use since Henry Ford rolled out the Model T more than a century ago. At least that's what I thought until I spent a week with the Tesla Model S.'

Green agrees: 'It is probably the most significant car since the Model T. It has revolutionised the motor industry, just as the Model T did ... The Model S proved that electric cars could be highly desirable, good to drive and popular, and paved the way for the EV revolution that's coming.'

Berman described the car as 'stylish, efficient, roomy, crazy fast, high-tech and all electric'. He also compared the look of the car to Maseratis, Jaguars and Aston Martins. It had the best drag coefficient in the world, better even than the Prius, which nobody would ever compare to an Aston Martin. 'Crazy fast' meant the car Berman drove could hit 60 mph in 5.6 seconds. The more powerful version could do that in 4.4 seconds. (In 2021 the Plaid version of the Model S was announced; it has 1,020 hp and its 0–60 speed is around 2 seconds.) Berman also noticed the way the power was delivered in 'silent, near instantaneous bursts'.

This was a high-end car. The price started at $77,000. Its technology had been tried out on two Mercedes CLSs that Tesla had eviscerated in order to fit in the batteries. And the big Mercedes market was the one the S targeted. Imitating Apple, whose computers and phones are more expensive but much more beautiful than those of its competitors, Tesla was aiming to break into the car market from the top. Something like a mass-market car, the Model 3, did not arrive until 2017. It became the bestselling all-electric car ever; half a million were delivered by spring 2020.

And, above all, the S was not just exciting to drive; it was morally exciting to own, socially exciting for the status-seeker and sexually

exciting for the horny. Scott Galloway says the S owner is simultaneously saying 'I'm rich' and 'I have a conscience'. But he is also saying
he is an innovator and he has 'genes paramount to the survival of
the species'. The lawyer who drives an S isn't merely a lawyer, he is
a 'visionary rebel'. Moreover, the glamour of the entire enterprise
and the high-risk swagger of Musk made Detroit look slow-witted
and outdated.

The S was the gold standard or, rather, the game changer. When I
drove one, I first noticed the giant 17-inch iPad-like object that was
the dashboard. But I found the silent-burst phenomenon the most
startling feature of the car. An internal-combustion engine does not
deliver all its power at once – it has to run through the gears to
attain higher speeds. The power, the torque, of an electric engine is
all there at once so it needs no gears. The combination of the electronics, the silence and this all-there-all-at-once quality made me
realise that the age of the ICE car really was ending. The high-end
S was terminating the car culture created by the T, the people's car.

But it wasn't just the car. In the same year the S was launched,
Tesla began building a network of Supercharger stations. The
Supercharger was and remains the fastest recharging system; there
are now 20,000 around the world. At one level this was simply a
marketing device. Range anxiety – the fear of finding yourself stuck
in the middle of nowhere without so much as a domestic electrical
point – is the most glaring disincentive to buying an EV. Furthermore, charging takes time, adding hours to a long journey. The
Superchargers are fast and increasingly available.

At another level, Musk was creating an ecosystem in which his
cars could function. At this point he was simply replacing the petrol
pump with a charger. In years to come this ecosystem will expand to
include aids to autonomy and roads and cities will be redesigned yet
again, this time to service vehicles driven by artificial intelligence.
Everything about the S proclaimed the approaching full digitisation
of automotive culture. This was, like the Prius, the great precursor.

'Driving it felt like being in a video game,' said Neil Cosgrove, the
friend whose S I drove, 'with scenery rushing at you but no noise or
other feel of speed. I loved the fact that it was a faster, more exciting
and cheaper family car than many high-end gas-guzzling supposed
sports cars.'

But there have been questions raised about Tesla reliability and service back-up. The most spectacular expression of this was at the Shanghai Auto Show in 2021. A woman leapt on top of a ruby red Tesla Model 3 and cried out that the car's brakes were faulty. Her action was defended by Xinhua, the state news agency: 'China is one of the world's largest auto markets, and it is an important market for which renowned global carmakers are vying. No matter which carmaker, it must have a respect for the Chinese market and accept the supervision from the consumers.'

This is, to say the least, suspicious. With three big Chinese companies aiming to compete with Tesla, a stunt like this could be just what they needed.

Nevertheless, for Musk and the investors who have driven his share price skyward, service back-up and good reliability are essential. Electric cars need very little servicing compared to ICE cars so it is not necessary to build a huge network of garages and parts warehouses. But it is necessary to provide *enough* service to keep the customers happy and loyal. The old car makers already have those networks and they are now working on or producing electric cars. They may not need to be quite as good or exciting as Teslas but they only need to provoke less anxiety to attract buyers.

7

It is, however, possible that electric cars might not be the future. Hydrogen power – in the form of a new kind of ICE or a fuel cell – could still win in the end. But, for the next decade, too much money has been spent by too many people for electric to fail. There can be little doubt that by 2030 electric cars will be dominant. This will be aided by price drops. There is currently what Bill Gates calls a 'green premium' on electric cars – they cost significantly more than their ICE equivalents. But Gates estimates this premium will have dropped to zero by 2030.

Toyota, which has so far stuck to hybrids rather than full electrics, might again change the game in this period. It is still hedging its bets with FCVs – fuel-cell vehicles in which power is provided by hydrogen – but the company is also working on solid-state batteries. Lithium-ion is a kind of gel; solid-state batteries are solid. They last longer, are less of a fire risk, charge quicker – not much longer than a petrol fill-up – and provide better range. Toyota says ten minutes' charging will get you 500 kilometres. There are problems. The batteries are not so good in cold conditions and they might not be as durable as lithium-ion. Nevertheless, Toyota is close to selling a solid-state SUV and both Nissan and Volkswagen are heading in the same direction.

Most governments currently agree with the 2030 date for electric cars to become dominant. In November 2020 the British government announced its intention to stop the sale of petrol and diesel cars by 2030. California and Japan are aiming to do the same by 2035, France by 2040, India by 2030 and so on. Globally it is expected that there will be up to 130 million EVs on the road by 2030, less than 10 per cent of the current world total but still a lot of cars. These are very ambitious targets and this is a very ambitious strategy – currently only about 0.3 per cent of cars in Europe are electric.

In addition, entire industrial and power-generating systems will have to be transformed. For a start there will be the cost of providing charging networks. In the UK this might cost £100 billion, a figure oil and energy companies might have no choice but to cover. Then there is the question of where all this new electricity will come from. A study by Transport for London suggested that all-electric vehicles in the city would consume five times as much as the London Underground. In the USA, California alone would need 50 per cent more electricity if all cars were electric.

This would be a high price to pay for carbon emission savings which some say would be much less than we think. An EV is still a car and as such will still need carbon-heavy production methods. The materials of batteries, meanwhile, are very carbon intensive to mine and transport. A study from the International Energy Agency suggested that an EV with a 400-kilometre range would have to be driven 60,000 kilometres just to pay off its emissions debt. In some contexts electric cars can actually increase carbon emissions. China is heavily dependent on coal for its power generation and it is the leading market for electric cars.

One strikingly original fix for this could be the Airo, an electric and potentially driverless car by the British designer Thomas Heatherwick, though this would be Chinese-built. Not only would this be emission-free, it would also suck up emissions from other vehicles.

As air flows under the car, it passes through a Hepa – high efficiency particulate air – filter, a device used to clean air in aircraft cabins. Whether people will be willing to pay for this act of automotive generosity remains to be seen.

But these emphases on emission reduction and customer acceptance of EVs could be the least of our problems. The real problem might be one that is seldom if ever discussed in debates about EVs. As Bob Hancké and Laurenz Mathei of the London School of Economics argue, the real issue is the political management of what could be disruptive carnage in the entire car-production chain.

EVs, they point out, are much simpler machines. They consist of only about 6,000 parts; petrol-powered cars have 20,000. The industrial-age glories of the internal-combustion engine will be replaced by an engine that is 'not qualitatively different' from the one in your washing machine. Only the software is complex and that is made not by factory workers in Germany or the UK, but by code-writers who usually live in Silicon Valley. Material skills are being replaced by dematerialised skills; a Tesla can be re-engineered from a laptop. And so these new machines require neither a skilled industrial work force to assemble them nor highly trained engineers in a long, complex supply chain.

The implications are seismic. Unions, engineers and managements might reasonably see the transition as a disruption too far: 'The foundations are laid for a failed transition, a social bloodbath, or an extinct European car industry.'

For Germany the problems will be most acute. Car production is a source of justified national pride. The high-productivity, high-skilled and highly paid parts producers of southern Germany are, say the authors, 'the envy of the world'. They employ 500,000 people. But 'without active shaping of the transition, they would go from among the wealthiest regions in the world to some of the poorest'. Hancké and Mathei conclude, 'The shift to electric cars is an instance where social calamities and political battles are almost easier to imagine than a cooperative solution.'

Such concerns are likely to be greeted with a shrug by the coders of Silicon Valley. Disruption to them is an unarguable virtue and their future is a text that is already written. Something similar has happened to other industries – coal mining, newspapers, retail – so what's the problem? And, in any case, the EVs are just the start.

8

Between 1949 and 1961 GM staged an annual 'Motorama'. This was intended to whip up enthusiasm for the company's future plans. The 1956 show was particularly spectacular and successful – it was seen in five cities and drew 2.2 million visitors. Cars – actual and possible – were the point of the show but so were all future domestic technologies. One ten-minute film – *Design for Dreaming* – captured the quaint, camp madness of it all.

A sleeping woman is woken by a man in white tie and tails who offers to take her to the place where tomorrow meets today, which turns out to be the Waldorf Astoria Hotel. Having first swooned over the cars on display, the woman is swept off to the kitchen of the future. This is comprehensively automated in the most bizarre and, as far as the actual future is concerned, inaccurate ways. What is striking is the loss of human agency in the cooking process. While the woman plays golf or tennis or dances, somehow the cake gets baked.

The woman performs the 'Dance of Tomorrow', which then segues into a series of cars accompanied by more swooning women. The climax of this process is the appearance of a car 'designed for the electronic highway of the future', the Firebird II. She flies, literally, into the car and is joined by the white-tie guy who takes off his mask to reveal that he is, I think, her husband. He announces, 'Firebird II to Control Tower, we are about to take off on the Highway of Tomorrow.' The language is that of flight and indeed the Firebird II looks like a plane with its glass dome and jet-engine-like intakes. Even the extravagant tail fins of the day have become a single gigantic fin that looks exactly like an aircraft's vertical stabiliser.

Most importantly, there is no steering wheel on the car – it navigates itself around the sweeping Jetson or possibly Flash Gordon landscape of electronic highways. The couple just smile and love every minute of it. Idle humans had found their driverless car amidst the fifties imagery of googie architecture, sci-fi comics and frictionless, controlled traffic.

There had been autonomous-car stillbirths before the war. Leonardo Torres y Quevedo justified his first name by becoming a polymath – an engineer and mathematician, he created a mechanical chess player, a new form of airship, a calculating machine and a radio-controlled, riderless tricycle. The latter would have seemed a pleasant enough diversion but it was a precursor of a wave that will soon engulf us.

More seriously, in 1921 the US Army revealed a strange, three-wheeled, coffin-like object in the streets of Dayton, Ohio. This too was radio-controlled and driverless.

More promising and certainly more sensational, however, was the American Wonder which appeared on the streets of Manhattan in 1925. This was a Chandler Sedan from whose roof projected a large aerial. It was closely followed by another car. This rig was the invention of an ex-army engineer named Francis P. Houdina. The Wonder was driverless, controlled by radio signals from the following car. It encountered all the problems encountered by contemporary AV (autonomous vehicle) designers. It did not, in short, go well. The car swerved uncontrollably, only narrowly avoiding serious collisions. Nevertheless, Houdina inspired imitators. But these seemed to be fairground attractions rather than useable cars. After all, if you had to drive along behind, why not dispense entirely with the driverless Wonder?

But the idea was now out there. In 1935 Chevrolet made a short film called *The Safest Place*. It begins, mysteriously, with a large sailing ship struggling in a storm followed by a man singing in his bath. As he climbs out he narrowly misses slipping on a bar of soap. After further near misses, the commentator announces you are not even safe at home. Then a couple walk up to a car: 'Here is the safest place to be,' intones the voice-over, 'in the modern home on wheels.'

Roads and cars are made as safe as possible but then there's the problem of the driver. This could be solved: 'With an automatic driving mechanism the car would always do what it should do when it got out on the road.' A driverless car is shown on the road, carefully following all possible safety procedures. But it turns out to be a stunt – the car does not exist. The remainder of the film exhorts drivers to drive as rationally and carefully as the fantasy Chevy AV.

The film is quaintly absurd but it is also prescient. It celebrates road design and the safety features of the car as ideal rule-makers which the human driver must obey. The very existence of the film suggests the driver is not expected to live up to these standards. This was reasonable enough – 35,000 people died on American roads in

1935. By 1956, when the Firebird II went on show, the figure had risen to 38,000.

The contrast between machine perfection and human blood-spilling fallibility was to provide the ostensible rationale for the overthrow not just of the ICE car but also of the human-driven electric car. We are just not good enough to be trusted with these machines that without humans at the wheel would be perfectly safe.

But driverlessness remained a dream state. Everybody had under-estimated the complexity of the task and nobody had the technology to make it work. This began to change in the mid eighties when Carnegie Mellon University's Navlab, funded by the Defense Advanced Research Projects Agency (DARPA), began work on AVs. In 1995 the NavLab 5, a Pontiac Trans Sport minivan, drove itself across America from Pittsburgh to San Diego. The average speed was 60 mph and only 50 of the 28,000 miles involved a human controller. In 2008 the minivan was inducted into the Robot Hall of Fame, another Carnegie Mellon project.

All of which was fun but driverlessness suddenly became serious when, on 17 January 2009, Google launched an AV project. This was supposedly secret but was exposed by the *New York Times* in October 2010: 'A Prius equipped with a variety of sensors and fol-lowing a route programmed into the GPS navigation system nimbly accelerated in the entrance lane and merged into fast-moving traffic on Highway 101, the freeway through Silicon Valley.'

The article included a brief but comprehensive report of all the claimed AV virtues: robots react faster than humans; they do not get sleepy or distracted; they will save lives and double the capacity of roads because they can drive close together; they can also be made lighter because crash protection will be unnecessary. And so on. The removal of risk was the big sell. Cars kill and maim people so who could argue with cars that couldn't? And, in fact, who could argue with Google, a company whose market capitalisation had just passed that of General Electric in 2009?

In 2014 Apple – market cap then $700 billion, that of General Motors $57 billion – secretly but really not so secretly launched Project Titan, with the aim of building an autonomous car. This has remained secret but not so secret ever since. Sometimes it's on; sometimes it's off. Sometimes the whole car is made by Apple; some-times it will be made by Hyundai.

Meanwhile, there had been what Daniel Yergin calls 'a whirlpool of hookups'. Toyota set up a $1 billion autonomous research partnership with MIT and Stanford. Google spun off its autonomous project as Waymo and has set up a driverless taxi service in Phoenix. Ford spent $1 billion on Argo AI. Apple put $1 billion into DiDi, a Chinese ride-hailing service. German car makers spent $3.1 billion on a mapping system from Nokia. GM put $500 million into Lyft and bought a start-up called Cruise Automation for $1 billion.

The blending of ride-hailing and driverless cars arises because of the huge financial interest the hailers have in the idea. Uber, Lyft and others will only really come into their own when they can dispense with drivers. But it is also easier to make AVs that work as taxis rather than handing them over to the vagaries of families and commuters.

But the real problem of developing an AV is not software, it is philosophy.

9

Philippa Foot was a British philosopher; she died in 2010, the year we all learned about Google's AV project. She was one of the leading figures in virtue ethics, a form of moral philosophy derived from Aristotle. Other forms of moral philosophy tend to be based on calculations like the greatest good for the greatest number (utilitarianism) or on rule-following (deontology). In virtue ethics there is no calculation and no duty, there is primarily just virtue, a moral posture within the individual directed towards goodness. At the centre of this is the concept of eudaimonia, a state of human flourishing or blessedness. Eudaimonia is the only aspect of moral philosophy that I do not find ridiculous in that it seems to refer to the way lives are actually lived.

AVs come crashing into these apparent abstractions when we come to one of Foot's most celebrated inventions (with Judith Jarvis Thomson), now known as the 'Trolley Problem'. A trolley – I prefer tram – is out of control; it is heading for five people who are tied to the tracks and unable to move. You are watching and you have a lever which operates points that will switch the direction of the tram. If you do nothing, the tram will kill all five people; if you switch the tracks, it will kill one other person you have just noticed.

You may think the solution is obvious – you kill one person as opposed to five. This is the utilitarian solution. But imagine, argues Foot, you are a judge. Rioters are demanding action for a crime – they want a man they believe to be guilty to be executed; if he isn't, they will kill five other people. The judge knows the man is innocent. What does he do? Clearly, to execute the innocent man the judge must abandon everything that he stands for. Doing nothing is most closely aligned to his primary virtue – assuming he is an honest judge – but it will result in the death of five people.

Unless you are a complete non-driver, you will see where this is heading. Driving does not seem a complex activity because drivers do it so much that they do not need to engage consciously with everything they are doing from moment to moment. They have an unconscious sense of everything that is happening around them – every movement of every car, pedestrian, cyclist or motorcyclist, every obstruction, every sound – that only becomes conscious when something goes wrong: a cyclist swerves or a pedestrian steps blindly out into the road. And when something does happen, the driver might find himself in the midst of a Trolley Problem. Only it needn't manifest as such – the driver is most likely to react quickly and without thought. In other words, the driver needs to be human.

The problem AV engineers face is that for all the noise and hype about artificial intelligence, robotics and computing power, nobody has yet designed anything remotely human or intelligent. Machines may seem to interact with you, they may seem to do so affectionately or seriously, but they know nothing. They don't even know you exist nor indeed that they or the world exists. It is easy to say they will get there – and they might – but much more difficult to see how.

AV research has been coping with this by piling on ever more computing power. This is getting out of hand. One scientist pointed out that 'the amount of software these processors run is greater than the combined amount of software in the Chevy Volt, the F-35 fighter jet and Facebook'. Or machines – more credibly – will learn by experience in more or less the same way that humans do.

Either way, getting there is proving dangerous as well as difficult. In Heibei, China, Gao Yuning, a 23-year-old, was killed when his Tesla running its Autopilot software crashed into a stationary truck. In Florida another Tesla running Autopilot hit a semi, killing Joshua

Brown. In Texas two men died, neither of them in the driving seat, while taking a Model S out for a spin – there is, at the time of writing, confusion about whether the Autopilot AV system was engaged. In Arizona a driverless Uber car hit and killed Elaine Herzberg. And so on.

One answer to that is: cars with drivers kill people all the time so what's the big deal? But, of course, the unique selling proposition for AVs is that they are safer than humans. If they are not, what's the point? And getting killed or maimed by a robot somehow feels a good deal more annoying than by a human.

Nevertheless, money is being poured into making driverless cars work. There is a frenzy in the air, a gold rush. Drivers may soon be able to take their hands off the wheel on motorways, allowing automated lane keeping systems – ALKS – to take over. This is surely premature. Insurers are nervous that drivers will become over-confident in these systems. Furthermore, who has to pay up when fully autonomous cars crash – the driver, the software designers, the car company? If it is the driver, then that will be a powerful incentive not to use autonomous systems.

But doubtless something workable will emerge. The interior decorators seem pretty convinced.

10

There are five levels of driverlessness: one might be power steering or cruise control; two is when the car itself can take over a limited amount of control if the driver tells it to; in three the car detects the environment and makes a few decisions for itself; four is self-driving mode, mainly in urban conditions and with some human interventions; five is fully autonomous – no steering wheel, etc.

Ikea is already working on level five. It has a division called Space10, a 'future living lab where we explore better, more meaningful and more sustainable ways of living—based on the needs of people'. One of those needs is something to do in a vehicle in which everybody is a passenger. One possibility is changing it into something other than a car – a 'Space on Wheels'. This might be a café, an office, a hotel or a shop.

'The day fully autonomous vehicles hit our streets,' said Bas van de Poel of Space10, 'is the day cars are not cars anymore – they could be anything.' So the death of the car might lead to the death of anything remotely resembling a car.

Also in Scandinavia, Volvo has designed a self-driving sleeping cabin and in Germany Audi is working on a long-wheelbase A8 redesigned as a 'Long Distance Lounge'. It has a single large door and a wooden floor. You can move the seats around. There's also augmented-reality technology with foldable screens.

Advertising executive and journalist Rory Sutherland, who pines for the days when there were picnic tables in Rolls-Royces, is familiar with this idea of the car as accommodation and leisure vehicle. He tried to persuade Ford to go down to Elkhart, Indiana, 'the RV [recreational vehicle] capital of the world': 'I said to Ford the car as accommodation and leisure vehicle – and mobile office even – will have a future . . . There's something about RV design. It's fascinating because there's an intelligent and efficient use of space, unlike home architecture which is incredibly wasteful. And you also notice that every RV now on the passenger side in the front has a massive fold-down desk.' This suggests that vehicles like the Dormobile and the Microbus are no longer relics of a forgotten past – they are portents of the driverless future.

'In future commutes,' says Robin Li, CEO of Chinese tech company Baidu, 'you won't have to focus much on driving anymore. You'll be able to have hot pot and sing karaoke on the ride.'

Yet there is something creepy about this level-five world in which driving has been banished entirely. Moving about has become a passive activity. For tough-minded driving lovers like Matthew Crawford, this is not a small thing. AVs represent a freedom-destroying victory over the driver's experience of serendipity, contingency, and faith and joy in their own competence.

11

Level-fivers would be passive spectators, led by algorithms through a dematerialised landscape and 'smart cities' where traffic movement, zoning and almost everything else will be centrally controlled. These smart cities represent a reversal of the finest urban thought of the twentieth century. Most influentially, Jane Jacobs spoke out in favour of urban areas that grew out of human interactions. 'Cities,' she said, 'have the capability of providing something for everybody only because and only when they are created by everybody.' And Lewis Mumford said, 'Forget the damned motor car and build cities for lovers and friends.'

These would be laughable sentiments to believers in smart cities – they are sometimes chillingly called 'ubiquitous cities'. The new thinking is literally inhuman, as it is based not on human behaviour but on technical capability. They are, in essence, big data systems from which are derived planning, transport, security and building programmes. There are already smart cities being built from the ground up – Songdo in South Korea, Masdar in Abu Dhabi – but elements of smartness are being introduced in many large cities around the world.

The advocates of smartness say they are doing these things 'for' people whereas in truth they are doing things 'to' people. In a brilliant critique of the idea the sociologist Richard Sennett detected a link between the smart city and Ford's mass production system: 'Urbanites become consumers of choices laid out for them by prior calculations of where to shop, or to get a doctor, most efficiently. There's no stimulation through trial and error; people learn their city passively.'

For Sennett a city is not a suffocating, all-controlling machine. Instead it should be a place where everything works well enough and is open to 'the shifts, uncertainties, and mess which are real life'.

But the techno-babble deafens people to such thought with talk of low-latency connectivity, autonomous drones as air taxis, smart urban agriculture and intelligent traffic management. Smart cities are the ultimate eco-systems for driverless vehicles. Just as once cities changed to accommodate the car, so they are now changing to make way for AVs and air taxis. These are all systems of surveillance and control; ultimately no movement in the smart city will go unlogged.

This will not be freedom; these will not be cars. So, as Audi's living rooms and Ikea's mobile hotels and cafés glide by, I hope I shall not be alone in shouting, 'Get a car!'

Epilogue

The car was born and its infancy spent in the Gilded Age in America and La Belle Époque in Europe. These were optimistic years of peace at home, economic growth, and literary and artistic radicalism. The nineteenth century was being swept away in a wave of creativity. Change became normal and desirable. Complacency reigned until, in Sarajevo on 28 June 1914, Gavrilo Princip shot Archduke Franz Ferdinand. Change can be good or bad but frequently it is total and catastrophic.

We are in another age of peace and plenty. Complacency, in spite of all our fussing and fighting about competing values, reigns. Change, now called disruption, is again celebrated as an unquestionable – in fact, the ultimate – good. And the car is being changed out of existence. Perhaps this time we can make better choices about what comes next.

We are back in 1885 and this time Karl Benz and Bertha Ringer have been replaced by Elon Musk, the creator and promoter of a new age. The age of the horse lasted six millennia; that of the internal-combustion-powered car will have lasted a mere century and a half. What comes next will be nothing like what came before. It might be better or it might be worse. Technological change offers promises but no guarantees.

The transition from horse to car was not smooth. Jobs and craft traditions were all but destroyed and an entire vision of how the world worked, how humans navigated space and time, was wiped out. No wonder people were affronted by the appearance of early cars. No wonder they cried, 'Get a horse!' as they passed. What they really meant was: let us continue in the way of life we know.

Horses, in their decline, were condemned, found guilty of causing death, disease and ecological disaster. Cars are now being similarly condemned. The technological, political, cultural and environmental convergence that will end the reign of the fossil-fuel-powered, human-driven car and its replacement by ever-increasing forms of algorithmic control precisely mirrors the overthrow of the horse.

We might shrug. Change happens. We might even embrace the disruptive code of Silicon Valley: all change is good. This is obviously self-serving, usually false and, like all change, it can be catastrophic. In any case, the shift from horse to car and the brevity of the car's reign indicate that we have entered a new phase in which change is accelerating. Ways of life in the future might last a few years, months or even days – the faster the better for Silicon Valley's bottom line.

The car has been the great precursor of an age in which technology – not politicians, not armies, not religions, not poets or artists – will end ways of life and start new ones. In a world subject to constant technology-driven change each way of life becomes a mere stepping stone on the way to the present and the future; the past is cancelled. The post-car, algorithm-driven world order will arrive trailing clouds of glory signalling a new golden age but one day soon this too will be condemned and its cancellation celebrated. All that endures is the difference between the approved now and the cancelled then.

What, we can hope, should endure after the advent of a new way of life is an understanding of what just happened, of what has been gained and what lost. Ways of life cannot simply be dismissed as mistakes – they are the choices whereby people make sense of the world. We should know how and why they chose as they did. As Ulrich Raulff puts it, 'To describe the separation of man and horse is one thing, to seek to find meaning and purpose in their former cohabitation is something else entirely.'

The former cohabitation of humans and cars is now what is to be understood. For the age of the horse Raulf found three purposes and meanings: it converted grass into energy; it created knowledge and conveyed experience; it inspired emotions of 'pride and admiration, desire for power and lust for freedom, fear, joy and compassion'. Replace grass with oil and all three could also be said of the car.

Freedom is the primary meaning in that it makes all the others possible. The horse certainly conferred freedom on those few who could afford one; the train conferred a qualified freedom on more

people; the car conferred almost unfettered freedom, thanks initially
to Henry Ford, on billions more. The car emancipated the masses
far more effectively than any political ideology; that it did so at a
cost should not obliterate the importance of that freedom.

Some, perhaps all, of that freedom might be lost if the new vehicles
and smart cities become, as now seems likely, tools of surveillance
capitalism or autocratic surveillance states. Who then will be able to
claim that the post-car world is an unalloyed improvement?

The car also gave us new ways of seeing and a new sense of
space: the countryside unfurling as we pass, the possibility of
the almost endless road, journeys shrunk from days or weeks to
hours, all accomplished by a few movements of the driver's feet
and hands. Furthermore, the creation and evolution of the car was
a spectacular display of human ingenuity and intelligence. The
internal-combustion engine is an extraordinary, improbable device
in which tightly controlled flames reliably produce smooth, flexible
power. The entire drive train is miraculous, the suspension system
a delight, the bodywork full of aerodynamic cunning. We forget all
about those things simply because they work so well.

They should be a source of wonder. They once were. E.B. White
said about the Ford Model T, 'Mechanically uncanny, it was like
nothing that had ever come to the world before.' Soichiro Honda
as a toddler chased after the first car he saw. People were stunned,
thrilled or horrified by the sight and sounds of Bertha's Motorwagen
as it passed. In Britain a man in front with a red flag was required to
mitigate the threat of this new machine.

For some, first contact with a car might have inspired the cry, 'Get
a horse!' but for many more it inspired amazement and wild sur-
mise. How could such things be? No matter how much Elon Musk
and his successors might impress us in the future, it is unlikely they
can compete with the shocking simplicity of a new machine that
moved freely without rails, wind, human or animal power.

Perhaps cars will end up in museums, a sad fate. Cars never look
right in museums – they look dead. This is where automotive aesthetes miss the point. They coo, all of them, about the beauty of
the same cars – the Ferrari GTO, the Bugatti Royale, the Bentley
R-Type, the Jaguar E-Type, the '61 Lincoln Continental, the Lamborghini Miura – as if to elevate the mere shapes of things to a new
canon of high art. But a car is not just a shape – it is movement

in space and air and an exquisite mechanical ballet. If cars can be art – and I don't doubt that they can be – they must be about more than the way they look.

The truth is that once cars became ubiquitous, artists and the rest of us stopped noticing them. They were everywhere and nowhere. Streets filled with cars had become an aspect of nature like forests or clouds. To notice cars at all had become a childish masculine obsession, an unattractive eccentricity or an unacceptable vulgarity, a clear sign of proletarian taste. After Nader, however, there were the first signs of a new interest in cars. This accelerated in the seventies with the appearance of explicit anti-car sentiment and, finally, in the eighties mere sentiment was hardened by science when global warming was announced to the world.

Then new technologies, actual and promised – ride-hailing, electric cars, autonomous cars, smart cities – were seized upon as the cure for the existential crisis brought on by the car. General Motors' Motorama of 1956 with its driverless Firebird II cars sweeping along the Highway of Tomorrow might have been premature but only by a few decades.

Suddenly it became reasonable, even fashionable, to think, talk about and notice cars. Dare I go electric? It's a question asked by people who know that one day soon they will have no choice. Now cars and their likely replacements are routinely discussed online, in print and in conversation.

The tenor of this discourse is largely negative – the gist is that the internal-combustion car is certainly a bad thing and we now have the technology to replace it. Seldom discussed are the threats to freedom embodied in this technology, nor do many discuss the unique delights of the fossil-fuel-powered car. Though these machines are still overwhelmingly dominant, they are already being seen as part of an unacceptable past.

So, Bertha's wild ride to Pforzheim was the start of a story that is now ending. But there is also another, larger story. The industrialisation of the nineteenth century, from which sprang the car, was accompanied by what Matthew Arnold called a 'melancholy, long, withdrawing roar'. This was the loss of faith in a secure, transcendent realm that sustained the material world and consoled us in our suffering. Raulff calls this 'one of the most unsettling experiences faced by nineteenth century man' and adds that twenty-first-century people now face 'a similar discomfort, finding themselves in the process of losing their grip on the physical realm'.

This is most precisely embodied in the changes that now afflict the car. It was the supreme product of the industrial age and the most effectively world-changing symptom of the Anthropocene. Now, as Tesla's upgrades are simply dropped into their vehicles from the cloud, the heavy, oily, industrial sheen of the fossil-fuelled car suddenly looks disgustingly twentieth century. Now our characteristic machines – phones, laptops, etc. – are not complete in themselves; they work only because of their ethereal attachments, the requests, notifications, search terms and alerts without which they are nothing.

In spite of the fact that it is the essence of the car not to be so dependent, so incomplete, they will soon be entrapped. The autonomous cars will not in fact be autonomous – they will be driven by the cloud. As level five approaches, they will cast off the capricious exigencies of human control and surrender to the demands of government or corporate clouds. This will have undoubted benefits – fewer people will, doubtless, die; traffic jams might become a thing of the past – but the joys of driving will be lost forever, as will, if we make the wrong choices, our freedoms.

We might make the right choices if we do not scorn but rather respect the age that is now passing. That is why the intention of this book has been to celebrate the internal-combustion, human-controlled car. For all its crimes it was – and still, for the moment, is – a marvellous thing.

So no matter how the history is rewritten, we should still say it was a great day when Bertha Benz set off for Pforzheim, when Emil Jellinek created the Mercedes 35hp, when Ford rocked in his chair and specified the Model T, when Ned Jordan wrote his ad for the Playboy, when Major Ivan Hirst saved the Beetle, when Harley Earl showed off the Buick Y-Job, when Billy Durant met Louis Chevrolet, when the Toyopet Crown disembarked at Long Beach, when Taiichi Ohno detected *muda* in Detroit, when Horatio Nelson Jackson drove into New York, when John Steinbeck blagged a truck off GM, when Dr Bob Hieronimus unveiled his Magic Bus, when Kanye West chopped his Maybach, when Gordon Murray drove a Honda NSX and even when Elon Musk launched the Tesla S. Together they made a way of life that was worth living.

Acknowledgements

I could not have written this book without my wife, Christena. It was her idea. She suggested, reasonably enough, that I should write about something in which I was genuinely interested. She is also a great editor and she guided and consoled me throughout the whole process.

I would also like to thank the many friends and indulgent strangers with whom I have discussed cars.

In particular I'd like to thank Michael Burleigh, Paul Claydon, John Gray, Gavin Green and Rudi Volti for reading all or parts of the book and helping me correct errors and uncertainties.

For longer discussions I am grateful to Patrick Collins, Brendan Cormier, Matthew Crawford, Neil Cosgrove, David Edgerton, Gordon Murray, Emma Rothschild, Rory Sutherland, Nassim Nicholas Taleb and Nigel H.M. Wilson.

For their belief in this book I also owe everything to my agent Sam Copeland and publisher Alan Samson, Maddy Price and Lucinda McNeile.

I would also like to thank, very selectively, the internet:

Wikipedia.org – primarily for the invaluable footnotes.
Jalopnik.com – a laddish but funny and massively informative car site.
Imcdb.org – a spectacularly thorough identifier of the cars that appear in films and television.
Carsandracingstuff.com – a well-organised journal of car wisdom and information from the Crittenden Automotive Library in Illinois.
Card.com – a source of detailed car specifications.

Thousands of other sites have been involved but these have been most helpful and, on cross-checking, accurate.

Bibliography

The following are quoted in the text but have no work in this bibliography: Peter Drucker, Shoshana Zuboff, Rodney Dale, John Lienhard, Herbert Osbaldeston Duncan, Edward Bernays, Walter D. Scott, Brooks Stevens, Ruth Benedict, Nassim Nicholas Taleb, Seisi Kato, Keith Bradsher, John T. Schlebecker, William O'Neill, James Gilbert

Ballard, J.G., *Crash*, Harper Perennial, London, 2008.
Bayley, Stephen, *Cars: Freedom, Style, Sex, Power, Motion, Colour, Everything*, Conran, London, 2008.
Bayley, Stephen, *Death Drive: There Are No Accidents*, Circa Press, London, 2018.
Bayley, Stephen, *Design Heroes: Harley Earl*, Grafton, London, 1992.
Benedict, Ruth, *The Chrysanthemum and the Sword*, Routledge & Kegan Paul, London, 1967.
Bentley, Jon, *Autopia: The Future of Cars*, Atlantic Books, 2019.
Bradsher, Keith, *High and Mighty*, Public Affairs, US, 2002.
Brandon, Ruth, *Auto Mobile: How the Car Changed Life*, Macmillan, London, 2002.
Bruckberger, R.L., *Image of America*, Longmans, London, 1959.
Burleigh, Michael, *The Third Reich: A New History*, Macmillan, London, 2000.
Calvino, Italo, *Six Memos for the Next Millennium*, Penguin, London, 2016.
Carroll, John, *Pickup Trucks*, Regency House Publishing, Broxbourne, 1998.
Casey, Robert, *The Model T: A Centennial History*, Johns Hopkins, Baltimore, 2008.
Choi, Eric and Richard, *Auto Empire: Highlights from M&As that Changed History*, CreateSpace, 2016.

Clarkson, Jeremy, *Clarkson on Cars*, Penguin, London, 2004.

Crawford, Matthew, *Why We Drive: On Freedom Risk and Taking Back Control*, Bodley Head, London, 2020.

Duncan, Dayton, *Horatio's Drive: America's First Road Trip*, Knopf, New York, 2003.

Drucker, Peter, *The Future of Industrial Man*, John Day, New York, 1942.

Eckermann, Erik, *World History of the Automobile*, SAE International, Warrendale, 2001.

Edwardes, Tickner, *Lift-Luck on Southern Roads*, Methuen, London, 1910.

Flink, James J., *America Adopts the Automobile, 1895–1910*, MIT Press, Cambridge, 1970.

Flink, James J., *The Car Culture*, MIT Press, Cambridge, 1975.

Ford, Henry, *My Life and Work*, Enhanced Media, 2017.

Gates, Bill, *How to Avoid a Climate Disaster: The Solutions We Have and the Breakthroughs We Need*, Allen Lane, London, 2021.

Hamilton, Patrick, *The Gorse Trilogy*, Abacus, London, 2017

Hiott, Andrea, *Thinking Small: The Long, Strange Trip of the Volkswagen Beetle*, Ballantine Books, New York, 2012.

Holroyd, Michael, *On Wheels: Five Easy Pieces*, Chatto & Windus, London, 2013.

Houellebecq, Michel, *The Map and the Territory*, Vintage, London, 2012.

Jacobs, Jane, *The Death and Life of Great American Cities*, Vintage, London, 2016.

James, Wanda, *Driving from Japan: Japanese Cars in America*, McFarland & Co, Jefferson, 2003.

Jellinek, Guy, *My Father Mr Mercédès*, G.T. Foulis, London, 1966

Jerome, John, *The Death of the Automobile: The Fatal Effects of the Golden Era, 1955–1970*, W.W. Norton, New York, 1972.

Jun, Zhang, *Driving Toward Modernity: Cars and the Lives of the Middle Class in Contemporary China*, Cornell University Press, Ithaca, 2019.

Keats, John, *The Insolent Chariots*, J.B. Lipincott, New York, 1958.

Kerouac, Jack, *On the Road*, Penguin Modern Classics, London, 2000.

King, Peter, *The Motor Men: Pioneers of the British Car Industry*, Quiller Press, London, 1989.

Lacey, Robert, *Ford: The Men and the Machine*, Heinemann, London, 1986.

Marquis, Samuel, *Henry Ford: An Interpretation*, Wayne State University Press, Detroit, 2007.

McShane, Clay, *Down the Asphalt Path: The Automobile and the American City*, Columbia University Press, New York, 1994.

Miller, Daniel (ed.), *Car Cultures*, Berg, Oxford, 2001.

Moraglio, Massimo, *Driving Modernity: Technology, Experts, Politics and Fascist Motorways, 1922–1943*, Berghahn, New York, 2017.

Muir, John, *The Wilderness Essays*, Gibbs M. Smith, Utah, 2015.

Mumford, Lewis, *The Myth of the Machine: The Pentagon of Power*, Harcourt Brace Jovanovich, New York, 1970.

Nader, Ralph, *Unsafe at Any Speed*, Grossman, New York, 1965.

Nixon, St John C., *Romance Among Cars*, G.T. Foulis, London, 1927.

Nixon, St John C., *The Antique Automobile*, Cassell, London, 1956.

Norton, Peter D., *Fighting Traffic: The Dawn of the Motor Age in the American City*, MIT Press, Cambridge, 2008.

Nye, David E., *America's Assembly Line*, MIT Press, Cambridge, 2013.

O'Toole, James, *Leading Change: Overcoming the Ideology of Comfort and the Tyranny of Custom*, Jossey-Bass, San Francisco, 1995.

Parissien, Steven, *The Life of the Automobile: A New History of the Motor Car*, Atlantic Books, London, 2013.

Pelfrey, William, *Billy, Alfred and General Motors*, HarperCollins Leadership, New York, 2006.

Raulff, Ulrich, *Farewell to the Horse: The Final Century of Our Relationship*, Allen Lane, London, 2018.

Reich, Charles, *The Greening of America*, Random House, New York, 1997.

Rieger, Bernard, *The People's Car: A Global History of the Volkswagen Beetle*, Harvard University Press, Cambridge, 2013.

Roszak, Theodore, *The Making of a Counter Culture: Reflections on the Technocratic Society and its Youthful Opposition*, Faber & Faber, London, 1971.

Rothschild, Emma, *Paradise Lost: The Decline of the Auto-Industrial Age*, Allen Lane, London, 1973.

Ruiz, Marco, *The Complete History of the Japanese Car, 1907 to the Present*, Bay Books, Sydney, 1986.

Sachs, Wolfgang, *For the Love of the Automobile: Looking Back into the History of Our Ideas*, University of California Press, Oakland, 1992.

Setright, L.J.K, *Drive On: A Social History of the Motor Car*, Granta Books, London, 2003.

Simister, John (ed.), *The Story of the Supercar: From Miura to McLaren*, Emap National Publications, London, 2000.

Sinclair, Upton, *The Flivver King: A Story of Ford-America*, Charles Kerr, Chicago, 1986.

Sloan, Alfred P., Jr, with Boyden Sparkes, *Adventures of a White Collar Man*, Doubleday, New York, 1941.

Sloan, Alfred P., Jr, *My Years with General Motors*, Doubleday, New York, 1963.

Sloman, Lynn, *Car Sick: Solutions for Our Car-Addicted Culture*, Green Books, 2006.

Sobel, Robert, *Car Wars: The Untold Story*, E.P. Dutton, New York, 1984.

Steinbeck, John, *Travels with Charley: In Search of America*, Penguin, London, 1971.

Stevenson, Heon, *Selling the Dream: Advertising the American Automobile 1930–1980*, Academy Books, London, 1995.

Strand, Ginger, *Killer on the Road: Violence and the American Interstate*, University of Texas Press, Austin, 2012.

Taylor, Frederick Winslow, *The Principles of Scientific Management*, Akasha Classics, London, 2008.

Townsend, Anthony M., *Ghost Road: Beyond the Driverless Car*, W.W. Norton, New York, 2020.

Updike, John, *Rabbit Is Rich*, Penguin, London, 2006.

Vance, Ashlee, *Elon Musk: How the Billionaire CEO of SpaceX and Tesla Is Shaping Our Future*, HarperCollins, New York, 2015.

Volti, Rudi, *Cars & Culture: The Life Story of a Technology*, Johns Hopkins, Baltimore, 2006.

Wagner, Rob Leicester, *Pick-Up Trucks*, Metro Books, New York, 1998.

Watts, Steven, *The People's Tycoon: Henry Ford and the American Century*, Vintage Books, New York, 2005.

Wells, H.G., *The Wheels of Chance*, Musaicum Books, 2017.

White, E.B., *Essays of E.B. White*, Harper & Row, New York, 1977.

Williams, Heathcote, *Autogeddon*, Jonathan Cape, London, 1991.

Wolfe, Tom, *The Kandy-Kolored Tangerine-Flake Streamline Baby*, Vintage, London, 2018.

Womack, James P., Jones, Daniel T. and Roos, Daniel, *The Machine That Changed the World*, Free Press, New York, 1990.

Wood, Jonathan, *Wheels of Misfortune: The Rise and Fall of the British Motor Industry*, Sidgwick & Jackson, London, 1988.

Yergin, Daniel, *The New Map: Energy, Climate and the Clash of Nations*, Allen Lane, London, 2020.

Yergin, Daniel, *The Prize: The Epic Quest for Oil, Money and Power*, Simon & Schuster, London, 2009.

Zeller, Thomas, *Driving Germany: The Landscape of the German Autobahn 1930–1970*, Berghahn Books, Oxford, 2006.

Zuboff, Shoshana, *The Age of Surveillance Capitalism*, Profile Books, London, 2019.

Filmography

Metropolis, 1927, dir. Fritz Lang.
Slippery Pearls (aka *The Stolen Jools*), 1931, dir. William C. McGann.
It Happened One Night, 1934, dir. Frank Capra.
Modern Times, 1936, dir. Charles Chaplin.
The Hitch-Hiker, 1953, dir. Ida Lupino.
Rebel Without a Cause, 1955, dir. Nicholas Ray.
Hud, 1963, dir. Martin Ritt.
Bonnie and Clyde, 1967, dir. Arthur Penn
La Bande à Bonnot, 1968, dir. Philippe Fourastié
The Italian Job, 1969, dir. Peter Collinson
Easy Rider, 1969, dir. Dennis Hopper.
Duel, 1971, dir. Steven Spielberg.
American Graffiti, 1973, dir. George Lucas.
Badlands, 1973, dir. Terrence Malick
Christine, 1983, dir. John Carpenter.
Repo Man, 1984, dir. Alex Cox.
The Hitcher, 1986, dir. Robert Harmon.
Who Framed Roger Rabbit?, 1988, dir. Robert Zemeckis.
Roger & Me, 1989, dir. Michael Moore.
Thelma & Louise, 1991, dir. Ridley Scott.
Crash, 1996, dir. David Cronenberg.
Gone in 60 Seconds, 2000, dir. Dominic Sena.
Horatio's Drive: America's First Road Trip, 2003, dir. Ken Burns.
The Tiger Brigades, 2006, dir. Jérôme Cornuau.
Little Miss Sunshine, 2006, dir. Jonathan Dayton, Valerie Faris
Cars, 2006, dir. John Lasseter, Joe Ranft
Death Proof, 2007, dir. Quentin Tarantino.
Iron Man, 2008, dir. Jon Favreau
Drive, 2011, dir. Nicholas Winding Refn.
Revenge of the Electric Car, 2011, dir. Chris Paine.
Rush, 2013, dir. Ron Howard.

Baby Driver, 2017, dir. Edgar Wright
El Camino: A Breaking Bad Movie, 2019, dir. Vince Gilligan
Le Mans 66 (aka *Ford v Ferrari*), 2019, dir. James Mangold

Index

Picture Credits